Preface: Alpha

As God Loves Me
Some see you dark as the darkest night.
Others see you white as the purest light.
But God sees a mind of great teaching;
A heart within reaching.
I love you, dear friend,
Not like most, you see,
I love you, as God loves me.

REVEREND DR. JACQUELINE HARDY HARRIS

OMEGA

If we never heard His voice in our hearts, we would never know the face of hope.

If we never felt His hand upon our shoulders, we would walk towards the goodness of love.

If we never tasted the sweetness of hope, we would never discover victory.

Our eyes have seen and our ears have heard of your goodness. We stand as living testimonies of your works. All praise and honor is due unto you, Oh mighty King of Kings. Our hearts will forever sing because we know the Lord, our God.

Dedication

I dedicate this book to my parents Reverend Roosevelt and Dorothy Hardy, who kept me in Christ Jesus and my loving son Minister Eric Thomas.

I love you, as God loves me.

REVEREND DR. JACQUELINE HARDY HARRIS

Table of Contents

    Preface: Alpha i
    Omega ii
    As God Loves Me iv

1. Jesus, The Way, The Truth and The Life 1
2. The Lord's Supper: Holy Communion 8
3. I'm Glad I Don't Look Like What I've Been Through . 16
4. Qualities of A Good Soldier 22
5. Beatitudes 29
6. Where There is Life, There is Hope 36
7. Spiritual Gifts 44
8. Behold Your Mother 53
9. Stay in the Word 60
10. Baby's Daddy 69
11. If the Lord Never Does Anything Else for Me, He's Done Enough 76
12. Doers of the Word 82
13. Disorderly Conduct 89
14. Drop Your Net 95

15. Fire Baptized 101
16. God Ain't Through With Me Yet 108
17. Grandma Told Me to Try Jesus 114
18. Fasting 121
19. Don't Count Me Out 130
20. GPS 136
21. Don't Give Up Your Rights 143
22. Will You Be Ready When Jesus Comes? 150
23. You Don't Love God? 158
24. Tithes, Offerings and Alms 164
25. Why Seek the Living Among the Dead? 170
26. Watch Your Tongue 175
27. Three Wise Decisions 181
28. You Can Lead A Horse to Water 187
29. Too Blessed to Be Stressed 194
30. Who Let the Dogs Out? 201
31. He Saw the Best in Me 207
32. One Nation Under God 213
33. I'd Rather Have Jesus 220
34. Respect Yourself 226
35. Many Are Called, Few Are Chosen 233
36. Christmas, It's Not About Us, It's About Jesus 241
37. The Blood of Jesus 248
38. Prayer 253
39. What Must I Do To Get Eternal Life? 262

40. The Bible is Right, Somebody's Wrong 270
41. A Servant of God's Gospel 278
42. A New Year, A New Attitude 288
43. I Shall Not Be Moved 296
44. The Dream Will Never Die 302
45. Don't Hate, Participate 309
46. Church Folk Involved in A Killing 317
47. An Obedient Child of God 323
48. How Deep Are You in the Spirit? 332
49. I Know I've Been Changed 340
50. Evangelize 346
    Epilogue 352
    Endnotes 353
    About the Author 355

Jesus, The Way, The Truth, and The Life!

SCRIPTURE: John 14: 1-6
KEY VERSE: John 14: 6
SUBJECT: Jesus is the Way, the Truth, and the Life

INTRODUCTION:
"Let not your heart be troubled." In part one of this text, Jesus instructed us that God gave us the power to Let or Let Not. We all are given a free will. We can cleave to the infallible Word of God or lay hold to the death wish of Satan. We can let individuals control our spiritual walk, or we can simply let them go! We can give in to temptations, trials, and tribulations, or we can let them be stepping stones down the narrow path of righteousness.

In today's text, we will explore three key points and I pray we all will come to this conclusion: Jesus, Is The Way, The Truth and The Life!

> (1) "Let not your heart be troubled; you believe in God, believe also in Me. (2) In My Father's house are many mansions; if it were not so, I would have told you. I go to prepare a place for you. (3) And if I go and prepare a place

for you, I will come again and receive you to Myself; that where I am, there you may be also. (4) And where I go you know, and the way you know." (5) Thomas said to Him, "Lord, we do not know where You are going, and how can we know the way?" (6) Jesus said to him, "I am the way, the truth, and the life. No one comes to the Father except through Me.

JOHN 14: 1-6 NKJV

"THE WAY"

When we simply turn on the t.v., we can see that many of the people of God are headed down the wrong way. The scriptures remind us to "Enter by the narrow gate, for wide is the gate and broad is the way that leads to destruction, and there are many who go in by it" (Matthew 7:13).

You can follow the ways of Buddhism, Mormonism, Jehovah's Witness, Islam, or Christian Science to name a few, but I guarantee those wide and heavily occupied roadways, will not lead you into the Kingdom of God.

WIDE GATES AND BROAD-WAYS

BUDDHISM: They serve a tiny god name Buddha; they deny "God the Father" and identify Jesus as only a good teacher.

MORMONISM: They believe as God is, Man can become; which was taught by their founder Joseph Smith. They do not believe in the Holy Trinity (God The Father, God

The Son, God The Holy Spirit), and they believe adamantly that heaven is for Mormons only.

JEHOVAH'S WITNESS: They find it difficult to believe in the *Holy Trinity (God The Father, God The Son, God The Holy Spirit)*. They do not believe that Jesus rose from the dead. They believe hard work earns them "Paradise", and they believe that there is no Hell.

ISLAM: They believe that Allah is "One", that Christ was just a Prophet and did not die for man's sins. They also believe that each person can earn their own salvation.

CHRISTIAN SCIENCE: They believe the Scriptures can only be interpreted by their leader Mary Barker. They believe that healings "prove" that Christian Science is authentic. They do not believe in the *Holy Trinity (God The Father, God The Son, God The Holy Spirit)*, or the atoning death and resurrection of Jesus Christ. They teach that the sinner makes his own hell by doing evil, and the saint makes his own heaven by doing right.

Do not be deceived. These religions or new cults are not the true way for the saints of God! I challenge you to research and recognize those who are undermining and attacking the very foundation of Biblical Christianity. Just because everybody is doing it, or going over there to that big fancy church, don't necessarily mean that this is the right decision for you. Watch whom and what you are following. Know those who labor among you!

I really like that old saying the young folk used to say, "What Would Jesus Do?". The humility, integrity, and unselfish ways of Christ are the only examples we should follow. Jesus Christ is the essence of our faith!

"THE TRUTH"

The great *Apostle Paul* touched on this subject in his second epistle to his protégé Timothy: (2nd Timothy 4:1-5)

> "(1) I charge you therefore before God and the Lord Jesus Christ, who will judge the living and the dead at His appearing and His kingdom: (2) Preach the word! Be ready in season and out of season. Convince, rebuke, exhort, with all longsuffering and teaching. (3) For the time will come when they will not endure sound doctrine, but according to their own desires, because they have itching ears, they will heap up for themselves teachers; (4) and they will turn their ears away from the truth, and be turned aside to fables. (5) But you be watchful in all things, endure afflictions, do the work of an evangelist, fulfill your ministry."

In other words preach the tried and true word! Tell them the truth! That's where most preachers go wrong. They do not stick to sound doctrine. We are instructed to study the Word of God, present ourselves acceptable unto God, and rightly divide the Word of Truth.

For you see, "all Scripture is given by inspiration of God, and profitable for doctrine, for reproof, for correction, and for instruction in righteousness." (2nd Timothy 3:16)

My beloved now is the time, in this present age, that we must continually preach about Jesus, His crucifixion and resurrection, "for there is none other name under heaven given among men, whereby we must be saved." (Acts 4:12)

"THE LIFE"

Jesus said these profound words, "The thief does not come except to steal, and kill, and destroy. I have come that you may have life, and that they may have it more abundantly." (John 10:10)

Of the many events of Jesus' earthly life the most significant, without a doubt, are His death and resurrection. On these two pivotal, historical incidents rests the validity of the entire Christian faith. It is vital then to understand the nature of these two events.

The death of Christ was first of all a humiliating physical death. More than that, for a brief time it constituted a spiritual separation from God (Matt. 27:46). Within this moment, there occurred the inexplicable mystery of the Father punishing the Son for the sins of the whole world (1 Pet. 3: 18; 2 Cor. 5:21).

This event, though it was the greatest crime of human history, was in the plan of God, and thus became the basis of salvation for all sinners. "But He was wounded for our transgressions, He was bruised for our iniquities: the chastisement of our peace was upon Him; and with His stripes we are healed." (Isaiah. 53:5)

Saints, the power of the death of Jesus Christ would be nullified without His bodily resurrection. While skeptics have denied the bodily resurrection of Christ, the historical evidence for it is overwhelming: the many separate accounts of His post resurrection appearances, the empty tomb, and the transformed disciples.

Every life that has been dramatically and wonderfully changed by believing in Christ since the first century is a testimony to its historical reality. Furthermore, it is the power of the resurrection that marvelously empowers us today to live a Christian life.

The Apostle John said it plain in the scriptures written "that you may believe that Jesus is Christ, the Son of God, and that believing you may have life in His name." (John 20:31)

In other words, Jesus Is The Way, The Truth and The Life!

CONCLUSION

My beloved Brothers and Sisters, I have come to the conclusion that Buddha, Joseph Smith, Mary Barker, or Farrakhan, will never be able to show me the way to the kingdom of God. Jesus is the only one.

Christ has paved the way down this narrow path of righteousness and reminds us that, "strait is the gate, and narrow is the way, which leadeth unto life, and few there be that find it." (Matthew 7:14)

Saints, if we persevere, hang in there, don't give in, hold out, be steadfast in His word, and keep the faith, Jesus promised us this:

"Blessed are they that do His commandments that they may have right to the tree of life, and may enter in through the gates into the city." (Revelation 22:14)

I don't know about you but I just want to see King Jesus and personally thank Him for all that He's done for me! I especially want to thank *God the Father* for showing me, Jesus, The Way, The Truth, and The Life!

The Lord's Supper: Holy Communion

SCRIPTURE: 1st Corinthians 11: 23-30
SUBJECT: Institution of the Lord's Supper

INTRODUCTION:
The Apostle Paul wrote this letter to the small Church of God in Corinth, which he started during his second missionary journey. The church was struggling from the beginning with the Corinthians' pagan lifestyle and their worship of idol gods such as the "Goddess of Love". In the Temple of Aphrodite (where they consecrated prostitutes) corrupt pleasure seekers would come to spend money on a holiday of entertainment in sin and vice. The city became so notorious for its evils that the term "Korin-thia-zomia" (to act like a Corinthian) became the synonym for decadence and prostitution. This is similar to what they say about going to New Orleans or Las Vegas (cities of sin).

   The Apostle Paul had his challenges in this church at Corinth. Nevertheless, he continued to preach the Word of God, telling a dying world that the wages of sin would be death, but the gift of God is eternal life through Christ Jesus our Lord!

Which brings us to our text today, Paul is forced to exercise his apostolic authority as he firmly deals with problems concerning improper observance of the Lord's Supper. Paul reminded them that it was the Lord's Supper not their own. This became a very serious matter that we will address today.

Some of the Corinthian Church members made a lot of foolish and out right dumb mistakes; so, like that old T.V. car commercial about the benefits from wearing your seat belt, perhaps we too "can learn a lot from a dummy."

1 CORINTHIANS 11: 23-30
(NEW KING JAMES VERSION)

23 For I received from the Lord that which I also delivered to you: that the Lord Jesus on the same night in which He was betrayed took bread; 24 and when He had given thanks, He broke it and said, "Take, eat; this is My body which is broken for you; do this in remembrance of Me." 25 In the same manner He also took the cup after supper, saying, "This cup is the new covenant in My blood. This do, as often as you drink it, in remembrance of Me." 26 For as often as you eat this bread and drink this cup, you proclaim the Lord's death till He comes. Examine Yourself 27 Therefore whoever eats this bread or drinks this cup of the Lord in an unworthy manner will be guilty of the body and blood of the Lord. 28 But let a man examine himself, and so let him eat of the bread and drink of the cup. 29 For he who eats and drinks in an unworthy manner eats and drinks judgment to himself, not discerning the

Lord's body. 30 For this reason many are weak and sick among you, and many sleep.

Sermon

VERSES 23, 24:

"For I received from the Lord that which I also delivered to you; that the Lord Jesus on the same night in which He was betrayed took bread; and when He gave thanks, He broke it and said, Take, eat; this is my body which is broken for you; do this in remembrance of me.

THIS IS MY BODY WHICH IS BROKEN FOR YOU...

Jesus was physically and spiritually broken down for our sake. The bread when broken symbolizes the extreme sacrifice Jesus made for us in His flesh.

Isaiah the Prophet said it best,

"Surely He has borne our griefs and carried our sorrows; yet we esteemed Him stricken, smitten by God, and afflicted. But He was wounded for our transgressions, He was bruised for our iniquities; the chastisement for our peace was upon Him, and by His stripes we are healed."

VERSES 25, 26:

In the same manner He also took the cup after supper, saying, this cup is the new covenant in my blood. This do, as often as you drink it, in remembrance of Me. For as often as you eat this bread and drink this cup, you proclaim the Lord's death till He comes.

THIS CUP IS THE NEW COVENANT IN MY BLOOD...

According to the Apostle Paul, God ushered a new era through the death of His beloved Son. Under the old covenant, people, such as Abraham, were justified by believing God and looking forward to the promise of the Messiah.

Today, we are under the new covenant and are justified, or declared righteous before God, through faith in Jesus Christ and His atoning death on the cross.

And not only are we justified by grace through faith, but Paul tells us in Romans 5:9 that, "having now been justified by His blood, we shall be saved from wrath through Him".

Somebody say Amen!

And if we continue a perpetual memory of Jesus' broken body and shed blood, we can all share the true meaning of this old hymn...

VERSES 27-30

His blood reaches to the highest mountain and it flows to the lowest valley.

His blood that gives me strength from day to day, It will never, never lose its power!

Therefore whoever eats this bread or drinks this cup of the Lord in an unworthy manner will be guilty of the body and blood of the Lord. But let a man examine himself, and so let him eat of that bread and drink of that cup. For he who eats and drinks in an unworthy manner eats and drinks judgment to himself, not discerning the Lord's body. For this reason many are weak and sick among you, and many sleep.

Saints I need you to really pay attention to these verses. They can hold serious consequences to your health and life.

Now what the Corinthian Church did wrong was 1. First, they did not take The Lord's Supper (Holy Communion) seriously and did not participate in the ritual of having the Lord's Supper. In fact during their fellowship meal, they would be eating all sorts of foods. Some of them over-indulged, while others were left hungry and humiliated.

You can understand how this could become a problem. For example: imagine that some of the down-home cooking members of the church bring in some of their country fried chicken and fish, potato salad, collard greens and cornbread and start serving all of that during the time that we are supposed to be having Holy Communion.

Come on yall, not a one of you would be thinking about Jesus or what He's done for you on Calvary's cross, in the midst of smelling those delectable southern aromas. I know I'm right about this!

So, the Apostle Paul rebuked them, and said if you are hungry eat that kind of food at home before or after you have the Lord's Supper. And for God's sake, stop being so self-indulgent!

2. Second, they were guilty of coming to the Lord's Supper with anger in their hearts toward family or friends,

not showing love or charity with their neighbors, and had not repented of their sins.

They would come to that sacred table, eat and drink of the symbolic broken body and shed blood of Christ and not realize that they were causing sickness and death to come to them in their own physical bodies.

It would have been better not to have taken the Lord's Supper at all!

Saints this is one of the most holy sacraments of the church. Jesus gave us a commandment to "do this in remembrance of Me."

Right before we give the Lord's Supper, we the ministers of God, bid to the church these words:

> *"Ye that do truly and earnestly repent of your sins, and are in love and charity with your neighbor, and intend to lead a new life, following the commandments of God, and walking, henceforth in His Holy ways, draw near with faith and take this holy sacrament to your comfort; and make your humble confession to Almighty God, by meekly kneeling or standing."*

And because we all have missed the mark; we prayerfully recite the "General Confession" which covers all of our shortcomings and sins done by thought, word or deed.

"GENERAL CONFESSION"

> *Almighty God, Father of our Lord Jesus Christ, maker of all things, judge of all men, we acknowledge and bewail our manifold sins and wickedness which we from time to time most grievously have committed by thought,*

word, and deed against Thy Divine Majesty, provoking most justly Thy wrath and indignation against us. We do earnestly repent and are heartily sorry for these our misdoings; the remembrance of them is grievous unto us. Have mercy upon us, have mercy upon us, most merciful Father for your Son our Lord Jesus Christ's sake; forgive us all that is past and grant that we may ever hereafter serve and please Thee in newness of life, to the honor and glory of Your name, through Jesus Christ our Lord, Amen.

David said it best in the 51st Psalm NKJV:

"1 Have mercy upon me, O God, According to Your loving-kindness; According to the multitude of Your tender mercies, Blot out my transgressions. 2 Wash me thoroughly from my iniquity, And cleanse me from my sin. 3 For I acknowledge my transgressions, And my sin is always before me. 4 Against You, You only, have I sinned, And done this evil in Your sight— That You may be found just when You speak, And blameless when You judge."

David went on to say…

" 7 Purge me with hyssop, and I shall be clean; Wash me, and I shall be whiter than snow. 8 Make me hear joy and gladness, That the bones You have broken may rejoice. 9 Hide Your face from my sins,
And blot out all my iniquities. 10 Create in me a clean heart, O God,

And renew a steadfast spirit within me. 11 Do not cast me away from Your presence, And do not take Your Holy Spirit from me."

Saints, we must repent of our sins before we take this Holy sacrament! This is very serious!

CONCLUSION

My brothers and my sisters, as Christians we really shouldn't need anyone to remind us of the seriousness of this sacred day of Holy Communion.

We must never forget what Jesus has done for us, because if it wasn't for the finished work at that Old Calvary's cross, not one of us would be here today!

We should never get so preoccupied, self-indulgent, sophisticated, or prosperous that we forget that it was the shed blood of Jesus Christ that saved us, and that we could not save ourselves.

The songwriter said it best...

It was nothing but the blood; it was nothing but the blood, it was nothing but the blood that saved me, that saved me!

One day when I was lost, Jesus died upon the cross and it was nothing but the blood that saved me!

I don't know about you, but it was at the cross, at the cross, where I first saw the light and the burden of my heart rolled away. It was there by faith I received my sight and now I am happy all the day!

I'm Glad I Don't Look Like What I've Been Through

SCRIPTURE: Job 13:1-15
KEY VERSE: Job: 13:15
SUBJECT: Trusting God in Sickness

INTRODUCTION:

The patriarch Job, teaches us through his providence experiences that we can trust and praise God in all circumstances; death of family, lost of personal property, lost of health (sickness), lost of loved-ones, and even lost of friends. Yes, the text for today clearing shows us that through all these circumstances God is in control and helping us to boldly declare, "I'm Glad I Don't Look Like What I've Been Through!"

Sermon

JOB 13: 1-15 NKJV

(1) "Behold, my eye has seen all this; my ear has heard and understood it. (2) What you know, I also know; I am not inferior to you. (3) But

I would speak to the Almighty, and I desire
to reason with God. (4) But you forgers of
lies, you are all worthless physicians. (5) Oh,
that you would be silent, and it would be your
wisdom! (6) Now hear my reasoning, and
heed the pleadings of my lips. (7) Will you
speak wickedly for God, and talk deceitfully
for Him? (8) Will you show partiality for
Him? Will you contend for God? (9) Will
it be well when He searches you out? Or can
you mock Him as one mocks a man? (10) He
will surely rebuke you if you secretly show
partiality. (11) Will not His excellence make
you afraid, And the dread of Him fall upon
you? (12) Your platitudes are proverbs of
ashes; your defenses are defenses of clay. (13)
"Hold your peace with me, and let me
speak; then let come on me what may! (14)
Why do I take my flesh in my teeth, and put my
life in my hands? (15) Though He slay me, yet
will I trust Him. Even so, I will defend my own
ways before Him.

JOB 13:15

"Though He slay me,
yet will I trust Him"

With these profound words, we can learn a lot about
Job. There is an old saying, "God will not put on you no
more than you can bear". This saying held true for Job.
You see the Lord God knew Job was a righteous and holy
man, who shunned the appearance of evil. God knew
that Job trusted Him and praised Him for all things and

that he prayed not only for himself and his family but for his extended family, friends and strangers. Job prayed earnestly for those who perhaps had sinned by thought, word or deed. Yes, God knew whatever He allowed old Satan to do to Job, that he would continue to trust and praise God!

"I'M GLAD I DON'T LOOK LIKE WHAT I'VE BEEN THROUGH!"

But how many of you find that when you are really sick and down and out, some of your friends relentlessly accuse you of commenting some great sin. Like Job's friends, they insisted that he must have done something to make God angry.

Parenthetically I'd like to touch on these scriptures James 5:13-16:

(13) Is anyone among you suffering? Let him pray. Is anyone cheerful? Let him sing psalms. (14) Is anyone among you sick? Let him call for the elders of the church, and let them pray over him, anointing him with oil in the name of the Lord. (15) And the prayer of faith will save the sick, and the Lord will raise him up. And if he has committed sins, he will be forgiven. (16) Confess your trespasses to one another, and pray for one another, that you may be healed. The effective, fervent prayer of a righteous man avails much.

Oh, if we would just do what the Word of God compels the saints to do and stop talking about people and just pray for them!

And when you visit the sick, don't come in with any other agenda except to pray and encourage them in the Lord. Check this out, an individual visited a person in the hospital and found out that they were diagnosed with a certain condition; this individual then stated to the very sick patient, "You know my mother had the same condition and she died".

Saints, please do not go into a sickroom and bring more sickness. You're looking at me kind of funny, let me see if I can put it another way, remember what James instructed us to do: Is anyone among you suffering? Let him pray. Is anyone cheerful? Let him sing psalms; when you come into a sickroom, come with the joy of the Lord! And for God sake, don't stay there all day; the sick need their rest, Amen!

"I'M GLAD I DON'T LOOK LIKE WHAT I'VE BEEN THROUGH!"

Now back to Job; how can someone who is deathly ill be capable of trust, let alone praise? You see, at one point Job felt like the songwriter…

> *There's a leak in this old building, and my soul's got to move*
> *My soul's got to move, my soul's got to move,*
> *There's a leak in this old building, and my soul's got to move*
> *To a building not made my hand!*
> *This old building keeps on leaning, and my soul's got to move*
> *My soul's got to move, my soul's got to move,*
> *To a building not made my hand!*

But I believe that Job reached back into the memory banks of his sanctified soul, and recalled that, "God is our refuge and strength, a very present help in trouble" (Psalm 46:1) And just like David, he proclaimed deep within his heart...

> (1) Bless the Lord, O my soul: and all that is within me, bless his holy name. (2) Bless the Lord, O my soul, and forget not all his benefits: (3) Who forgiveth all thine iniquities; who healeth all thy diseases.
> (Psalm 103:1-3 KJV)

CONCLUSION

My brothers and my sisters, what I really admire about Job is that he did not begin to trust God when he became sick, he always trusted God. There comes a point in one's life that your mind, body and soul realizes that God is in control; that you exist only because He allows you to. To trust God, means that you depend on Him, you believe in Him, you have faith in Him, and last but not least, you have hope only in Him.

> "I'M GLAD I DON'T LOOK LIKE
> WHAT I'VE BEEN THROUGH!"

Job's patience in his troubles is an example for our encouragement to follow. His troubles began in Satan's malice, which God restrained; his restoration began in God's mercy, which Satan could not oppose.

Mercy did not return when Job was disputing with his friends, but when he was praying for them. God is served and pleased with our devotions, not with our disputes. (Repeat)

My beloved, Job was not concerned about earthly possessions, "Naked came I out of my mother's womb, and naked shall I return thither: the Lord gave, and the Lord hath taken away; blessed be the name of the Lord." (Job 1:21 KJV) We may lose much for the Lord, but we shall not lose any thing by Him. Whether the Lord gives us health and temporal blessings or not, if we patiently suffer according to his will, in the end we shall be blessed. Job's estate increased. The blessing of the Lord makes us rich; it is He that gives us power to get wealth, and gives success in honest endeavors. The last days of a good man/woman sometimes prove his/her best, their last works-their best works, their last comforts-their best comforts. The scriptures declared, "After this lived Job an hundred and forty years, and saw his sons, and his sons' sons, even four generations."

(JOB 42:16 KJV)

Brother Job boldly declared, "I'm Glad I Don't Look Like What I've Been Through!"

Qualities of A Good Soldier

SCRIPTURE: 2nd Timothy 2: 1-15
KEY VERSE: 2nd Timothy 2: 3
SUBJECT: Qualities of a Good Soldier of Christ Jesus

INTRODUCTION:

Every year we celebrate Veteran's Day. We take this precious time to remember our Veterans, the fallen, disabled, retired, dedicated, and courageous soldiers of the Armed Forces. We also give honor to the men and women soldiers that continue to stand in harms way for the safety and protection of this United States of America.

In today's text, the Apostle Paul while in prison encourages Timothy, regarding the "Qualities of a Good Soldier". I dedicate this sermon in memory of all our fallen veterans.

Sermon

2ND TIMOTHY 2:1-15 NKJV

(1) You therefore, my son, be strong in the grace that is in Christ Jesus. (2) And the things that you have heard from me among many witnesses, commit these to faithful men who will be able to teach others also. (3) You

therefore must endure hardship as a good soldier of Jesus Christ. (4) No one engaged in warfare entangles himself with the affairs of this life, that he may please him who enlisted him as a soldier. (5) And also if anyone competes in athletics, he is not crowned unless he competes according to the rules. (6) The hardworking farmer must be first to partake of the crops. (7) Consider what I say, and may the Lord give you understanding in all things. (8) Remember that Jesus Christ, of the seed of David, was raised from the dead according to my gospel, (9) for which I suffer trouble as an evildoer, even to the point of chains; but the word of God is not chained. (10) Therefore I endure all things for the sake of the elect that they also may obtain the salvation which is in Christ Jesus with eternal glory.

(11) This is a faithful saying: For if we died with Him, we shall also live with Him. (12) If we endure, we shall also reign with Him. If we deny Him, He also will deny us. (13) If we are faithless, He remains faithful; He cannot deny Himself. (14) Remind them of these things, charging them before the Lord not to strive about words to no profit, to the ruin of the hearers. (15) Be diligent to present yourself approved to God, a worker who does not need to be ashamed, rightly dividing the word of truth.

"QUALITIES OF A GOOD SOLDIER"

"And the things that thou hast heard of me among many witnesses, the same commit thou to faithful men, who shall be able to teach others also." (2:2)

A "Good Soldier" teaches what he or she has learned from role models such as Grandparents, Parents, Pastors (spiritual leaders), and their own life experiences. In other words, if it worked back then for you, use it now! Share the information and training you have learned and what worked best for you with this generation. And for God sake don't forget to tell of your past blunders so that they will not make the same mistakes that you did.

> "And also if anyone competes in athletics, he is not crowned unless he competes according to the rules." (2:5)

I really like how the scripture compares a "Good Soldier" as being like an athlete. For you see we are all competitors in this race of life and if we follow the rules (The Commandments), we will at the end, be rewarded with a "crown of righteousness". (2nd Timothy 4:8)

Nevertheless, this race is quite different from the Olympics, for you see the "race of life" is not to the swiftest but to those who endure unto the end. Every disciplined athlete prepares all his or her life to reach their goal of being a champion.

Paul stresses that a "Good Soldier" does the same; hold fast to sound doctrine, beware of false teachings, be strong, shun arrogance, endure hardships, be diligent to present yourself approved, pursue righteousness, avoid wickedness, discontinue foolish quarrels, flee youthful lusts and speculations, stay in the Word of God which will equip and give you power to combat the enemy now and in the future!

"Remind them of these things, charging them before the Lord not to strive about words to no profit, to the ruin of the hearers. Be diligent to present yourself approved to God, a worker who does not need to be ashamed, rightly dividing the word of truth." (2: 14,15)

Dr. Calvin H. Sydnor, III, Editor of "The Christian Recorder" said these prophetic words, "The military and the ministry have a lot in common." When Dr. Sydnor attended the U.S. Army Command and General Staff College at Fort Leavenworth, Kansas throughout his classes on military strategy, the term "doctrine" was used repeatedly. The instructors used the term so much and emphasized the importance of knowing and following military doctrine that it almost sounded like you were in church.

Dr. Sydnor further stated that "doctrine" was stressed so much that you came to understand that following doctrine in the military was not a recommendation, but a commandment and that the military and religion intertwined.

Our veterans can understand this, when taking on a military objective, every commander and chain of command in every sector of the operation has to know the rules of engagement and the doctrine in how that military objective is to be accomplished.

One commander cannot say of a common military objective, "I will do it this way" and another commander participating in the same military operation say, "I will accomplish the objective in my own way."

My beloved, that kind of thinking does not follow military doctrine and nearly always results in failure. If commanders in different sectors are on one-accord, following the same military doctrine, most often victory will be the result!

Which brings me to another point, every African Methodist Episcopal Church should follow the Doctrine of the A. M. E. Church. Pastors and members cannot "do their own thing". We are the A.M.E. Church not Burger King; "you can't have it your way".

All denominations and churches know the importance of doctrine and when they neglect the discipline of doctrine, it is the beginning of the downfall of that religious institution.

"As the military was taught from religion, the churches have a lot to learn from the military."

For example, one of the first things that one learns upon entering the military is the chain of command. Every soldier, sailor, airman, marine, or coast guard understands the chain of command and the consequences of disrespecting the chain of command.

In some local churches, the laity does not exhibit respect for pastors, presiding elders or bishops. Some pastors show little respect for presiding elders and others show little respect for Episcopal leadership. This disrespectfulness does not enhance the body of Christ or the work of the Church.

Everybody in the military is responsible and accountable to someone; from the private to the general. And every "good soldier in the army of the Lord" is responsible and accountable to God; "so be diligent to present yourself approved to God, a worker who does not need to be ashamed, rightly dividing the word of truth."

CONCLUSION

One of this nation's most respected Soldiers, Retired U.S. Secretary of State, General Colin Luther Powell who endorsed President Barack Obama, said these profound words...

> "There are no secrets to success: Don't waste time looking for them. Success is a result of perfection, hard work, learning from failures, loyalty to those for whom you work, and persistence."

We have been given our marching orders by our Lord and Savior Jesus Christ. He is looking for a few good men and women who will fight the good fight of faith. For we realize that we do not wrestle merely against flesh and blood; but against principalities, against powers, against rulers of the darkness of this age, and against spiritual host of wickedness in high places.

Therefore, as a "Good Soldier in the Army of the Lord", I compel you to take up the whole armor of God, so that you may be able to withstand in the evil day, having done all, to still stand!

Stand therefore, having girded your waist with truth, having put on the breastplate of righteousness, and having shod your feet and strapped up your boots with the preparation of the gospel of peace.

Don't forget to take your shield of faith so you will be able to quench all the fiery darts of the wicked one. Now, whatever you do, for God sake take the helmet of salvation, and the sword of the Spirit, which is the Word of God!

Don't give up, don't give in, and for God sake don't throw in the towel, in fact throw the towel up in the air and allow the breath of the living God, the Holy Ghost, to anoint the towel, then wipe your brow one more time, hold your head up, stick your chest out, stand at attention, and order arms!

The songwriter said it best when asking...

HYMN 410-AM I A SOLDIER OF THE CROSS

> Am I a soldier of the cross, a follower of the Lamb,
> And shall I fear to own His cause, or blush to speak His name?
> Must I be carried to the skies on flowery beds of ease,
> While others fought to win the prize, and sailed through bloody seas?

SAINTS, THE ANSWER IS...
Sure, I must fight if I would reign: Increase my courage, Lord;
I'll bear the toil, endure the pain, supported by Thy word!

WHY?
Because I'm A Good Soldier in the Army of the Lord!
A Sanctified Soldier in the Army of the Lord!
And if I die, let me die,
A Good Soldier in the Army of the Lord!

Beatitudes

SCRIPTURE: Matthew 5:1-12
Matthew 5:48
SUBJECT: The Blessed of God

INTRODUCTION:

Beatitudes are the opening sentences (Introduction) of Jesus' Sermon on the Mount, which describe the quality of life of all Christians. The word "Beatitude" comes from a Latin word meaning "happy" or "blessed".

I say Jesus was a Methodist Preacher, because the Sermon on the Mount (Matthew 5th -7th Chapters), takes approximately 15 minutes to read by the average reader. Jesus wasn't long winded (Smile).

The traditional site of the Sermon is marked today by a little church, the Chapel on the Mount of Beatitudes, one of the major stopping points for tourist who visit the Holy Land.

The Sermon on the Mount, starting with the Beatitudes, sets forth the spiritual principles of the kingdom of God. They clearly define the character of a child of the King.

Now the Beatitudes are not separate blessings, no, they are to be applied and developed by all believers.

Today we will discuss these (8) Beatitudes, which the Lord and Savior Jesus Christ clearly reminds us that, "You shall be perfect, just as your Father in heaven is perfect". (Matthew 5:48)

MATTHEW: 5:2-10

"Then He opened His mouth and taught them saying:
Blessed are the poor in spirit, for theirs is the kingdom of heaven.
Blessed are those who mourn, for they shall be comforted.
Blessed are the meek, for they shall inherit the earth.
Blessed are those who hunger and thirst for righteousness, for they shall be filled.
Blessed are the merciful, for they shall obtain mercy.
Blessed are the pure at heart, for they shall see God.
Blessed are the peacemakers, for they shall be called the sons of God.
Blessed are those who are persecuted for righteousness' sake, for theirs is the kingdom of heaven."

Sermon

MATTHEW 5:3

"Blessed are the poor in spirit, for theirs is the kingdom of heaven."

The "poor in spirit" denotes the fact of sin. The word poor used in this verse means less of you and more of the Holy Spirit.

During my studies of the New Testament, sin is interpreted as "unbelief". A person who does not believe in the Lord and Savior Jesus Christ or resist the truth that is revealed through the power of the Holy Spirit is consider spiritually blind.

This spiritual blindness causes them to become slaves to sin or transgressions (to step cross the line); lawlessness, uncleanness, vicious criminal and sexual acts, and almost any action in opposition to God's standards of righteousness.

The consequences of sin are that it separates us from God. This separation need not be permanent, but if a person dies not having corrected this problem by believing and trusting Jesus Christ, then the separation does become permanent; Romans 6:23 says, "For the wages of sin is death, but the gift of God is eternal life in Christ Jesus our Lord."

So, what shall we do? "Believe on the Lord Jesus Christ and you will be saved." (Acts 16:31)

MATHEW 5:4

> Blessed are those who mourn, for they shall be comforted.

The term "those who mourn", means those who repent of their sin.

The Apostle Paul said this, "godly sorrow produces repentance to salvation, not to be regretted."

As Christians, we must admit our sin, regret the actions of our sin, plead the blood of Jesus Christ, and believe that God has indeed done what He promised, namely, to cleanse us from all unrighteousness and restore and comfort us with His Holy Spirit.

MATTHEW 5:5

> Blessed are the meek, for they shall inherit the earth.

"The meek" describes not the weak, but rather strength that is surrendered to God in the new birth experience.

The Apostle Peter said this, "Likewise you younger people, submit yourselves to your elders. Yes, all of you be submissive to one another, and be clothed with humility, for God resist the proud, but gives grace to the humble. Therefore humble yourselves under the mighty hand of God, that he might exalt you in due time." (1st Peter 5:5, 6)

Young people respect your elders! Saints, respect each other, don't keep putting your brothers and sister down!

MATTHEW 5:6

> Blessed are those who hunger and thirst for righteousness, for they shall be filled.

"To hunger after righteousness" signifies the strong desire to be more like Christ.

MATTHEW 5:7

> Blessed are the merciful, for they shall obtain mercy.

"The merciful" are those who show an attitude of forgiveness.

Jesus taught his disciple, "Forgive us our trespasses, as we forgive those who trespass against us."

MATTHEW 5:8

> Blessed are the pure at heart, for they shall see God.

"The Pure at heart" are those individuals who strive daily to live a clean and holy life.

MATTHEW 5:9

> Blessed are the peacemakers, for they shall be called the sons of God.

I really like this one. At the age of nine year's old I told my parents I wanted to be a Police Officer. People used to ask me how can you be a Police Officer, isn't it against the will of God? Well I direct them to this passage of scripture which clearly states that "The peacemakers exert a calming influence in the storms of life. Every time I came on the scene of an incident I would bring with me the peace of the Lord!

MATTHEW 5:10

> Blessed are those who are persecuted for righteousness' sake, for theirs is the kingdom of heaven.

"Those who are persecuted" denotes those individuals who are faithful under stressful situations. Those who in spite of circumstances continue to trust God!

CONCLUSION

My beloved, each one of the Beatitudes carries with it a strong promise of ultimate good for those who develop them. As Christians, we must try and do our best to live the life Jesus outlined for us. When we fail, while trying to do our best, we need not despair; for God is a God of grace and forgiveness to all who confess and repent of their sins. We are not perfect yet, but we should always strive for perfection; each day we should be just a little holier than yesterday.

Also, we should realize that we cannot live this holy life by our own powers and abilities; we have to yield to the power of the Holy Spirit. We must offer ourselves to the Lord as living sacrifices; allowing the Holy Spirit to work within and control us.

Yes, the Beatitudes are Jesus' expectations of those who are washed in the Blood of the Lamb, those who persevere in spite of persecution, those who are talked about, criticized, ostracized, falsely accused, and called everything but a child of God for Christ's sake.

Our Lord and Savior, Jesus Christ concluded with this, "Rejoice and be exceedingly glad, for great is your reward in heaven; for so they persecuted the prophets who were before you."

SONG:
Lord, I want to be a Christian, in my heart, in my heart!
Lord, I want to be like Jesus, in my heart, in my heart!

Where There Is Life, There Is Hope

SCRIPTURE: 1st Kings 3: 16-28
SUBJECT: Take Me to the King!

INTRODUCTION:

I would like to dedicate this sermon to all the Mothers of the world, especially to my beloved mother (Dorothy Mae Hardy) and to those mothers who have given life and hope to this world. I personally want to thank them for their many tears, long-suffering, laboring both day and night, giving up their last meal so that their children can eat, going without so that their children can have, and for nurturing and caring for us when we could not do it for ourselves. An Economist on CNN stated the other day that if we add up all that mothers have done; their salary would be that of most Corporate Executives about $117,000 a year (six figures); in other words, most of us could never pay Momma back. That's why Shirley Caesar sang that old song "No Charge". Yes, these wonderful gifts from God, called mothers, realized through nine months of true patience and agape love that where there is life, there is hope!

DR. JACQUELINE HARDY HARRIS

1 KINGS 3:16-28 (NEW KING JAMES VERSION)

(16) Now two women who were harlots came to the king, and stood before him. (17) And one woman said, "O my lord, this woman and I dwell in the same house; and I gave birth while she was in the house. (18) Then it happened, the third day after I had given birth, that this woman also gave birth. And we were together; no one was with us in the house, except the two of us in the house. (19) And this woman's son died in the night, because she lay on him. (20) So she arose in the middle of the night and took my son from my side, while your maidservant slept, and laid him in her bosom, and laid her dead child in my bosom. (21) And when I rose in the morning to nurse my son, there he was, dead. But when I had examined him in the morning, indeed, he was not my son whom I had borne."
(22) Then the other woman said, "No! But the living one is my son, and the dead one is your son." And the first woman said, "No! But the dead one is your son, and the living one is my son." Thus they spoke before the king. (23) And the king said, "The one says, 'This is my son, who lives, and your son is the dead one'; and the other says, 'No! But your son is the dead one, and my son is the living one.' (24) Then the king said, "Bring me a sword." So they brought a sword before the king. (25) And the king said, "Divide the living child

in two, and give half to one, and half to the other." (26) Then the woman whose son was living spoke to the king, for she yearned with compassion for her son; and she said, "O my lord, give her the living child, and by no means kill him!" But the other said, "Let him be neither mine nor yours, but divide him." (27) So the king answered and said, "Give the first woman the living child, and by no means kill him; she is his mother." (28) And all Israel heard of the judgment which the king had rendered; and they feared the king, for they saw that the wisdom of God was in him to administer justice.

Sermon

In our text, there are three key personalities:
Good mother -loving, caring, concerned, compassionate
Solomon - represents The King of kings, Jesus Christ
The living child - Your child/children

3:16 "HARLOTS"

Harlots or Prostitutes lived in taverns all together with their children during this time. I'm so glad that through divine intervention our forefathers of this great country realized that, "We hold these truths to be self-evident that all men, women, boys and girls are created equal and that we are endowed with certain unalienable rights." Yes, even a prostitute has rights! My beloved, we all, the great and small, the good, the bad and the ugly will have to stand before God the Righteous Judge, in that great Day of the Lord.

3:20 "IN THE MIDDLE OF THE NIGHT" ...

While you are asleep comfortably in your bed, the enemy is plotting, scheming and thinking of ways to not only harm you, but your family too! But I'm so glad we serve a God that neither slumbers nor sleeps and watches over us.

David said in Psalm 121: 4 indeed, he who watches over Israel will neither slumber nor sleep. 5 The Lord watches over you— the Lord is your shade at your right hand; 6 the sun will not harm you by day, nor the moon by night. 7 The Lord will keep you from all harm— he will watch over your life;

3:21 "IT WAS NOT MY SON" ...

A good mother knows her child. In fact, mothers, I admonish you to examine and observe your children carefully.
- What they are wearing?
- What are their habits, likes and dislikes?
- Are they speaking or being silent?
- What and whom are they watching on the internet?
- Are they texting or sexting? Tweeting or Twerking?
- Who are they hanging out with?
- Do they have any special birthmarks or new tattoos?

- Mothers in this day and age you must know everything you can about your child!

3:26 "GIVE HER THE LIVING CHILD" ...

Sometimes my beloved you will have to give your child up temporarily to someone or someplace that you just don't feel good about, a gut wrenching feeling that only a mother senses.

Here are just a few examples:

1. You may have to give your child up, temporarily, to the Division of Child and Family Services, because maybe you were deemed an unfit mother (drugs, alcohol, abuse). In Miami, a mother parked her car near the Biscayne Bay, called her fiancée on her cell phone and screams, "They're not going to take my babies, I ain't gonna give them up to no foster care."

   She then drives her car into the bay and drowns not only herself but her 5-year-old daughter and her 3-month-old son. Saints, I believe this mother loved her children, but how many of you know that she didn't love herself?

   You don't hear me. I'd rather have my babies be alive in a foster home, than dead floating in a bay! Listen to me mothers!

2. You may have to give your child up temporally to a correctional facility, because they committed a crime.

3. You may have to give your child up temporally to a drug rehabilitation center, because they tried crack, or ecstasy, just once and got hooked!

Yes, my beloved, you may have to give your child up temporarily, but for God sake don't give up on them…

- Keep on praying! Keep on fasting!
- Don't give in, Don't give out, Hold on, and Hang in there!
- Mothers, tell the devil he's a liar, that's my baby! That's my child! As long as the blood is running warm in their veins, there is hope! For Where There Is Life, There Is Hope!

CONCLUSION

My beloved, God the Father loved us so much that He too gave up his only son, Jesus Christ, so that we could have the right to eternal life. Saints, Christ lives and reigns forever. He is alive and is our only Hope! We must remember that there is no hope in the grave. Once your spirit separates itself from your body, once you give up the ghost, and the mortician glues your tongue to the roof of your mouth, there is no more hope for you. There are no more opportunities to make choices or a change in your life, what's done is done!

All that will be left is judgment day. We will all (living and dead) will have to stand before God and give an account of our works.

Mothers, there will come a time in your life when you too, will have a difficult decision like the woman in this text today. You will have to bring this monumental problem to the King of Kings. It's just too much for you.

But then you remember what your Momma said, "Baby there's absolutely nothing too hard for God".

You see a good mother knows when she places her child in the hand of the King of kings, Lord of lords, Great and Mighty Councilor, I'm talking about Jesus Christ, that even if her child ends up in the valley of the shadow of death, they want have to fear no evil for God will be with them!

The Word and His Holy Spirit will comfort them! God will even prepare a table before them in the presence of their enemy! God will anoint their heads with oil and their cup will run over! And surely, surely, Goodness and Mercy shall follow them all the days of their natural life!

And Mothers, I've got the faith to believe that your child and my child will dwell in the house of the Lord forever and ever!

I believe the songwriter said it best…

Take Me To The King
I don't have much to bring
My heart is torn in pieces
It's my offering.

DR. JACQUELINE HARDY HARRIS

Lay me at the throne
Leave me there alone
To gaze upon Your glory
And sing to You this song
Please Take Me To The King!

MY BELOVED MOTHERS REMEMBER THIS;
WHERE THERE IS LIFE, THERE IS HOPE!

Spiritual Gifts

SCRIPTURE: 1st Corinthians 12:1-12; 28-31vs
SUBJECT: Spiritual Gifts of the Holy Spirit

INTRODUCTION:
Next to the Master Teacher Himself (Jesus Christ), the apostle Paul is probably the most eloquent and persuasive teacher in the bible. Many of the doctrines he expounded are considered the hallmarks of the Christian faith.

For example in 1st Corinthians Chapter 12, Paul speaks of the church as a body, reminding Christians their various gifts were to be used in building up the body of Christ and that we should work together for the common good of the Christian cause. Paul went on to teach that the Holy Spirit was a more effective power for holy living in the Christian's life than the old Jewish Law had ever been. For you see the Law told the people what to do, but it could not provide the will or power to do it. But praise be to God for His Holy Spirit which provides the necessary power and motivation to do God's will and God's work!

I will, with the help of the Holy Spirit, teach on the Spiritual Gifts. Now Spiritual Gifts are different from the Fruits of the Spirit:

1. "Fruits of the Spirit" are like delicious fruit from a tree that grow and develop in it's season:

   (GALATIANS 5: 22-26)

   22   But the fruit of the Spirit is love, joy, peace, longsuffering, kindness, goodness, faithfulness, 23 gentleness, self-control. Against such there is no law. 24 And those who are Christ's have crucified the flesh with its passions and desires. 25   If we live in the Spirit, let us also walk in the Spirit. 26 Let us not become conceited, provoking one another, envying one another.

I often tell people, you don't have to tell me you are saved the Fruits of the Spirit will tell on you!

2.   "Spiritual Gifts" are given by God through the manifestation (demonstration/materialization) of the Holy Spirit:

   I CORINTHIANS 12:1-12VS, 28-31 VS.

   1   Now concerning spiritual gifts, brethren, I do not want you to be ignorant: 2 You know that you were Gentiles, carried away to these dumb idols, however you were led. 3 Therefore I make known to you that no one speaking by the Spirit of God calls Jesus accursed, and no one can say that Jesus is Lord except by the Holy Spirit.

   4   There are diversities of gifts, but the same Spirit.

5   There are differences of ministries, but the same Lord.

6   And there are diversities of activities, but it is the same God who works all in all. 7 But the manifestation of the Spirit is given to each one for the profit of all: 8 for to one is given the word of wisdom through the Spirit, to another the word of knowledge through the same Spirit, 9 to another faith by the same Spirit, to another gifts of healings by the same Spirit, 10 to another the working of miracles, to another prophecy, to another discerning of spirits, to another different kinds of tongues, to another the interpretation of tongues.

11 But one and the same Spirit works all these things, distributing to each one individually as He wills. 12 For as the body is one and has many members, but all the members of that one body, being many, are one body, so also is Christ.

28 And God has appointed these in the church: first apostles, second prophets, third teachers, after that miracles, then gifts of healings, helps, administrations, varieties of tongues.

29 Are all apostles? Are all prophets? Are all teachers? Are all workers of miracles? 30 Do all have gifts of healings? Do all speak with tongues? Do all interpret?

31 But earnestly desire the best gifts. And yet I show you a more excellent way.

DR. JACQUELINE HARDY HARRIS

SPIRITUAL GIFTS

1. WISDOM:

The gift of wisdom is the special ability that God gives to certain members of the body of Christ to know the mind of the Holy Spirit in such a way as to receive insight into how given knowledge may be best applied to specific needs arising in the body of Christ.

> 1ST CORINTHIANS 2:1-12
> 1ST CORINTHIANS 12:8
> PSALM 111:10
> ACTS 6:3-10

2. KNOWLEDGE:

The gift of knowledge is the special ability that God gives to certain members of the body of Christ to discover, accumulate, analyze and clarify information and ideals which are pertinent to the growth and well-being of the body.

> 1ST CORINTHIANS 12:8
> ACTS 5: 1-11,
> 1ST CORINTHIANS 2:14,
> 2ND CORINTHIANS 11:6,
> COLOSSIANS 2:2-3

3. FAITH:

The gift of faith is the special ability that God gives to certain members of the body of Christ to discern with extraordinary confidence the will and purpose of God for His work.

> 1ST CORINTHIANS 12:9
> HEBREW 11

AS GOD LOVES ME

ACTS 11:22-24
ROMANS 4:18-21

4. HEALING:

The gift of healing is the special ability that God gives to certain members
of the body of Christ to serve as human intermediaries through whom it pleases
God to cure illness and restore health apart from the use of natural means.

1ST CORINTHIANS 12:9, 28

5. MIRACLES:

The gift of miracles is the special ability that God gives to certain
members of the body of Christ to serve as human intermediaries through whom it
pleases God to perform powerful acts that are perceived by observers to have altered the ordinary course of nature.

1ST CORINTHIANS 12:10, 28

6. PROPHECY:

The gift of prophecy is the special ability that God gives to certain
members of the body of Christ to receive and communicate an immediate
message of God to His people, through a divinely-anointed utterance.

1ST CORINTHIANS 12; 10,
28 EPHESIANS 4:11-14
LUKE 7:20, ACTS 15:32

7. DISCERNING OF SPIRITS:

The gift of discerning of spirits is the special ability that God
gives to certain members of the body of Christ to know with assurance whether certain behavior purported to be of God is in reality divine, human or satanic.

1ST CORINTHIANS 12:10 ACTS 5:1-5
ACTS 16:16-18 1ST JOHN 4:1-6
MATTHEW 16:21-23

8. TONGUES:

The gift of tongues is the special ability that God gives to certain members
of the body of Christ to (a) speak to God in a language they have never learned and/or (b) receive and communicate an immediate message of God to His people through a divinely anointed utterance in a language they have never learned.

1ST CORINTHIANS 12:10, 30
1ST CORINTHIANS 14:13-19
ACTS 2:1-13, MARK 16:17

9. INTERPRETATION:

The gift of interpretation is the special ability that God gives to certain
members of the body of Christ to make known in the vernacular the message of one who speaks in tongues.

1ST CORINTHIANS 12:10, 30
1ST CORINTHIANS 14:26-28

10. PASTOR:

The gift of pastor is the special ability that God gives to certain
members of the body of Christ to assume a long-term personal responsibility for the spiritual welfare of a group of believers.

> EPHESIANS 4:11-14
> TIMOTHY 3: 1-7

11. TEACHING:

The gift of teaching is the special ability that God gives certain
members of the body for Christ to communicate information relevant to the health and ministry of the body and its members in such a way that others will learn.

> 1ST CORINTHIANS 12:28
> EPHESIANS 4:11-14
> ROMANS 12:7

12. HELPS:

The gift of helps is the special ability God gives to certain members of
the body of Christ to invest the talents they have in the life ministry of other members of the body, thus enabling those others to increase the effectiveness of their own spiritual gifts.

> 1ST CORINTHIANS 12:28 ROMANS 16:1, 2

13. GIVING:

The gift of giving is the special ability that God gives to certain

members of the body of Christ to contribute
their material resources to the work of the Lord
with liberality and cheerfulness!

ROMANS 12:8
2ND CORINTHIANS 8:1-7
MARK 12:41-44

14. MISSIONARY:

The gift of missionary is the special ability that
God gives to certain
members of the body of Christ to minister
whatever spiritual abilities they have in a second
culture.

1ST CORINTHIANS 9:19-23
ACTS 22:21
ROMANS 10:15

15. EVANGELIST:

The gift of evangelist is the special ability that
God gives to certain
members of the body of Christ to share the
gospel with unbelievers in such a way
that men, women and children become Jesus'
disciples and responsible members
of the body of Christ.

EPHESIANS 4:11
2ND TIMOTHY 4: 1-5

CONCLUSION

My Brother and Sisters, through the quickening power of the Holy Spirit which comes to every individual who is born again; we begin to realize in our soul that we cannot live without God the Father, The Son and The Holy Spirit. Some of us tried to resist His love, struggled hopelessly to escape His loving arms. Then suddenly you begin to long for forgiveness, to be cleansed, to be set free from sin.

You desire and need peace in your life that only God can give. My beloved, no amount of money can buy it, no degree of intellect can procure it, wisdom cannot attain it, and you can never by your own efforts secure it; My beloved,

Forgiveness, Peace, Salvation, and Spiritual Gifts are offered only from God. All you have to do is reach out your hands toward heaven and grasp a hold of them.

These are free gifts from God, paid in full by our Lord and Savior Jesus Christ!

HYMN 191 COME HOLY SPIRIT, HEAVENLY DOVE

Come Holy Spirit, Heavenly Dove, With all Thy quickening powers;
Kindle a flame of sacred love In these cold hearts of ours.
Look how we grovel here below, Fond of these earthly toys; Our souls,
how heavenly they go To reach eternal joys.
Come Holy Spirit, Sweet Heavenly Dove, With all Thy quickening
powers; Come shed abroad a Saviour's love, And that shall kindle ours.
Amen

Behold Your Mother!

SCRIPTURE: John 19: 25-30
SUBJECT: A Tribute to Mother

INTRODUCTION:
The archangel Gabriel brought the good news to Mary that she would give birth to the Messiah, the Savior of the world. The New Testament reveals that angels guided, instructed and protected God's people. Angels still exist today but are not as obviously active because of the larger role that the Holy Spirit plays in the lives of Christians.

Although the angel Gabriel made it plain and clear to Mary her very sacred role and that she was highly favored of God; she still had to be later reminded by Jesus himself that "He must be about the Father's business" (Luke 2:49-51). Mothers we too are reminded today that our children do not belong to us; they are precious gifts from God! So before we give them up to the babysitters, daycare centers, public or private schools, we must first give them back to God. Present them to His alter, get them baptized, get them in Sunday school. Amen!

This selected scripture text is one of the most beautiful tributes to a mother found in biblical history.

Although Jesus had the weight and the sins of the whole world on His shoulders, He took some time out on Calvary's Cross to make very sure that:

Everyone knew that Mary was in fact "His" mother, giving her honor, respect, and reverence as the mother of the Son of God.

Making sure that all Mary's needs were met, Financially, Physically and Spiritually.

JOHN 19:25-30
(NEW KING JAMES VERSION)

25 Now there stood by the cross of Jesus His mother, and His mother's sister, Mary the wife of Clopas, and Mary Magdalene.

26 When Jesus therefore saw His mother, and the disciple whom He loved standing by, He said to His mother, "Woman, behold your son!"

27 Then He said to the disciple, "Behold your mother!" And from that hour that disciple took her to his own home.

28 After this, Jesus, knowing that all things were now accomplished, that the Scripture might be fulfilled, said, "I thirst!

29 Now a vessel full of sour wine was sitting there; and they filled a sponge with sour wine, put it on hyssop, and put it to His mouth.

30 So when Jesus had received the sour wine, He said, "It is finished!" And bowing His head, He gave up His spirit.

DR. JACQUELINE HARDY HARRIS

JOHN 19: 25, 26

> "Now there stood by the cross of Jesus His mother, and His mother's sister, Mary the wife of Clopas, and Mary Magdalene. When Jesus therefore saw His mother, and the disciple whom He loved standing by, He said to His mother, "Woman, behold your son!"

"WOMAN BEHOLD YOUR SON"

Jesus loved his mother very much and he absolutely knew she loved him too. So he said these profound words to her, "Woman behold your son"; spiritually interpreted, Mother look upon your baby boy one more time for in three days your beloved son will be Savior and Redeemer of the whole world!

Jesus gave his mother a precious moment in time to embrace her son for the last time. Mothers, you understand how this must feel, to finally let your child go, to allow them to be all that they can be. But for some reason it still hurts and leaves a small hole in your heart that will never quite be filled.

But I could imagine Mary looked upon her son Jesus and said to herself, 'This is much bigger than me', in other words it's not about me. She finally realized that she had to let her baby boy finish the work he came to do.

Mothers, we too must allow our children to grow and go. Teach them to be independent and not dependant. Train them up in the (Lord) the way they should go, while they are young and when they become old they will not depart from it. Amen!

JOHN 19: 27

27 Then He said to the disciple, "Behold your mother!" And from that hour that disciple took her to his own home.

"BEHOLD YOUR MOTHER!"

We claim that we are so busy and can't take care of mom. We say, "I have a wife and children or girlfriend/boyfriend, I've got all kinds of responsibilities on my job; for goodness sake I can only do so much!

Our Lord and Savior Jesus Christ showed us a paradigm in His tribute to His beloved mother. He admonished us in this passage of scripture to take time out to tell mom how much you appreciate her, how much you love and care for her. When mom gets older and can no longer take care of herself, it is up to you and me to make sure that she is provided for, physically, financially and spiritually.

I really like what Jesus did; He made sure that his mother was with someone who was a believer, someone who had the fear of God, and an overwhelming love for Christ.

This type of person was perfect for Jesus' mother and would be excellent for your mother too.

Another thing Jesus showed me, this person(s) doesn't necessarily have to be a family member.

You are looking at me kind of funny; Let me explain this statement. Yes, there are some individuals whom God has chosen to minister to the elderly, the motherless, the fatherless, and the sick and shut-in. Such as Deaconess Arminta Ricks Curtis and Sister Juanita Miller, I told them that their ministry is so powerful and rewarding; I pray that the Lord continues to shower down blessings from heaven upon their good works! For the word of God says, "He that hath pity upon the poor lendeth unto the LORD; and that which he hath given will he pay him again." (Proverbs 19:17)

It is a fact that everyone has a mother; even our Lord and Savior Jesus Christ. Yes, Everyone has a mother; some of you may not have known your mother, or even liked her, but you still, thank God you have a mother.

Most of us like Jesus cherish our mothers and give tribute to them everyday. We treasure her wisdom as we ourselves grow older.

- Now to the individuals who have a mother who did not know how to love and care for you; do not have a pity party, stop concentrating on your broken dreams. Find ways to help other mothers, who like yours, need some parenting skills.
- To my sisters who can not conceive, or maybe you lost a child; please do not dread "Mother's Day" but embrace it as a time to reflect on, serve, and honor your own mother.

- If your mother is no longer with you do not despair. She is as close as your memory. Think about the good times and not the loss. Was mom a good cook? Did she like to read? Was she a great student? Was she a meticulous housekeeper? Was she a classy dresser who liked beautiful hats and shoes to match? Did she tell jokes and make you laugh?
- These are inherited qualities you can develop to show honor and love to mother.
- Love, honor and respect does not end at the grave of your mother. As long as the blood is running warm in your veins, you must continue to give your mother honor and respect. By doing this, you also give honor and respect to our heavenly Father who commanded that we must "Honor our Mothers and Fathers".

CONCLUSION

JOHN 19: 30

"So when Jesus had received the sour wine, He said, "It is finished!" And bowing His head, He gave up His spirit."

My brothers and my sisters, just before Jesus gave up His spirit, just before His death on Calvary's cross; He gave His beloved mother Mary the highest honor and respect by saying these profound words to the world, "Behold thy Mother!" Look, that's my Beloved Mother!

In other words, Jesus was saying...

- Mother I love you!
- Mother I appreciate you!
- Mother I honor and respect you!
- Mother you are more precious to me than silver or gold, than diamonds or pearls!
- Mother I thank you, because if it had not been for you, I would not be here today!
- Mother with all my heart and soul, I pray that God the Father and the precious Holy Spirit continues to bless and keep you!
- Mother, I've got to go now but don't you worry about anything. I go to prepare a place for you and where I go you can go too.
- Saints, behold your mother!

SONG: My Mother told me to try Jesus, He's alright!

SERMON DEDICATION: To Mother Dorothy Hardy

Stay In The Word

SCRIPTURE: Luke 8:4-15 John 8:31
SUBJECT: The Parable of the Sower

INTRODUCTION:
This parable, is an earthly story with a heavenly meaning, of the "Sower" who sowed his seeds. This is one of three parables that are recorded in the Synoptic Gospels: Matthew, Mark, and Luke. Jesus used parables as a means of teaching. They were particularly effective and easy to remember, because he used familiar scenes. Although parables clarified Jesus' teachings, they always had hidden meanings, needing further explanation. These hidden meanings revealed truths to the "believers" and concealed them from unbelievers. From parables, Jesus' enemies could find no direct statements to use against him.

Now in this beautiful text today, you will notice that the same kind of seed fell on various types of soil, producing different results. The first type of soil is hard, the second is shallow, the third is overgrown with thorns and the fourth type, unlike the other three, is fine and good soil. According to Jesus, the seed is the Word of God, and the soil represents people with different conditions of the heart. This parable of the sower is a powerful illustration of Jesus' statement in John 8:31vs:

> "If you continue in my word, then you are my disciples indeed."

1 LUKE 8:4-15 NEW KING JAMES VERSION
THE PARABLE OF THE SOWER

4   And when a great multitude had gathered, and they had come to Him from every city, He spoke by a parable:

5   "A sower went out to sow his seed. And as he sowed, some fell by the wayside; and it was trampled down, and the birds of the air devoured it.

6   Some fell on rock; and as soon as it sprang up, it withered away because it lacked moisture.

7   And some fell among thorns, and the thorns sprang up with it and choked it.

8   But others fell on good ground, sprang up, and yielded a crop a hundredfold." When He had said these things He cried, "He who has ears to hear, let him hear!"

9   Then His disciples asked Him, saying, "What does this parable mean?"

10   And He said, "To you it has been given to know the mysteries of the kingdom of God, but to the

rest it is given in parables, that' Seeing they may not see, And hearing they may not understand.'

11   "Now the parable is this: The seed is the word of God.

12   Those by the wayside are the ones who hear; then the devil comes and takes away the word out of their hearts, lest they should believe and be saved.

13   But the ones on the rock are those who, when they hear, receive the word with joy; and these have no root, who believe for a while and in time of temptation fall away.

14   Now the ones that fell among thorns are those who, when they have heard, go out and are choked with cares, riches, and pleasures of life, and bring no fruit to maturity.

15   But the ones that fell on the good ground are those who, having heard the word with a noble and good heart, keep it and bear fruit with patience.

Sermon

VERSE #5

"A sower went out to sow his seed. As he sowed, some fell by the wayside and it was trampled down, and birds of the air devoured it."

The first type of soil that the seed falls on is that which is alongside the road, where the seed is trampled down. Soil alongside a road that leads through a grain field is hard packed by the flow of pedestrian traffic.

In this illustration Jesus shows, those who allow the comings and goings of the world to impose undue demands on their time and energy may find that they are too preoccupied to develop any heartfelt appreciation for the Word of God. They hear it, but they fail to meditate on it. Before they develop a love for it, the Devil comes and takes the word away from their hearts in order that they may not truly believe and be saved.

How can this be prevented?

1. Make time to study and meditate on God's word.
2. Do not become preoccupied with mundane things.
3. Reflect on the more important things in life.

VERSE #6

"Some fell on rock and as soon as it sprang up, it withered away because it lacked moisture."

When the seed falls on the second type of soil, it does not just remain on it, as in the first case. It takes up root and sprouts. But then when the sun rises, the sprout is scorched by the heat of the sun and withers.

The reason the sprout withers is not the heat.

Jesus says in [Matthew 13: 5, 6] that the sprout withers because of not having depth of soil and not having moisture. A rock-mass situated right under the layer of the topsoil, prevents the seed from sinking its roots deep enough to find moisture for stability. The sprout then withers because the soil is shallow.

Jesus illustrates here individuals who receive the word with joy and eagerly follow Jesus for a season. But, when exposed to the blazing sun of tribulation or persecution, they become so fearful that they lose their joy and soon give up following Christ.

The reason these individuals become fearful and fall away is because of the rock-like condition of their heart, which prevents them from meditating deeply enough on positive and spiritual things. Their appreciation of the Word of God is too feeble to withstand opposition, trials or tribulation.

WHAT ARE SOME OF THESE ROCK LIKE OBSTACLES?

1. Deep seated bitterness, Self-interest
2. Sexual immorality, Idolatry
3. Hatred, Dissension and Jealousies

The Apostle Paul in Galatians 5 said these are the "works of the Flesh". I tell people you don't have to tell me you are saved; the fruits of the Holy Spirit will tell on you! And what are these fruits: love, joy, peace, longsuffering, kindness, goodness, faithfulness, gentleness, self-control. Gal 5:19-26vs

What can we do to prevent these rock-like obstacles?

Rest assured, if some of these rock-like obstacles are present in your heart the power exerted by Word of God can break it up! Prayerful meditation again stimulates the implanting of the Word deep down in your heart providing you with the strength and courage to cope despite your trials or tribulations.

VERSE #7

> "And some fell on thorns, and the thorns
> sprang up with it and choked it."

The third type of soil, the one with thorns, especially deserves our attention because in some ways it is similar to the fine soil. Like the fine soil, the thorny soil lets the seed take root and sprout.

Initially there is no difference in the growth of the new plant in these two types of soil. However, with time, a condition develops that eventually chokes the plant. Unlike the fine soil this soil becomes overgrown with thorns. As the young plant rises from the soil, it faces competition from the thorns that grow up with it. For a while both vie for nutrition, light, and space, but eventually the thorns overshadow the plant and choke it off. Jesus shows in this verse those individuals that have heard the Word of God, but by being carried away by anxieties, riches and the pleasures of this life, they are completely choked and bring nothing to maturity.

Just as the sower's seed and the thorns grow in the soil at the same time, so do some individuals try to take in the Word of God and the pleasures of this world at the same time. The truth of God's word is sown in their heart, but it faces stiff competition from other worldly pursuits. In other words, their heart is divided. My beloved you cannot serve two Masters!

In Matthew 6:24, Jesus said, "No one can serve two masters; for either he will hate one and love the other, or else he will be loyal to the one and despise the other. You cannot serve God and mammon (riches)." How can we prevent this choking?

1. By giving spiritual matters precedence over material/worldly things
2. Never neglect bible reading/study and reflect upon what you read
3. Make time for concentrated and prayerful meditation on the Word of God in your home
4. Simplify your life as much as possible; do you really need all that?

Saints we must give sufficient time to the Word of God, if we do not, we will lack the enduring power to fight the thorns of this world.

CONCLUSION

VERSE #8

"But others fell on good ground, sprang up, and yielded a crop a hundredfold"

JOHN 8: 31VS

"If you continue in my word, then you are my Disciples indeed."

My brothers and my sisters, with these last two verses, Jesus is pointing out that you and I have an opportunity to be his true disciples; provided that we remain in his word. Jesus viewed endurance as such an important quality for his followers that in his last conversation with his disciples, recorded in the Gospel, twice he urged, "Follow Me"

(JOHN 21: 19,22)

My beloved all of us, young and old, must make sure that we remain in the Word of God and endure as Christ's disciples! We must make a vow this day that the soil of our figurative heart never becomes hard, shallow or overgrown but remains soft and deep; so that we can continue to absorb the Word of God fully and bear fruit with endurance.

My favorite bible verse is...

PSALM 40:8

I delight to do thy will, Oh my God, And your law is within my heart.

When I start feeling rejected and neglected...

HEBREWS 13:5

I will never leave you nor forsake you."

So we may boldly say: "The LORD is my helper. I will not fear. What can man do to me?"

When my money starts looking a little funny...

MALACHI 3:10

Bring ye all the tithes into the storehouse, that there may be meat in mine house, and prove me now herewith, saith the LORD of hosts, if I will not open you the windows of heaven, and pour you out a blessing, that there shall not be room enough to receive it.

When I get old, tired in this old body; I believe the songwriter said it best, "There's a leak in this old building and my soul gots to move to another building not made by man". Then I'm assured in the Word of God...

JOHN 14: 1-4

Let not your heart be troubled: ye believe in God, believe also in me. In my Father's house are many mansions: if it were not so, I would have told you. I go to prepare a place for you. And if I go and prepare a place for you, I will come again, and receive you unto myself; that where I am, there ye may be also.

Everything you need is in the Word of God; Stay In The Word!

Baby's Daddy

SCRIPTURE: Matthew 1:18-25
SUBJECT: Joseph: The Righteous Daddy of Jesus

INTRODUCTION:
This passage of scripture today encourages all the single women to know that there are some righteous good men out there who are obedient to the voice of the God. These God fearing men are loving, kind, and generous. These amazing men of God are also willing to protect and take care of you and your children. Genealogy indicates that Joseph descended from King David, this explains in what sense this son of David (1:20) became Jesus' legal father by adoption. Today, we will center on one of the most phenomenal "Baby's Daddy" in human history, Joseph the righteous daddy of Jesus.

MATTHEW 1:18-25

(18) Now the birth of Jesus Christ was as follows: After His mother Mary was betrothed to Joseph, before they came together, she was found with child of the Holy Spirit. (19) Then Joseph her husband, being a just man, and not wanting to make her a public example, was minded to put her away secretly. (20) But

while he thought about these things, behold, an angel of the Lord appeared to him in a dream, saying, "Joseph, son of David, do not be afraid to take to you Mary your wife, for that which is conceived in her is of the Holy Spirit. (21) And she will bring forth a Son, and you shall call His name JESUS, for He will save His people from their sins." (22) So all this was done that it might be fulfilled which was spoken by the Lord through the prophet, saying: (23) "Behold, the virgin shall be with child, and bear a Son, and they shall call His name Immanuel," which is translated, "God with us (24) Then Joseph, being aroused from sleep, did as the angel of the Lord commanded him and took to him his wife, (25) and did not know her till she had brought forth her firstborn Son. And he called His name JESUS.

Sermon

LESSONS FROM A RIGHTEOUS MAN

The mystery of Christ's becoming man is to be adored, and not curiously inquired about. You will never be able to comprehend the mind of God. Let me see if I can put it another way. God is what you and I are not! God is the creator, provider and sustainer of life!

Parents, it is much easier to explain to your child where he/she comes from than to articulate where baby Jesus came from.

In our passage of scriptures, Matthew portrays a righteous young man and woman as models for Christian living. Luke focuses on God's revelation to Mary. Matthew focuses on the revelation to Joseph.

Jewish men in Joseph's day generally married around the age of eighteen or twenty, after working to save some money. Jewish women could marry as young as twelve or fourteen, after reaching puberty. Greek and Roman women, they could be married much older.

By calling Joseph righteous, (1:19) Matthew invites us to learn from Joseph's character about fidelity, discipline and preferring God's honor above our own. Like most first century Jewish people, Joseph was faithful to his future spouse in advance. He was awaiting marriage, and he expected the same in return.

Matthew points out that even after Joseph and Mary were married, they refrained from marital relations until Jesus' birth (1:25). This would have taken considerable self-control, because many simply assume that "if a man and woman are alone together for more than twenty minutes, they have had intercourse". The self-control of this young couple challenges those today who doubt their ability to control their passions.

Now for Joseph to "put Mary away" (1:19, literally) meant for Joseph to divorce her (NIV). Ancient Mediterranean fathers generally arranged their daughters' marriages through a custom called betrothal. Betrothal was much more serious than our modern practice of engagement. It left the survivor of the man's death a widow, and if both partners lived, it could be ended only by divorce.

At the same time, we should observe that the circumstances under which Joseph was planning to divorce Mary were hardly light. Unlike today, Joseph had no option of giving Mary a second chance, even if he wanted to. Jewish and Roman law both demanded that a man divorce his wife if she were guilty of adultery.

Roman law actually treated a husband who failed to divorce an unfaithful wife as a panderer (Pimp) exploiting his wife as a prostitute. A wife's adultery, could imply the husband's inadequacy or his family's poor choice of a mate. Mary's apparent unfaithfulness, shamed Joseph as well.

Under these circumstances, Joseph would be righteous in divorcing Mary. To fail to do so would violate law and custom, bring enduring reproach on his household and constitute embracing one who had betrayed him in the worst manner conceivable in his culture.

Society offers little sympathy for Joseph's pain. Our culture encourages marital betrayal that wounds trusting hearts, devastating homes where children should be nurtured in love. Too often, families are crushed with the despair of abandonment amidst betrayal.

We treat divorce harshly, yet often excuse adultery. Some of the same Christians who clamor for greater punishment for violent crimes or drug dealing, counsel betrayed or abused spouses to be perpetually patient as if no consequences were appropriate for the betrayers or abusers.

By calling Joseph righteous, Matthew challenges both our culture and our church in their lax views of sexual fidelity. The evil of divorce is in the breaking apart of what God has put together. A person who abandons, betrays or abuses his or her spouse has already done just that. Matthew does not permit us to punish the innocent party in a divorce any more than we should punish the innocent party in a rape (Deut 22:25-27) or any other crime.

Joseph was righteous, not because he was divorcing Mary (although, as noted, this did not make him unrighteous); Joseph was righteous for divorcing Mary quietly or privately, Joseph was righteous for not bringing unnecessary shame on her. He knew much suffering already awaited her. Her premarital pregnancy had likely already ruined any chance of her ever marrying, and placed her in line for a horrible fate in an economically and honor driven male centered society.

I have known of some churches that publicly shamed a young woman who became pregnant, usually leaving the less obvious father of the child concealed from public reproach. Joseph's "justness" or "righteousness" reminds us that justice is not merely a matter of punishment and shame, but also a matter of mercy. Joseph was going to divorce Mary, and although he felt wounded, he still did everything in his power to minimize her shame.

CONCLUSION

When God reveals the truth to Joseph, he immediately believes and obeys God's will. This is unbelievable because many unmarried men today refuse to take responsibility even when they are the father!

Joseph trusted God enough to obey him. Such obedience was costly. Joseph married Mary, and outsiders would assume that he had gotten Mary pregnant before the wedding. Joseph would remain an object of shame in a society dominated by the value of honor. This was a stressful way to begin a marriage! Joseph chose to embrace shame and to humbly preserve the sanctity of God's call.

Joseph's obedience to God even cost him the right to value his own reputation. Joseph did as the angel of the Lord had bidden him, speedily, without delay, and cheerfully, without dispute.

Many Christians today, probably much older than Joseph and claiming the power of the Holy Spirit in their lives, have yet to learn his lesson.

Matthew teaches us about the power and authority of scripture through the Prophet Isaiah and about fidelity (loyalty), commitment and obedience through Joseph.

Last but certainly not least, Mathew also provides a teaching about salvation from sin through our Lord and Savior Jesus Christ. Even while Jesus is in Mary's womb, the angel declares that his name will be (translated *"Joshua"* in the Old Testament and Jesus in the New), which means *"salvation"*. Jesus would bear this name because he would save his people from their sins (1:21).

More than anything today, we need to hear the Bible made "relevant" and "practical" . Matthew teaches us through the example of Joseph. Nothing Matthew tells us is more practical, than the way he reveals the heart and character of our Lord and Savior Jesus Christ.

As we get to know Jesus better through the Scriptures, we get to know the Scripture's author (God the Father), and our character becomes more and more like His (2 Corinthians 3:14-18). Matthew invites us today to consider and worship the God who accepted the ultimate vulnerability. Born as an infant to poor and humiliated parents, into a world hostile to his presence.

> MY BROTHERS AND SISTERS, THERE'S A NEW TWIST TO AN OLD SAYING, "ANYONE CAN BE A FATHER", BUT IT'S TAKES A REAL RIGHTEOUS, OBEDIENT MAN TO BE A "BABY'S DADDY".

If The Lord, Never Does Anything Else For Me, He's Done Enough!

SCRIPTURE: John 20:10-18
SUBJECT: Mary Magdalene: A Living Witness

INTRODUCTION:
Today we will lift up a blessed woman of the bible named Mary Magdalene. Mary, from Magdala near ancient Galilee, was exorcised of seven demons by Jesus. Demon possession was a physical and spiritual illness and Mary was extremely sick until her encounter with Jesus Christ. But, after being set free, she became a part of an inner circle of women-supporters of Christ - who followed Jesus all the way to Calvary's Cross and beyond. Yes, Mary Magdalene, if she was here today would boldly proclaim, If The Lord, Never Does Anything Else For Me, He's Done Enough!

JOHN 20: 10-18 NIV

(10) Then the disciples went back to their homes, (11) but Mary stood outside the tomb crying. As she wept, she bent over to look into the tomb (12) and saw two angels in white, seated where Jesus' body had been, one at the head

and the other at the foot. (13) They asked her, "Woman, why are you crying?" "They have taken my Lord away," she said, "and I don't know where they have put him." (14) At this, she turned around and saw Jesus standing there, but she did not realize that it was Jesus. (15) "Woman," he said, "why are you crying? Who is it you are looking for? Thinking he was the gardener, she said, "Sir, if you have carried him away, tell me where you have put him, and I will get him." (16) Jesus said to her, "Mary." She turned toward him and cried out in Aramaic, "Rabboni!" (which means Teacher). (17) Jesus said, "Do not hold on to me, for I have not yet returned to the Father. Go instead to my brothers and tell them, 'I am returning to my Father and your Father, to my God and your God." (18) Mary Magdalene went to the disciples with the news: "I have seen the Lord!" And she told them that he had said these things to her.

Sermon

Mary Magdalene, was once possessed by Satan, then repossessed by Christ. We can find her story in all four gospels, where she is mentioned by name (14) times - this is significant, since many women of the Bible are nameless. She was from Magdala, a town known for vice and violence. But no where in the Bible or my research of the scriptures states that Mary Magdalene was a prostitute. Nevertheless in Paul's letter to the Corinthians there is a passage of scriptures that declares if you lay down with a harlot you will obtain a "harlot spirit". (1st Corinthians 6:16) This may very well explain why Mary Magdalene had so many demons (spirits) in her, considering the sexually immoral life style of the city where she lived.

Young people you "hook-up" with people who are sexually active and you say, "I'm not sexually active". Some of you run with thieves, yet you say "I don't steal". You hangout with drug addicts, yet you say "I don't use drugs". You socialize with individuals who are gay, yet you say, you're not gay.

I'd like to interject another passage of scripture parenthetically:

EPHESIANS 5:3-7

> "But fornication and all uncleanness or covetousness, let it not even be named among you, as fitting for saints; neither filthiness, nor foolish talking, nor coarse jesting, which are not fitting, but rather give thanks. For you know that no fornicator, unclean person, nor covetous man, who is an idolater, has any inheritance in the kingdom of Christ and God. Let no one deceive you with empty words, for because of these things the wrath of God comes upon the sons of disobedience. Therefore do not be partakers with them." Therefore do not be partakers with them! (Repeat)

We may never know the whole background story of Mary Magdalene but she made biblical history as a leader among women. This faithful, devoted and dedicated follower of Christ was the first to witness His resurrection.

DR. JACQUELINE HARDY HARRIS

CAN I TELL MARY'S STORY?

Yes, early Sunday morning, Mary Magdalene saw the stone had been removed from the entrance of the tomb; she hurried to Jerusalem and convinced Peter and John to come and see the empty tomb. What intrigued me about this leader among women, is that she clearly was respected by her fellow disciples because they wasted no time running back with her to the tomb.

But what I really admire about Mary Magdalene is that even after the death of Christ, she never left his side. She remained weeping outside of the tomb, unwilling to abandon her Savior. Because nobody really knew all that he'd done for her, but her! Nobody knew how far he had brought her, how long he had kept her!

My beloved there will be some valleys in your life and if you have not stumbled into one, you just keep on living.

Maybe you have never been sick, I mean really sick and the doctors gave up on you. Your own family called you helpless and hopeless. Even your so-called friends turned their backs on you and walked away.

Then just when you were about to drown in your own tears you hear a gentle and soothing voice call out your name: "Mary", why are you crying?" Who is it you are looking for?

Do you remember when He heard your cry? Do you remember when he answered your prayer? Do you remember when he saved you?

Do you remember when He reached out of I don't know where, with

I don't know what, and made a way out of no way just for you?

Saints, I remember and that's why I can boldly say, If The Lord, Never Does Anything Else For Me, He's Done Enough!

CONCLUSION

My beloved, before Jesus returned to his heavenly home, He gave Mary Magdalene an assignment: "Go to my brothers and tell them, 'I am returning to my Father and your Father, to my God and your God." Mary took her mission very serious. This first Itinerant Elder preacher (smile) ran and took the good news of the gospel to the other disciples, "I have seen the Lord!" God's not dead, He is alive!

Song writer said, *Oh Mary don't you weep, go tell Martha not to moan!*

Today's text is a personal, undeniable testimony, setting an example for you and me today. Like Mary Magdalene we are called to be living witnesses of Jesus Christ.

So just like Mary Magdalene, "If you can't tell it, let me tell it" ...

God has been so good to me! He forgives all my sins, redeemed my life from the very pit of hell, crowns me with His loving-kindness and His tender mercies; He satisfies my mouth with good things so that my youth is renewed like the eagle's.

Yes, He saved me, He washed me with His blood, He sanctified me with His love, He has made me whole, and He has made me bold!

Because I know, good God almighty, I know that my Redeemer lives!

And He shall stand at last on this old earth.

And after I've labored in His field and done all that the good Lord has asked me to do, *when my skin is destroyed, this I know, that in my flesh I shall see God, Whom I shall see for myself, and my eyes shall behold Him, and not another!*

If The Lord, Never Does Anything Else For Me, He's Done Enough!

Doers Of The Word Of God

SCRIPTURE: James 1:19-27   Luke 6:46-49
SUBJECT: Doers of the Word of God

INTRODUCTION:
This Epistle of James was addressed to the Jewish Christians who were beset with problems that were testing their faith; James was concerned that they were succumbing to impatience, bitterness, materialism, disunity, and spiritual apathy.

James encouraged and instructed them that genuine faith in regards to trials, tribulations and tests are designed to produce mature endurance and a sense of dependence upon God. He goes on to say that a righteous response to tests requires that one be "swift to hear, slow to speak, and slow to wrath".

This brings us to our text today, which summarizes the remaining of James' Epistle; quickness of hearing involves one thing: obedience to God's Word! In other words, true hearing means more than just listening; the Word must be applied. True faith in the Word of God produces Godly reactions. We must be Doers of God's Word, Amen!

DR. JACQUELINE HARDY HARRIS

JAMES 1:19-27 NEW KING JAMES VERSION

19 So then, my beloved brethren, let every man be swift to hear, slow to speak, slow to wrath; 20 for the wrath of man does not produce the righteousness of God. 21 Therefore lay aside all filthiness and overflow of wickedness, and receive with meekness the implanted word, which is able to save your souls. 22 But be doers of the word, and not hearers only, deceiving yourselves. 23 For if anyone is a hearer of the word and not a doer, he is like a man observing his natural face in a mirror; 24 for he observes himself, goes away, and immediately forgets what kind of man he was.

25 But he who looks into the perfect law of liberty and continues in it, and is not a forgetful hearer but a doer of the work, this one will be blessed in what he does. 26 If anyone among you thinks he is religious, and does not bridle his tongue but deceives his own heart, this one's religion is useless. 27 Pure and undefiled religion before God and the Father is this: to visit orphans and widows in their trouble, and to keep oneself unspotted from the world.

Sermon

JAMES 1:19, 20, 21:

"Therefore, my beloved brethren, let every man be swift to hear, slow to speak, slow to wrath; for the wrath of man does not produce

> the righteousness' of God. Therefore lay aside all filthiness and overflow of wickedness, and receive with meekness the implanted word, which is able to save your souls."

The Apostle Paul said this in Romans,

> "How then shall they call on Him in whom they have not believed? And how shall they believe in Him of whom they have not heard. And how shall they hear without a preacher?"

In other words, we the ministers of God must first study to show ourselves approved unto God, a workman who needs not be ashamed, rightly dividing the Word of Truth; which is the Word of God. Then we must teach this engrafted Word to the people of God.

Why, simply because the Word of God is living and powerful, sharper than any two-edged sword, piercing even to the division of the soul and spirit, and joints and marrow, and is a discerner of the thoughts and intents of the heart.

My beloved, "Faith comes by hearing, and hearing by the Word of God." (Romans 10: 17)

So, as we mature in our faith, the Word of God, through the indwelling help of the Holy Spirit, begins to produce a change in our attitudes, speech, and temperament.

You don't do what you use to do, you don't say what you use to say, you don't go where you use to go, you just can't be with who you use to be with, and praise be to God, you're not as quickly infuriated or angered like you use to be!

Somebody say Amen!

JAMES 1: 22, 23, 24:

> "But be doers of the word, and not just hearers only, deceiving yourselves. For if anyone is a hearer of the word and not a doer, he is like a man observing his natural face in a mirror; for he observes himself, goes away, and immediately forgets what kind of man he was."

The key word in this passage is "Doer". True faith should always result in actions. A faith that produces no change is not a saving faith. The Apostle Paul said, "Faith without works is dead."

The Lord has given each saint of God spiritual gifts, to be used for the upbuilding of His kingdom. And I say to you, God is not unjust to forget your work and labor of love which you have shown toward His name.

I encourage you to not become sluggish or slothful, but keep the faith and continue to do good works. So that when you look into the mirror each day you will know who you are; "For we are His workmanship created in Christ Jesus for good works, which God prepared beforehand that we should walk in them." (Ephesians 2:10)

If you sing, sing to the glory of God! If you dance, then dance to the glory of God! Amen!

JAMES 1: 25, 26, 27:

> "But he who looks into the perfect law of liberty and continues in it, and is not a forgetful hearer but doer of work, this one will be blessed in what he does.

If anyone among you thinks he is religious, and does not bridle his tongue but deceives his own heart, this one's religion is useless.

Pure and undefiled religion before God and the Father is this: to visit orphans and widows, in their trouble, and keep oneself unspotted from the world."

CONCLUSION

My brothers and my sisters, James brings the text to a conclusion with these final verses.

First, James challenges our outward test of faith. We must be obedient doers of the Word of God.

Second, He admonishes us that if we say we are religious, then we should act and sound like we are religious-Christians.

And last but not least, James gives us examples of pure and untainted religion:

1. Visit the orphans and widows in their time of trouble
2. Keep yourselves unspotted from the world

Saints, the strong pulls of worldliness and wealth create conflicts that are harmful to the growth of our faith. The world system is at enmity with God, and the pursuit of its pleasures only produces covetousness, envy, fighting, and arrogance.

As believers, our only alternative is submission to God in a humble and repentant spirit.

This meek and repentant spirit will produce a transformed attitude towards others as well. We can begin to sincerely care for the oppressed, downtrodden, sick and shut-in, elderly, widows, and the fatherless and motherless.

Jesus said, in (Matthew 25:40) "Inasmuch as you have done it unto one of the least of these my brethren, you have done it to me"

I tell people that I'm no better than you, I just know better. Since, I know better, I am compelled to do better. You're looking at me kind of funny, let me see if I can put it another way;

Yes, I'm no better than you, I just know better;

- I know better than to trust any other god but my God!
- I know better than to worship any other god but my God!
- I know better than to use my God's name in vain!
- I know better than to be doing anything but thinking about Jesus on the Sabbath Day!
- I know better than to disrespect or dishonor my parents!
- I know better than to kill!
- I know better than to mess with somebody else's husband/wife!
- I know better than to take anything that belongs to others!
- I know better than to lie about others!

- I know better than to be anxious about anything, but to be content and satisfied with what the good Lord has given me!

What about you? Do you know better? Are you a Doer of the Word?

The songwriter said it best...

Since I met this blessed Savior,
Since He cleansed and made me whole,
I will never cease to praise Him; I'll shout it while eternity rolls;
He touched me, O He touched me,
And O the joy that floods my soul! Something happened,
And now I know, He touched me and made me whole!

I compel you to be Doers of the Word, and not just Hearers only!

Disorderly Conduct

SCRIPTURE: 2 Thessalonians 3:1-18
SUBJECT: Disorderly Conduct among the Saints

INTRODUCTION:
Disorderly Conduct: Virginia Code §18.2-415 makes it a class-1 misdemeanor for disorderly conduct when an individual, "with the intent to cause public inconvenience, annoyance or alarm, or recklessly creating a risk thereof. " The prohibited behavior must have occurred in a public place as opposed to a private venue. Furthermore, the conduct must have a direct tendency to cause acts of violence.

This is what the Virginia Law constitutes Disorderly Conduct; but what does the does the Word of God say about disorderly conduct?

The Apostle Paul again teaches and admonishes through the scriptures that we as Christians should try earnestly to behave ourselves. In other words, those who have received the gospel are to live according to the gospel.

He goes further and says this,"But we command you, brethren, in the name of our Lord Jesus Christ, that you withdraw from every brother who walks disorderly and not according to the tradition which he received from us."

Paul sternly reminds the saved Thessalonians that they must constantly be aware of who they are, "Followers of Christ", and that they must disassociate themselves from those engaging in Disorderly Conduct.

2 THESSALONIANS 3:1-18
(NEW KING JAMES VERSION)

1   Finally, brethren, pray for us, that the word of the Lord may run swiftly and be glorified, just as it is with you, 2 and that we may be delivered from unreasonable and wicked men; for not all have faith. 3 But the Lord is faithful, who will establish you and guard you from the evil one. 4 And we have confidence in the Lord concerning you, both that you do and will do the things we command you. 5 Now may the Lord direct your hearts into the love of God and into the patience of Christ. 6 But we command you, brethren, in the name of our Lord Jesus Christ, that you withdraw from every brother who walks disorderly and not according to the tradition which he received from us. 7 For you yourselves know how you ought to follow us, for we were not disorderly among you; 8 nor did we eat anyone's bread free of charge, but worked with labor and toil night and day, that we might not be a burden to any of you, 9 not because we do not have authority, but to make ourselves an example of how you should follow us. 10 For even when we were with you, we commanded you this: If anyone will not work, neither shall he

eat. 11 For we hear that there are some who walk among you in a disorderly manner, not working at all, but are busybodies. 12 Now those who are such we command and exhort through our Lord Jesus Christ that they work in quietness and eat their own bread. 13 But as for you, brethren, do not grow weary in doing good. 14 And if anyone does not obey our word in this epistle, note that person and do not keep company with him, that he may be ashamed. 15 Yet do not count him as an enemy, but admonish him as a brother. 16 Now may the Lord of peace Himself give you peace always in every way. The Lord be with you all. 17 The salutation of Paul with my own hand, which is a sign in every epistle; so I write. 18 The grace of our Lord Jesus Christ be with you all. Amen.

Sermon

2 THESSALONIANS 3:6

"But we command you, brethren, in the name of our Lord Jesus Christ, that you withdraw from every brother who walks disorderly and not according to the tradition which he received from us."

Saints, we are Christians, followers of Christ. This should be apparent in our speech, disposition and conduct. A follower of Christ should not be counted among the "I-aints", but among the "Saints". Not busybodies but busy doing the work of the Lord. A Christian does not have a slothful or idle countenance. The doctrine of the Lord's return requires a balance of waiting and working.

Paul warned the Thessalonians and he speaks to us today. The world is watching your Christian conduct. Is it disorderly? Are you behaving as a saint of God? Preachers, what are CNN reporters saying about your behavior? Let's get real. Are you a follower of the in-crowd, down-low crowd or Jesus Christ?

Much like the Apostle Paul, I really feel this way, "Follow me as I follow Christ"; in others words:

- I have no right telling you to be holy, if I'm not holy!
- I must walk the walk, before I can talk the talk!
- I must practice what I preach!

Why was Paul so hard on the Thessalonians?

Not long after the Thessalonians had received Paul's first letter exhorting on the coming *"Day of the Lord"* they fell prey to false teachers and their outright deceptions; thinking the day of the Lord had already come to past.

So, Paul wrote this second letter to correct and encourage them to continue the faith. Paul also reproves those who have decided to cease from working because they also believed the coming of Christ was near.

Paul corrects and assures the Thessalonians that the day of the Lord is yet in the future and will not arrive unannounced. This tactful apostle then gives a final sharp word of command to those who have been using the truth of Christ's return as an excuse for disorderly conduct.

14 And if anyone does not obey our word in this epistle, note that person and do not keep company with him, that he may be ashamed.

15 Yet do not count him as an enemy, but admonish him as a brother.

It is a great error and abuse of religion, to make it a cloak for idleness or any other sin. When we are idle, the devil and a corrupt heart will find something evil for you to do. The mind of mankind is a busy thing. If it is not employed in doing well, it will be employed in doing evil.

For example, have you ever hung-out with a thief? Did you notice that they are constantly thinking about what they can take from someone?

Have you been around individuals who are lazy, and insist they can not find any work?

Have you been around a person who gossips about everyone?

Have you had someone in your own home that eats everything but the kitchen sink and does not offer you a penny?

Paul is absolutely right when he said, *"do not keep company with them."* The act of disassociating yourselves from them will bring shame to them and hopefully with prayerful counsel, they will change their ways.

CONCLUSION

My brothers and my sisters, I know that it seems like Paul was harsh to the Thessalonians but from the confined walls of a prison he knew that their Christian integrity was in jeopardy. In fact, Paul said something scripturally phenomenal: "for not all have faith."

What Is Faith? "Now faith is the substance of things hoped for, the evidence of things unseen."

We must remember that we are Christians and "Faith" is the essence of our being; for we hope and wait patiently (doing good works), for the return of our Lord and Savior Jesus Christ!

We are Christians, followers of Christ, Saints of the most high God, saved, sanctified, being filled with the Holy Spirit; so we do not take matters into our own hands but take everything to God in prayer!

There is a beautiful hymn of the church and it goes like this...

HYMN # 410 AM I A SOLDIER OF THE CROSS

Am I a soldier of the cross a follower of the Lamb, and shall I fear to own His cause, or blush to speak His name?

Must I be carried to the skies on flowery beds ease, while others fought to win the prize, and sailed through bloody seas?

Sure I must fight if I would reign: increase my courage Lord; I'll bear the toil, endure the pain, supported by Thy word!

BENEDICTION:

Now may the Lord of peace Himself give you peace always in every way. The Lord be with you all.

Drop Your Net

SCRIPTURE: Matthew 4: 12-22
KEY VERSE: Matthew 4: 20
SUBJECT: Sacrificing All for Christ

INTRODUCTION:
Matthew teaches us through this text today that, servants of God must consider the responsibility and sacrifice of the ministry. Servants must be willing to come out of their comfort zones and move to an unfamiliar place. Sometimes that might mean quitting a job that pays well and has great benefits to work in a low-paying pastoral position. A true servant of God must be willing to make these drastic adjustments for the ministry. In other words *"Drop Your Net"* for the sake of Christ Jesus and kingdom building.

MATTHEW 4: 12-22
(NEW INTERNATIONAL VERSION)

(JESUS BEGINS TO PREACH)

12   When Jesus heard that John had been put in prison, he returned to Galilee. 13 Leaving Nazareth, he went and lived in Capernaum,

which was by the lake in the area of Zebulun and Naphtali— 14 to fulfill what was said through the prophet Isaiah: 15 "Land of Zebulun and land of Naphtali, the way to the sea, along the Jordan, Galilee of the Gentiles—16 the people living in darkness have seen a great light; on those living in the land of the shadow of death a light has dawned." 17 From that time on Jesus began to preach, "Repent, for the kingdom of heaven is near."

(THE CALLING OF THE FIRST DISCIPLES)

18 As Jesus was walking beside the Sea of Galilee, he saw two brothers, Simon called Peter and his brother Andrew. They were casting a net into the lake, for they were fishermen. 19 "Come, follow me," Jesus said, "and I will make you fishers of men." 20 At once they left their nets and followed him. 21 Going on from there, he saw two other brothers, James son of Zebedee and his brother John. They were in a boat with their father Zebedee, preparing their nets. Jesus called them, 22 and immediately they left the boat and their father and followed him.

Sermon

MOVING TO A BIGGER TOWN

John's imprisonment foreshadows Jesus' own suffering and becomes the signal for Jesus to begin his public ministry. The forerunner, John the Baptist, has now completed his mission of preparing the way.

Although Jesus had grown up in a relatively unpretentious town, the time had come for him to find a more suitable base for his urgent mission: Capernaum. Capernaum was a town with more people with greater notoriety and from which news would spread quickly around the perimeters of the lake of Galilee and perhaps also via the nearby trade route.

Although God may intend for some of us to serve in places like Nazareth for years, he is undoubtedly calling many of us to larger challenges at some point in our lives. I say "undoubtedly" because the vast majority of full-time Christian workers serve among people where the gospel is widely available, while fewer than thirty thousand serve the half of the world's population that has never received an adequate witness of the gospel, such as Africa and Haiti.

ABANDONING ALL FOR THE KINGDOM

Jesus' call to leave profession and family was radical. This was the type of demand that only the most uncompromising teacher would make. Jesus replied later in Matthew 8:20, *"Foxes have holes and birds of the air have nests, but the Son of Man has no place to lay his head."*

Although most scholars agree that Matthew's community included Christian scribes; Jesus did not call those professionally trained rabbis (who might have been so heavenly high that they were no earthly good) to be his disciples. He called skilled laborers and encouraged them that the talents they already had were serviceable in the kingdom.

This gives credence to the old saying, "God does not call the qualified he qualifies the called".

For you see my beloved, if God called shepherds like Moses and David to shepherd his people in Israel, why couldn't Jesus call fishermen to also be gatherers of the people of God? Even social workers, teachers and many others have skills and backgrounds from which we can draw and use in the church today. It is to our loss when congregations disregard the insights of these various professions among us.

JESUS' CALL SOMETIMES INVOLVES DOWNWARD MOBILITY (4:20)

Although skilled laborers had far less income than the wealthy (who made up perhaps 1 percent of the ancient population), they still were not among the roughly 90 percent of the population called peasants. Fishermen and family businesses like these were especially profitable. Even if the disciples followed Jesus only during certain seasons of the year, they could not easily return to their abandoned businesses. Therefore, the disciples paid a price economically to follow Jesus. Saints, could you just *"Drop Your Net?"*

The kingdom is like a precious treasure, worth the abandonment of all other treasures. Many of us today respond defensively, "I would abandon everything if Jesus asked me to, but he has not asked me to." Just maybe Jesus is asking but you are not listening... *He that if one has an ear, let them hear!*

DR. JACQUELINE HARDY HARRIS

THE CALL COSTS COMFORT AND CHALLENGES PRIORITY OF FAMILY

James and John abandoned not only the boat (representing their livelihood) but also their father and the family business (4:22).

In a society where teachers normally stressed no higher responsibility than the honor of parents, including economic responsibility for them; some people would view James' and John's behavior as scandalous.

Now Jesus is not saying kingdom building is an excuse to downplay our crucial responsibilities to our families. They too warrant our attention and our ministry, for *"charity begins at home"*.

God "calls" his servants, and that means we are not our own; we belong to God and we must first worship Him. The scripture clearly states "You shall not bow down to them or worship them; for I, the LORD your God, am a jealous God, punishing the children for the sin of the fathers to the third and fourth generation of those who hate me." EXODUS 20:5 NIV

Which brings me to this point, those of you who are single do not choose marriage partners who cannot bear your calling in the ministry. I'm speaking to someone over there, you know who you are. (Smile)

CONCLUSION

My brothers and my sisters, God's call to Christian servanthood demands faithfulness with or without popularity.

Popularity does not always translate into deep commitment in the end.

When the good Lord called his first Disciples, notice that they were already working, some laboring day and night. They were not lazy or idle. God is still calling those who are ready, willing and able to help in kingdom building.

This millennium, historians will record this decade as the point in time that America had to make sacrifices, witness the loss of jobs, businesses, homes, and schools, and the loss of lives due to wars. All of these things result in a significant negative change in the social and economic environment of every city and state. We have all been forced to hear a message saying: *"Drop Your Nets"*; whether we wanted to or not. So, I just made up my mind to do as the old songwriter:

All to Jesus I surrender, All to Him I freely give;
I will ever love and trust Him,
In His presence daily live.
All to Jesus I surrender, Humbly at His feet I bow,
Worldly pleasures all forsaken, Take me, Jesus take me now.
I surrender all, I surrender all, All to Thee my blessed Savior, I surrender all!

Fire Baptized!

SCRIPTURE: Matthew 3:1-17
KEY VERSE: Matthew 3:11
SUBJECT: Why do we baptize?

INTRODUCTION:
Today we will discuss one of the most holy Sacraments of the Church, Baptism; and through the help of the Holy Scriptures try to answer these questions:

1. Why do we baptize? 2. Who do we baptize? 3. Where do we baptize? 4. How do we baptize?

MATTHEW 3: 1-17
NEW KING JAMES VERSION

1   In those days John the Baptist came preaching in the wilderness of Judea,

2   and saying, "Repent, for the kingdom of heaven is at hand!"

3   For this is he who was spoken of by the prophet Isaiah, saying: "The voice of one crying in the wilderness: 'Prepare the way of the Lord; Make His paths straight.'"

4   Now John himself was clothed in camel's hair, with a leather belt around his waist; and his food was locusts and wild honey.

5   Then Jerusalem, all Judea, and all the region around the Jordan went out to him 6 and were baptized by him in the

Jordan, confessing their sins.

7   But when he saw many of the Pharisees and Sadducees coming to his baptism, he said to them, "Brood of vipers! Who warned you to flee from the wrath to come?

8   Therefore bear fruits worthy of repentance,

9   and do not think to say to yourselves, 'We have Abraham as our father.' For I say to you that God is able to raise up children to Abraham from these stones.

10 And even now the ax is laid to the root of the trees. Therefore every tree which does not bear good fruit is cut down and thrown into the fire.

11 I indeed baptize you with water unto repentance, but He who is coming after me is mightier than I, whose sandals I am not worthy to carry. He will baptize you with the Holy Spirit and fire.

12 His winnowing fan is in His hand, and He will thoroughly clean out His threshing floor, and

gather His wheat into the barn; but He will burn up the chaff with unquenchable fire."

Sermon:

After Malachi, there were no other prophets that came until "John the Baptist". He appeared first in the wilderness of Judea. This was not an uninhabited desert, but a part of the country not thickly populated. The doctrine John preached was repentance. The word repent - implies a total alteration in the mind, a change in judgment, disposition, and affections; to righteously consider your ways and change your mind. It is still as necessary this day to repent and humble ourselves, and to continue to "prepare the way of the Lord", as it was during the time of John the Baptist. There is still a great deal to be done to make way for Jesus Christ into the soul of mankind. Saints, nothing is more needful than the realization that we are all sinners and the conviction that we cannot be saved by our own righteousness. The way of sin and Satan is a crooked way; but to prepare a way for Christ, the paths must be made straight, (Hebrews 12:13).

John prepared the way for Christ. Many came to John's baptism, but few kept sacred the confession they made. Those who received John's doctrine and testified their repentance by confessing their sins, were ready to receive Jesus Christ's baptism of the Holy Spirit and Fire!

MATTHEW 3: 11

> "I indeed baptize you with water unto repentance, but He who is coming after me is mightier than I, whose sandals I am not worthy to carry. He will baptize you with the Holy Spirit and fire."

What is Baptism? Baptism is a ceremony in which one enters the Christian church family. It is an outward way of showing you are a believer in Jesus Christ. The baptism of a believer by water symbolizes the renewal and change in the believer's life. And it is a testimony to the Death, Burial, and Resurrection of Jesus Christ as the only way of salvation. Jesus said in Matthew 28:19,

> "Therefore go and make disciples of all nations, baptizing them in the name of the Father, and of the Son and of the Holy Spirit." Baptism is the critical step to discipleship! John the Baptist had the distinct privilege and honor of baptizing our Lord and Savior Jesus Christ: Matthew 3: 13-17; 13 Then Jesus came from Galilee to John at the Jordan to be baptized by him. 14 And John tried to prevent Him, saying, "I need to be baptized by You, and are You coming to me?" 15 But Jesus answered and said to him, "Permit it to be so now, for thus it is fitting for us to fulfill all righteousness. "Then he allowed Him. 16 When He had been baptized, Jesus came up immediately from the water; and behold, the heavens were opened to Him, and He saw the Spirit of God descending like a dove and alighting upon Him. 17 And

suddenly a voice came from heaven, saying, "This is My beloved Son, in whom I am well pleased."

John would immerse repentant sinners (those who had a "changed mind and heart"). John's baptism is still interpreted in the Christian church today:

1. Repentance: To regret, be remorseful of our sins
2. Confession: To plead or acknowledge guilt
3. Conversion: Believe in Jesus, the Resurrection and Eternal Life
4. New creature in Christ: Evidence of Changed Lives

JESUS' BAPTISM BY THE HOLY SPIRIT AND FIRE:

Now Jesus himself did not do the "water baptism" but this was done by his disciples. The scripture states in John 4:12 "The Pharisees heard that Jesus was gaining and baptizing more disciples than John, although in fact it was not Jesus who baptized, but his disciples." The Baptism of the Holy Spirit and Fire happens when you accept Jesus into your life. The Holy Spirit enters your heart with His saturating presence and purifies the believer. The Holy Spirit empowers and cleanses the believer in a spiritual baptism. The Baptism of the Holy Spirit testifies that you are washed, sanctified, set aside and justified in the name of the Lord Jesus and by The Spirit of God; you are uniquely born again! Now, I believe we know why and who gets baptized. So let's talk a little about where and how the African Methodist Episcopal Church baptizes. (Acts 8:26-40) As Phillip and the Eunuch went down the desert road, they came to some water. And the eunuch said, "See, here is water. What hinders me from being baptized?"

And so in the A. M. E. Church we offer these three choices of baptism:

1. Sprinkle: Church Infant- Adult
2. Pour: Church Infant-Adult
3. Immersion: Church Baptism Pool/Waterside: Youth-Adult

CONCLUSION:

My brothers and my sisters, when John the Baptist said, "He shall baptize you with the Holy Spirit and Fire", he simply meant that Jesus has the ability to immerse you and I into the presence of God the Father Almighty, so that we are uniquely aware of our sins and have a burning desire and need to be cleansed. Jesus said, "Most assuredly, I say to you, unless one is born of water and the Spirit, he cannot enter the kingdom of God. That which is born of the flesh is flesh, and that which is born of the spirit is spirit. Do not marvel that I said to you, 'You must be born again.' (John 3: 5, 6, 7)

To be Fire Baptized is to be convicted, converted and convinced that Jesus is Lord! To be signed, sealed and delivered by the Holy Spirit!

When Jesus said "You must be born again", He meant we must have a change of heart, mind, body, and soul and to simply become children of God. We must become as "newborn babes' like Gage Lincoln Mitchell, then "grow-up' and become great men and women in Christ Jesus.

Through the quickening power of the Holy Spirit, which comes to every individual who is born again, we begin to realize in our soul that we cannot live without God The Father, The Son and The Holy Spirit. Some of us tried to resist His love, struggled hopelessly to escape His loving arms. Then suddenly you begin to long for forgiveness, to be cleansed and to be set free from sin.

I believe the songwriter said it best...

I know I've been changed! I know I've been changed!
Cause the Angels in heaven done signed my name!
If you don't believe I've been redeemed;
Then follow me down to that old Jordan stream!
You see, I step in the water and the water was cold.
You know it chilled my body but not my soul!
Good God Almighty!
I know I've been changed! Saints, I know I've been changed!
Cause the Angels in heaven done signed my name!

God Ain't Through With Me Yet

SCRIPTURE: Psalm 51:1-17
KEY VERSES: Psalm 51:1-4
SUBJECT: God's Still Working on Me!

INTRODUCTION:
Every year, I've had the pleasure of watching the B. E. T. Gospel Celebration, hosted by the renowned comedian, philanthropist, T.V. and radio personality, author, proud husband and father, and West Virginia's very own Steve Harvey. What I liked most about the show is the great gospel singers such as Shirley Caesar, Marvin Sapp, Rance Allen and Fred Hammond just to name a few. Of course, I adore *Steve Harvey*; and what I love the most about him is his humility.

Steve always says before he starts the show, *"I'm a Christian, I am saved ya'll but God ain't through with me yet"*. In other words, Steve prepared us for maybe a few slip-ups in his vernacular (curse words) and that there were still some flaws in his personality and temperament. For over 13 years, the good Lord has been working on Steve and the B. E. T. Gospel Awards Show, Family Feud and the Steve Harvey Show. They have all been very successful!

Today through these inspirational scriptures in Psalm 51, I pray that each of us will realize as individuals, like *Steve Harvey* that… "God Ain't Through With Me Yet".

PSALM 51 (NEW KING JAMES VERSION)

1 Have mercy upon me, O God, According to Your lovingkindness; According to the multitude of Your tender mercies, Blot out my transgressions. 2 Wash me thoroughly from my iniquity, and cleanse me from my sin. 3 For I acknowledge my transgressions, And my sin is always before me. 4 Against You, You only, have I sinned, And done this evil in Your sight— That You may be found just when You speak, And blameless when You judge.

5 Behold, I was brought forth in iniquity, And in sin my mother conceived me. 6 Behold, You desire truth in the inward parts, And in the hidden part You will make me to know wisdom. 7 Purge me with hyssop, and I shall be clean; Wash me, and I shall be whiter than snow. 8 Make me hear joy and gladness, That the bones You have broken may rejoice. 9 Hide Your face from my sins, And blot out all my iniquities. 10 Create in me a clean heart, O God, And renew a steadfast spirit within me. 11 Do not cast me away from Your presence, And do not take Your Holy Spirit from me. 12 Restore to me the joy of Your salvation, And uphold me by Your generous Spirit. 13 Then I will teach transgressors Your ways, And sinners shall be converted to You. 14 Deliver me from the guilt of bloodshed, O God, The God of

my salvation, And my tongue shall sing aloud of Your righteousness. 15 O Lord, open my lips, And my mouth shall show forth Your praise. 16 For You do not desire sacrifice, or else I would give it; You do not delight in burnt offering. 17 The sacrifices of God are a broken spirit, A broken and a contrite heart— These, O God, You will not despise.

Sermon

Have you ever met anyone who acted like they were "holier than thou"? I'm sure you can recall some individuals whom you personally knew back in the day, your running partners, who have found *themselves* to be *saved* and now are so "heavenly high they are no earthly good". In other words, they have forgotten that they were just sinners saved by God's grace.

This text Psalm 51 classified as an "Individual Lament Psalm" is all about David the shepherd, musician, warrior, king and his cry to God of repentance.

Nathan the prophet went to David and made him aware of his sins of adultery with *Bathsheba* and the murder her husband *Uriah the Hittite*. Now David, being convinced of his sins, poured out his soul to God in prayer for mercy and grace and he was forgiven.

We can learn a lot from David. The first step to solving a problem is to admit that you have a problem:

> 3   For I acknowledge my transgressions, And my sin is always before me. 4 Against You, You

only, have I sinned, And done this evil in Your sight

David had such a deep awareness of his sin that he was continually thinking of it, with sorrow and shame. His sin was committed against God and His Commandments.

> 10 Create in me a clean heart, O God, And renew a steadfast spirit within me. 11 Do not cast me away from Your presence, And do not take Your Holy Spirit from me. 12 Restore to me the joy of Your salvation, And uphold me by Your generous Spirit.

David now saw, more than ever, what an unclean heart he had, and sadly laments it. He sees that it is not in his own power to amend it, and therefore begs that God would create in him a clean heart. He knew he had by his sin grieved the Holy Spirit, and provoked Him to withdraw.

The Holy Spirit will not dwell in an unclean place and David dreads this more than anything. Sin had made him weak; so, David prays, Lord please uphold me with thy Spirit.

My beloved, Confession is not only good for the soul, it saves the soul.

1ST JOHN 1: 9

> "If we confess our sins, He is faithful and just to forgive us our sins and to cleanse us from all unrighteousness."

Also, **ROMANS 10:9 SAYS,**

"that if you confess with your mouth the Lord Jesus and believe in your heart that God has raised Him from the dead, you will be saved".

Saints, I've come to know that those who have been through spiritual tests and trials, know how to have pity and pray for others who are afflicted because God brought them out. Like the songwriter Marvin Sapp ministers...

Never would have made it, never could have made it without you!
I would have lost it all, but now I see that you were there for me.
I'm stronger; I'm wiser, I'm better, so much better.
When I look back over all He brought me through,
I realize I had Him to bring me through!
Never would have made it, never could have made it without you!
I would have lost it all, but now I see that you were there for me.

CONCLUSION

17   The sacrifices of God are a broken spirit, A broken and a contrite heart— These, O God, You will not despise.

My brothers and my sisters, David was not perfect, he sinned before God by thought, word and deed. Yet, David still remained the "Apple of His Father's eye", because David always had a contrite, repentant and remorseful heart before God. You see David knew he was a "work in progress" and that God was not through with him yet.

Through David's story we now know that a "Saint is just a Sinner who fell down and got back up".

You will not be able to avoid the temptation of sin; not while the blood is running warm in your veins. You see temptation is not the dilemma. Yielding to the temptation is the sin. The Apostle Paul said this: (1st Corinthians 10:13 NKJV)

> "No temptation has overtaken you except such as is common to man; but God is faithful, who will not allow you to be tempted beyond what you are able, but with the temptation will also make the way of escape, that you may be able to bear it."

We have a Savior who has endured every temptation, suffering, and humiliation without one blot of sin. Jesus has proven to us that we can escape temptation but we need Him and the power of the Holy Spirit, our helper, keeper, and strengthener.

My brothers and my sisters, do not resist the Holy Spirit your very present help. Allow Him to mold you and shape you into the person God wants you to be. When folks start getting on your sanctified nerves by questioning your salvation, don't get mad and sin, just take a deep calm breath, then boldly say, "God Ain't Through With Me Yet!

THE SONGWRITER SAID IT BEST...

Yield not to temptation, for yielding is sin; Each victory will help you some other to win; Fight manfully onward, dark passions subdue; Look ever to Jesus, He'll carry you through.
Ask the Savior to help you, Comfort, Strengthen and Keep you He is willing to aid you, He will carry you through!

Grandma Told Me To Try Jesus

SCRIPTURE: 2nd Timothy 1: 1-14
KEY VERSE: 2nd Timothy 1: 5
SUBJECT: The Godly Care and Instructions of Grandparents

INTRODUCTION:

The apostle Paul knows as he writes this final epistle that his days on earth are quickly drawing to a close. He is about to relinquish his heavy burdens, so this godly apostle seeks to challenge and strengthen his somewhat timid but faithful associate, Timothy, in his difficult ministry in Ephesus. Paul expresses his thanksgiving for Timothy's genuine faith, and then encourages him to stand firm in the power of the gospel and to overcome any fear in the face of opposition. Paul urges his younger helper to overcome his natural shyness and boldly proclaim the gospel even if it means that he will suffer for doing so. Paul then declared that he thanked God for Timothy's faith, which dwelt first with his grandmother Lois and then with Timothy's mother Eunice. And the Spirit of a Living God persuaded Paul that this genuine faith continued to dwell in Timothy!

DR. JACQUELINE HARDY HARRIS

2ND TIMOTHY 1: 1-14 NKJV

(1) Paul, an apostle of Jesus Christ by the will of God, according to the promise of life which is in Christ Jesus, (2) To Timothy, a beloved son: Grace, mercy, and peace from God the Father and Christ Jesus our Lord. (3) I thank God, whom I serve with a pure conscience, as my forefathers did, as without ceasing I remember you in my prayers night and day, (4) greatly desiring to see you, being mindful of your tears, that I may be filled with joy, (5) when I call to remembrance the genuine faith that is in you, which dwelt first in your grandmother Lois and your mother Eunice, and I am persuaded is in you also. (6) Therefore I remind you to stir up the gift of God which is in you through the laying on of my hands. (7) For God has not given us a spirit of fear, but of power and of love and of a sound mind.

(8) Therefore do not be ashamed of the testimony of our Lord, nor of me His prisoner, but share with me in the sufferings for the gospel according to the power of God, (9) who has saved us and called us with a holy calling, not according to our works, but according to His own purpose and grace which was given to us in Christ Jesus before time began, (10) but has now been revealed by the appearing of our Savior Jesus Christ, who has abolished death and brought life and immortality to light through the gospel, (11) to which I was appointed a preacher, an apostle, and a teacher of the Gentiles. (12) For this reason I

also suffer these things; nevertheless I am not ashamed, for I know whom I have believed and am persuaded that He is able to keep what I have committed to Him until that Day. (13) Hold fast the pattern of sound words which you have heard from me, in faith and love which are in Christ Jesus. (14) That good thing which was committed to you, keep by the Holy Spirit who dwells in us.

Sermon

Lois, the grandmother and Eunice the mother of Timothy have been honored as model mentors for rearing children. They both had genuine faith and passed it on to Timothy. This grandmother and mother realized early in their lives that the scriptures were given by inspiration from God and that they are profitable for doctrine, for reproof, for correction, and for instruction in righteousness, that the man or woman of God may be complete and thoroughly equipped for every good work!

I'm lead to believe with this knowledge of the scriptures that grandmother Lois and mother Eunice teamed up on little Timothy and began to train him up in the way that he should go and they were assured by the Word of God that when Timothy got older he would not depart from it. (Proverbs 22: 15)

I could imagine that they both knew "Foolishness is bound in the heart of a child but the rod of correction shall drive it far from him". (Proverbs 22: 15)

Saints, I remember my grandmother saying, "Spare the rod, spoil the child". Proverbs 13: 24, also says, "He who spares his rod hates his son, but he who loves him disciplines him promptly".

In other words, it's timeout for "Time-Out". In fact the only time out my Grandmamma or Momma honored was the timeout they took to catch their breath between putting a whipping on my butt! Saints, you'd better get back to the ways of your grandparents before your children start doing real time in the County Jail.

You see the first thing my grandmother and parents instilled in me was to fear God! Because to fear God was the beginning of wisdom and the knowledge of the Holy One, Jesus Christ, is understanding.

I was also taught the Ten Commandments. Grandmother Anna Brown being an A.M. E. told me, "Baby the Ten Commandments were laws given by God as guidelines for daily living. These laws are called the Decalogue, from the Greek word "Ten Words". Church School Superintendent William Hayes often says, *"They are Ten Commandments not Ten Suggestions!"*

TEN COMMANDMENTS

1. Trust God only. (Ex. 20:3,4)
2. Worship God only. (Ex. 20:5,6)
3. Use God's name in ways to honor Him. (Ex. 20:7)

4. Rest on the Sabbath day and think about God. (Ex. 20:8-11)
5. Respect and obey your parents. (Ex.20: 12)
6. Protect and respect human life. (Ex. 20: 13)
7. Be true to your husband and wife. EX.20:14)
8. Do not take what belongs to others. (Ex. 20: 15)
9. Do not lie on others. (Ex, 20:16)
10. Be satisfied with what you have. (Ex. 20: 17)

About 1,300 years after God gave these commandments, Jesus upheld them. He actually placed them on a higher plane, demanding that the spirit, as well as the legal aspects of the law be observed. In fact HE placed his stamp of approval on the Commandments by declaring, "Do not think I came to destroy the Law or the Prophets. I did not come to destroy but to fulfill." (Matt. 5: 17)

CONCLUSION

My brothers and my sisters, God has not given us the spirit of fear, but the spirit of power, courage and resolution, to meet difficulties and dangers. HE has also given us the spirit of love for him, which will carry us through any opposition. Lastly, HE has given us the spirit of a sound mind, a made-up mind.

The Holy Spirit is not the author of a timid or cowardly disposition, or of slavish fears. I often say the Lord didn't choose any scary or lazy people, they were courageously and diligently doing something constructive when he called them! Those who cleave to the gospel need not be ashamed, the cause of the gospel will always bear them out. Those who oppose it, will ever be ashamed.

The apostle Paul had trusted his life, his soul, and eternal interests, to the Lord Jesus. He knew that no one else could deliver and secure his soul through the trials of life or death.

My beloved Grandmother Anna Brown was just like Timothy's grandmother Lois; I was about 11 years old when grandmother Anna Brown died, to this day I can not forget her words of wisdom and the first prayer she taught me;

> "Now I lay me down to sleep, I pray the Lord my soul to keep, If I should die before I wake, I pray the Lord my soul to take! Amen."

My grandmother prayed for me both night and day. I really thought she was going to be around forever. Like Paul, the time of her departure was at hand. She fought the good fight of faith and she finished her race. Finally, she can receive her crown of righteousness. The Lord, the righteous Judge, will give it to her on that great Day of the Lord, and not just her but to me and you and all who have loved the Lord. (2nd Tim. 4:6-8)

I compel you young people, to observe the commandments of your father. Forsake not the teaching of your mother or (Grandparents). Bind them continually in your heart, and tie them around your neck (like a yoke). When you walk about, they will guide you. When you sleep, they will watch over you, and when you awake they will talk to you. (Proverbs 6:20-23)

Grandma's Hands

I am reminded of a song by artist Bill Withers entitled, Grandma's Hands. It speaks to that sweet feeling of reuniting with Grandma in heaven and feeling the touch of her soft hands. The song also proves that the wisdom of grandma is more valuable than we can ever know. We must take heed to wisdom to live our greatest blessings.

Fasting: The Secret Weapon

SCRIPTURE: Matthew 17: 14-21   Matthew 6:17, 18
SUBJECT: The Preparation for Fasting

INTRODUCTION:

Why is fasting important? "Fasting" is the secret weapon for spiritual renewal, for guidance, for healing, for the resolution of problems, and for special grace to handle difficult situations. Through fasting and prayer we humble ourselves before God so the Holy Spirit will stir our souls, awaken our churches, and heal our land (2 Chronicles 7:14).

In our text, the disciples came to Jesus privately after they were unable to rebuke a demon from an epileptic child and said, "Why could we not cast it out?" Jesus said, "However, this kind does not go out except by prayer and fasting." Today we will learn (5) essential steps in preparation for fasting.

MATTHEW 17:14-21
(NEW KING JAMES VERSION)

14   "And when they had come to the multitude, a man came to Him, kneeling down to Him and saying, 15 "Lord, have mercy on my son,

for he is an epileptic and suffers severely; for he often falls into the fire and often into the water. 16 So I brought him to Your disciples, but they could not cure him." 17 Then Jesus answered and said, "O faithless and perverse generation, how long shall I be with you? How long shall I bear with you? Bring him here to Me." 18 And Jesus rebuked the demon, and it came out of him; and the child was cured from that very hour. 19 Then the disciples came to Jesus privately and said, "Why could we not cast it out?" 20 So Jesus said to them, "Because of your unbelief; for assuredly, I say to you, if you have faith as a mustard seed, you will say to this mountain, 'Move from here to there,' and it will move; and nothing will be impossible for you. 21 However, this kind does not go out except by prayer and fasting."

MATTHEW 6:17-18
(NEW KING JAMES VERSION)

17 "But you, when you fast, anoint your head and wash your face, 18 so that you do not appear to men to be fasting, but to your Father who is in the secret place; and your Father who sees in secret will reward you openly."

STEP 1: MAKE YOUR COMMITMENT

Pray about the kind of fast you should undertake. Jesus implied that all of His followers should fast (Matthew 6:16-18; 9:14, 15) For Him it was a matter of when believers would fast, not if they would do it. Before you fast, decide the following up front:

- How long you will fast - one meal, one day, a week, several weeks, forty days (beginners should start slowly, building up to longer fasts.)
- The type of fast God wants you to undertake (such as water only, or water and juices, what types of juices you will drink and how often).
- What physical or social activities you will restrict?
- How much time each day you will devote to prayer and God's Word?

Making these commitments ahead of time will help you sustain your fast when physical temptations and life's pressures tempt you to abandon it.

STEP 2: PREPARE YOURSELF SPIRITUALLY

The very foundation of fasting and prayer is repentance. Unconfessed sin will hinder your prayers. Here are several things you can do to prepare your heart:

- Ask God to help you make a comprehensive list of your sins.
- Confess every sin that the Holy Spirit calls to your remembrance and accept God's forgiveness (1 John 1:9).

- Seek forgiveness from all whom you have offended, and forgive all who have hurt you (Mark 11:25; Luke 11:4; 17:3,4).
- Ask God to fill you with His Holy Spirit according to His command in Ephesians 5:18 and His promise in 1 John 5:14, 15.
- Surrender your life fully to Jesus Christ as your Lord and Master and refuse to obey your worldly nature (Romans 12:1, 2).
- Meditate on the attributes of God, His love, sovereignty, power, wisdom, faithfulness, grace, compassion, and others (Psalm 48:9,10; 103:1-8, 11-13).
- Begin your time of fasting and prayer with an expectant heart (Hebrews 11:6).

STEP 3: PREPARE YOURSELF PHYSICALLY

Fasting requires reasonable precautions. Consult your physician first, especially if you take prescription medication or have a chronic ailment. Some persons should never fast without professional supervision.

Physical preparation makes the drastic change in your eating routine a little easier so that you can turn your full attention to the Lord in prayer.

- Do not rush into your fast. Prepare your body.

- Eat raw fruit and vegetables for two days before starting a fast.
- Eat smaller meals before starting a fast.
- Avoid high-fat and sugary foods.

Your time of fasting and prayer has come. You are abstaining from all solid foods and have begun to seek the Lord. Here are some helpful suggestions to consider:

- Avoid drugs, even natural herbal drugs and homeopathic remedies. Medication should be withdrawn only with your physician's supervision.
- Limit your activity. Exercise only moderately. Walk one to three miles each day if convenient and comfortable. Rest as much as your schedule will permit.
- Prepare yourself for temporary mental discomforts, such as impatience, crankiness, and anxiety.
- Expect some physical discomforts, especially on the second day. You may have fleeting hunger pains, dizziness, or the "blahs".
- Withdrawal from caffeine and sugar may cause headaches. Physical annoyances may also include weakness, tiredness, or sleeplessness.

The first two or three days are usually the hardest. As you continue to fast, you will likely experience a sense of well-being both physically and spiritually. However, should you feel hunger pains, increase your liquid intake.

STEP 4: PUT YOURSELF ON A SCHEDULE

For maximum spiritual benefit set aside ample time to be alone with the Lord. Listen for His leading. The more time you spend with Him, the more meaningful your fast will be.

MORNING
- Begin your day in praise and worship.
- Read and meditate on God's Word, preferably on your knees.
- Invite the Holy Spirit to work in you to do His good pleasure according to Philippians 2:13.
- Invite God to use you. Ask Him to show you how to influence your life, your family, your church, your community, your country, and beyond.
- Pray for His vision for your life and empowerment to do His will.

NOON
- Return to prayer and God's Word.
- Take a short prayer walk.
- Spend time in intercessory prayer for your community's and nation's leaders, for the world's unreached millions, for your family or special needs.

EVENING
- Get alone for an unhurried time of "seeking His face".
- If others are fasting with you, meet together for prayer.
- Avoid television or any other distraction that may dampen your spiritual focus.

When possible, begin and end each day with your spouse for a brief time of praise and thanksgiving to God. Longer periods of time with our Lord in prayer and study of His Word are often better spent alone.

TIPS ON JUICE FASTING
- Drinking fruit juice will decrease your hunger pains and give you some natural sugar energy. The taste and lift will motivate and strengthen you to continue.
- The best juices are made from fresh watermelon, lemons, grapes, apples, cabbage, beets, carrots, celery, or leafy green vegetables. In cold weather, you may enjoy a warm vegetable broth.
- Mix acidic juices (orange and tomato) with water for your stomach's sake.
- Avoid caffeinated drinks. And avoid chewing gum or mints, even if your breath is bad. They stimulate digestive action in your stomach.

When your designated time for fasting is finished, you will begin to eat again. But how you break your fast is extremely important for your physical and spiritual well-being.

STEP 5: END YOUR FAST GRADUALLY

Begin eating gradually. Do not eat solid foods immediately after your fast. Suddenly reintroducing solid food to your stomach and digestive tract will likely have negative, even dangerous, consequences.

Try several smaller meals or snacks each day. If you end your fast gradually, the beneficial physical and spiritual effects will result in continued good health.

HERE ARE SOME SUGGESTIONS TO HELP YOU END YOUR FAST PROPERLY:

- Break an extended water fast with fruit such as watermelon.
- Gradually return to regular eating with several small snacks during the first few days. Start with a little soup and fresh fruit such as watermelon and cantaloupe.
- Advance to a few tablespoons of solid foods such as raw fruits and vegetables or a raw salad and baked potato.

CONCLUSION:

Jesus said these profound words in Matthew 6:17-18 "But you, when you fast, anoint your head and wash your face, so that you do not appear to men to be fasting, but to your Father who is in the secret place; and your Father who sees in secret will reward you openly."

If you sincerely humble yourself before the Lord, repent, pray, and seek God's face; if you consistently meditate on His Word, you will experience a heightened awareness of His presence (John 14:21). The Lord will give you fresh, new spiritual insights. Your confidence and faith in God will be strengthened. You will feel mentally, spiritually, and physically refreshed. And last but not least, you will see answers to your prayers!

A single fast, however, is not a spiritual cure-all. Just as we need fresh infillings of the Holy Spirit daily, we also need new times of fasting before God. A 24-hour fast each week has been greatly rewarding for many pastors/ministers.

It takes time to build your spiritual fasting muscles. If you fail to make it through your first fast, do not be discouraged. You may have tried to fast too long the first time out, or your may need to strengthen your understanding. As soon as possible, undertake another fast until you do succeed. God will honor you for your faithfulness.

The Songwriter said it best. We can carry everything to God in prayer.

Don't Count Me Out!

SCRIPTURE: Matthew 26: 26-35, 69-75
SUBJECT: Complexities of the Apostle Peter

INTRODUCTION:
July 4, we celebrate our nation's birthday and anniversary of freedom and independence. We do this by having backyard barbecues, gatherings of family and friends to eat, dance, and watch games and fireworks. Speaking of games, the #1 sport in America is the game of baseball. This game can be very exciting, then again it can drag-on with scoreless innings for hours. The most important element of the game of baseball is that "three strikes and you're out".

    The Apostle Peter reminds us today, that thanks be to God and his beloved Son Jesus Christ that in the *game of life* even if we stumble and fall, we don't necessarily have to be counted out.

MATTHEW 26: 31-34, 69-75
JESUS PREDICTS PETER'S DENIAL

> 31   Then Jesus said to them, "All of you will be made to stumble because of Me this night, for it is written: 'I will strike the Shepherd, And the sheep of the flock will be scattered.' 32 But after I have been raised, I will go before you to

Galilee." 33 Peter answered and said to Him, "Even if all are made to stumble because of You, I will never be made to stumble." 34 Jesus said to him, "Assuredly, I say to you that this night, before the rooster crows, you will deny Me three times."

PETER DENIES JESUS, AND WEEPS BITTERLY

69 Now Peter sat outside in the courtyard. And a servant girl came to him, saying, "You also were with Jesus of Galilee." 70 But he denied it before them all, saying, "I do not know what you are saying." 71 And when he had gone out to the gateway, another girl saw him and said to those who were there, "This fellow also was with Jesus of Nazareth." 72 But again he denied with an oath, "I do not know the Man!" 73 And a little later those who stood by came up and said to Peter, "Surely you also are one of them, for your speech betrays you." 74 Then he began to curse and swear, saying, "I do not know the Man!" Immediately a rooster crowed. 75 And Peter remembered the word of Jesus who had said to him, "Before the rooster crows, you will deny Me three times." So he went out and wept bitterly.

Sermon

The scripture lesson begins with the *Lord's Supper* (Holy Communion) being introduced to the disciples. "Take, eat; this is My body." 27 Then He took the cup, and gave thanks, and gave it to them, saying, "Drink from it, all of you. 28 For this is My blood of the new covenant, which is shed for many for the remission of sins.

Every first Sunday the African Methodist Episcopal Church compels the congregation to eat the communion wafer, representing the act of partaking in the grace of Christ and the blessed fruits of the breaking of his body. The blood of Christ is signified and represented by the wine. He gave thanks, to teach us to look to God in every part of this sacred ordinance; for Jesus said, "This do in remembrance of me". (Luke 22: 19)

MATTHEW 26: 31, 32

> "Then Jesus said to them, "All of you will be made to stumble because of Me this night, for it is written: 'I will strike the Shepherd, And the sheep of the flock will be scattered. But after I have been raised, I will go before you to Galilee."

Jesus knew that his disciples would soon fall by the wayside. He tried to prepare them by teaching about faith, prayer and fasting but to no avail. They could not stay awake with him and pray, even in the garden of Gethsemane. Jesus' time of the "great passion" was approaching and his disciples were not ready for Christ's crucifixion on Calvary's cross. Which brings me to this point: pray for the Pastor, the head Shepherd of the flock of God that the Holy Spirit may continue to give them revelation, strength, knowledge and wisdom to provide leadership in the church.

MATTHEW 26: 33, 34

> Peter answered and said to Him, "Even if all are made to stumble because of You, I will never be made to stumble." Jesus said to him, "Assuredly, I say to you that this night, before the rooster crows, you will deny Me three times."

Inappropriate self-confidence, like that of Peter, is the first step to a great fall. Proverbs 16:18 "Pride goes before destruction, and a haughty spirit before a fall". There is a proneness in all of us to be overconfident. But for some reason, those who are the most confident in themselves fall the quickest. Satan is active to lead these individuals astray. He catches them off their guard. This would technically be called the first strike, but don't count Peter out yet.

MATTHEW 26: 74, 75

> "Then he began to curse and swear, saying, "I do not know the Man!" Immediately a rooster crowed. 75 And Peter remembered the word of Jesus who had said to him, "Before the rooster crows, you will deny Me three times." So, he went out and wept bitterly.

My brothers and sisters, Peter wept bitterly. His sorrow and repentance for this sin was not slight, but great and deep. This same Peter, who wept so bitterly for denying Christ, never denied him again, but confessed him often in the face of danger.

After the crucifixion and resurrection, Jesus Christ met the disciples as he had told them in Galilee. He gave them "The Great Commission": Matthew 28: 18-20

> "And Jesus came and spake unto them, saying, All power is given unto me in heaven and in earth. Go ye therefore, and teach all nations, baptizing them in the name of the Father, and of the Son, and of the Holy Ghost: Teaching them to observe all things whatsoever I have commanded you: and, lo, I am with you always, even unto the end of the world. Amen."

Then Jesus told the Disciples what they really needed to be successful in this great work of God: Acts 1: 8 "But ye shall receive power, after that the Holy Ghost is come upon you: and ye shall be witnesses unto me both in Jerusalem, and in all Judaea, and in Samaria, and unto the uttermost part of the earth."

The Lord Jesus knew they needed power! Power! This power comes from the Holy Spirit. You must be a clean vessel. This cleansing comes only from the Holy Spirit. You must be born again!

CONCLUSION

Peter clearly showed us that through the power of the shed blood and resurrected body of Christ and the gift of the Holy Spirit, you and I don't have to be "counted out."There is hope for us!

Jesus said these profound words to (Simon) Peter in Luke 22: 31, 32:

> 31 And the Lord said, Simon, Simon, behold, Satan hath desired to have you, that he may sift you as wheat: 32But I have prayed for thee, that thy faith fail not: and when thou art converted, strengthen thy brethren.

The Lord prayed for Peter and did not give up on him. He didn't throw him away, and he didn't write him off. And after the power of the Holy Spirit, this same ornery, bad tempered, cantankerous Peter became one of the most anointed and faithful disciples on this side of heaven.

In fact, what Jesus had proclaimed earlier in Matthew 16:18 came to pass:

> "And I say also unto thee, that thou art Peter, and upon this rock I will build my church; and the gates of hell shall not prevail against it."

In other words, Don't Count Me Out!

G. P. S. = God's Precious Son = Jesus

SCRIPTURE: Matthew 7:13-23
KEY VERSE: Matthew 7: 13, 14
SUBJECT: Travel the Road of Life with God's Precious Son

INTRODUCTION:
Have you ever been driving down on a lonely deserted back road and found yourself totally lost? I have and I thank God for the invention of the G P S.

When people talk about a "G P S", they usually mean a G P S receiver. The (G P S) a Global Positioning System is actually a constellation of 27 Earth-orbiting satellites (24 in operation and three extras in case one fails). The U.S. military developed and implemented this satellite network as a military navigation system, but soon opened it up to everybody else.

Each of these 3,000 to 4,000-pound solar-powered satellites circles the globe at about 12,000 miles (19,300 km), making two complete rotations every day. The orbits are arranged so that at any time, anywhere on Earth, there are at least four satellites "visible" in the sky. A GPS receiver's job is to locate four or more of these satellites, figure out the distance to each, and use this information to deduce its own location.

I'd like to introduce you to another Global Positioning System: (G. P. S.) = God's Precious Son = Jesus and the power of God's Precious Spirit. If we depend upon them both, then the road of life will be safe and secure!

MATTHEW 7:13- 23
NEW KING JAMES VERSION

13 "Enter by the narrow gate; for wide is the gate and broad is the way that leads to destruction, and there are many who go in by it. 14 Because narrow is the gate and difficult is the way which leads to life, and there are few who find it. 15 "Beware of false prophets, who come to you in sheep's clothing, but inwardly they are ravenous wolves. 16 You will know them by their fruits. Do men gather grapes from thorn bushes or figs from thistles? 17 Even so, every good tree bears good fruit, but a bad tree bears bad fruit. 18 A good tree cannot bear bad fruit, nor can a bad tree bear good fruit. 19 Every tree that does not bear good fruit is cut down and thrown into the fire. 20 Therefore by their fruits you will know them. 21 "Not everyone who says to Me, 'Lord, Lord,' shall enter the kingdom of heaven, but he who does the will of My Father in heaven. 22 Many will say to Me in that day, 'Lord, Lord, have we not prophesied in Your

> name, cast out demons in Your name, and done many wonders in Your name?' 23 And then I will declare to them, 'I never knew you; depart from Me, you who practice lawlessness!'

Sermon

> 13 "Enter by the narrow gate; for wide is the gate and broad is the way that leads to destruction, and there are many who go in by it. 14 Because narrow is the gate and difficult is the way which leads to life, and there are few who find it.

Christ came to teach us, not only what we are to know and believe, but what we are to do towards God and towards men. Christ also taught us what we are to do towards those of our party and persuasion, and towards mankind in general. The Decalogue says this: *"Hear what Christ Our Savior saith, thou shalt love the Lord thy God with all thy heart, and with all thy soul, and with all thy mind. This is the first and great commandment. And the second is like unto it; thou shalt love thy neighbor as thyself. On these two commandments hang all the Law and the Prophets"*.

We must do to our neighbor that which we ourselves acknowledge to be fit and reasonable. We must, in our dealings with mankind, treat others as we would like to be treated!

My brothers and sisters, there are but two ways: right and wrong, good and evil. In other words, the way to heaven and the way to hell in the one or the other, all are walking: there is no middle place now or hereafter.

(REVELATION 22:14, 15 NKJV)

"Blessed are those who do His commandments that they may have the right to the tree of life, and may enter through the gates into the city. But outside are dogs and sorcerers and sexually immoral and murderers and idolaters, and whoever loves and practices a lie."

1. The way of sin and sinners the gate is wide, and stands open. You may go in at this gate with all your lusts about you; it gives no check to appetites or passions. It is a broad way; there are many paths in it. There is a large company in this way; sometimes plenty money, form and fashion.

But the Word of God says, "For what is a man profited, if he shall gain the whole world, and lose his own soul? Or what shall a man give in exchange for his soul?" (Matthew 16:26 KJV)

2. The way to eternal life is narrow. We are not in heaven as soon as we go through the strait gate. Self must be denied, the body kept under, and corruptions mortified by the purging and cleansing power of the other G. P. S. = God's Precious Spirit. Daily temptations must be resisted and godly duties must be completed. We must watch in all things, and walk with care and we must go through much tribulation. That's why Jesus warned, "Every tree that does not bear good fruit is cut down and thrown into the fire. Therefore by their fruits you

will know them. Not everyone who says to Me, 'Lord, Lord,' shall enter the kingdom of heaven, but he who does the will of My Father in heaven."

A true disciple of Christ, has sometimes, been looked upon as an unfashionable and peculiar character, but I've come to notice that those who hung out with the in crowds and sided with the greater number, soon became lost on that broad road of destruction.

If we serve God, we must be firm in our religion. If we get off the path of righteousness, and find ourselves far from the straight gate and the narrow way, then we must consult our #1 G. P. S. = God's Precious Son = Jesus.

We've been reassured with these profound words, "Jesus saith unto him, I am the way, the truth, and the life: no man cometh unto the Father, but by me." (John 14:6 KJV)

Unfortunately, there are some things that prevent mankind from entering the strait gate, and becoming true followers of Christ, such as the carnal, soothing, flattering doctrines of those who oppose the truth.

These false prophets may be known by the drifting effects of their doctrines, but the faithful servant of God preaches or teaches the true doctrine. He or she does not try to dress up the word, turn it around to suite his/her purpose, or sugarcoat the word to make you feel better.

Sunday after Sunday, we try earnestly to teach you the right way to go. When we see you going down the wrong road, we become concerned. We are like those "post signs" on the highway of life, giving directions, instructions and information, to help you think clearly and make righteous decisions.

Besides what good is a mind if it doesn't think? What good is a heart if it doesn't feel? What good is a voice if it doesn't speak? What good is our faith if we do not share it?

CONCLUSION

A father wanted to read a magazine but was being bothered by his little girl. She wanted to know what the United States looked like? Finally, he tore a sheet out of his new magazine on which was printed the map of the country. Tearing it into small pieces, he gave it to her and said, "Go into the other room and see if you can put this together. This will show you our whole country today."

After a few minutes, she returned and handed him the map, correctly fitted and taped together. The father was surprised and asked how she had finished so quickly? "Oh, she said, on the other side of the paper was s a picture of Jesus. When I got all of Jesus back where He belonged, then the map of the country just came together."

I agree with that young lady, when we get the G. P. S. = God's Precious Son, Jesus, back where He belongs, our country will come together! Amen.

The Songwriter said it best…

HYMN 387 "JUST A CLOSER WALK WITH THEE"

Just a closer walk with Thee; Grant it Jesus, if you please,
Daily walking close with Thee, Let it be dear Lord, let it be.
I am weak but Thou art strong, Jesus, keep me from all wrong,
I'll be satisfied as long, as I walk, Let me walk close with Thee.

Don't Give-Up Your Rights!

SCRIPTURE: Genesis 25:19-34
KEY VERSES: Genesis 25: 29-34
SUBJECT: Don't Give-Up Your God-Given Birth Rights

INTRODUCTION:

BIRTHRIGHT

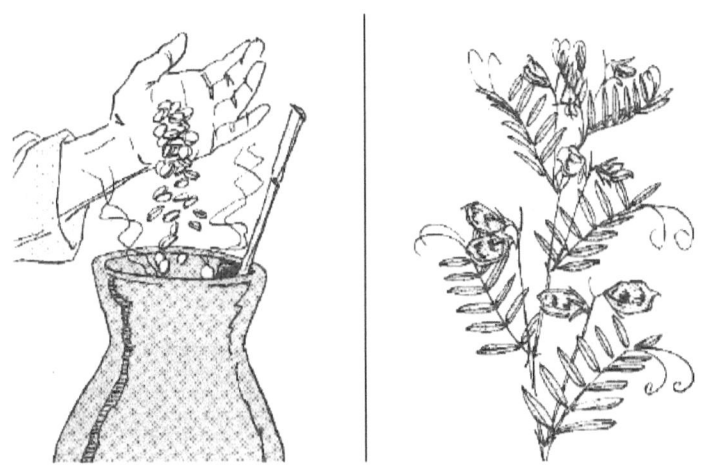

Lentils, from which Jacob made stew, was a common vegetable of Old Testament times. It grew in pods like peas or beans.

The term birthright appears several times in the Bible. The word refers to the inheritance rights of the firstborn son in a Hebrew family in Old Testament times. The property of a father was normally divided among his sons at his death. A larger amount, usually a double portion, went to the oldest son (Deut. 21:17), who assumed the care of his mother and unmarried sisters.

The birthright with its privileges and responsibilities could be forfeited by behavior that was offensive to the father or behavior in opposition of God's will. For example, Esau foolishly squandered his birthright by trading it to his brother Jacob for a bowl of stew made from lentils (Gen. 25:29-34; see illustration).

This ancient account about the birthright, reminds us today, that we can forfeit God's blessings, if we do not live responsibly as the heirs of God.

GENESIS 25:19-34
(NEW INTERNATIONAL VERSION)

19   This is the account of the family line of Abraham's son Isaac. Abraham became the father of Isaac, 20 and Isaac was forty years old when he married Rebekah daughter of Bethuel the Aramean from Paddan Aram and sister of Laban the Aramean. 21 Isaac prayed to the LORD on behalf of his wife, because she was childless. The LORD answered his prayer, and his wife Rebekah became pregnant. 22 The babies jostled each other within her, and she said, "Why is this happening to me?" So she went to inquire of the LORD. 23 The

LORD said to her, "Two nations are in your womb, and two peoples from within you will be separated; one people will be stronger than the other, and the older will serve the younger." 24 When the time came for her to give birth, there were twin boys in her womb. 25 The first to come out was red, and his whole body was like a hairy garment; so they named him Esau. 26 After this, his brother came out, with his hand grasping Esau's heel; so he was named Jacob. Isaac was sixty years old when Rebekah gave birth to them. 27 The boys grew up, and Esau became a skillful hunter, a man of the open country, while Jacob was content to stay at home among the tents. 28 Isaac, who had a taste for wild game, loved Esau, but Rebekah loved Jacob. 29 Once when Jacob was cooking some stew, Esau came in from the open country, famished. 30 He said to Jacob, "Quick, let me have some of that red stew! I'm famished!" (That is why he was also called Edom. 31 Jacob replied, "First sell me your birthright." 32 "Look, I am about to die," Esau said. "What good is the birthright to me?" 33 But Jacob said, "Swear to me first." So he swore an oath to him, selling his birthright to Jacob. 34 Then Jacob gave Esau some bread and some lentil stew. He ate and drank, and then got up and left. So Esau despised his birthright.

Sermon

Jacob and Esau were prayed for. Their parents, after being long childless, obtained them by the power of fervent prayer. The fulfillment of God's promise is always sure, yet it is often slow. In other words, you can't hurry God! The faith of believers is tried, and their patience is exercised. I've come to know that mercies long waited for, are more appreciated and welcomed when they come. In all our doubts and cares, we should inquire of the Lord by prayer. There is a song that we should heed as it encourages us to "take everything to God in prayer".

THE DIFFERENT CHARACTERS OF ESAU AND JACOB

Esau hunted the beasts of the field with dexterity and success, until he became a conqueror, ruling over his neighbors. Jacob was a plain man, and one that liked the true delights of retirement better than all pleasures. He was a stranger and a pilgrim in his spirit and a shepherd all his days. Isaac and Rebekah had but these two children. One was the father's darling, and the other the mother's "baby boy".

We can learn a lesson here. Although godly parents might feel their affections most drawn towards a godly child, they should not show partiality. As parents, our affections should always lead us to do what is just and equal to every child, or evils will arise. (Gen. 25:29-34)

> Once when Jacob was cooking some stew, Esau came in from the open country, famished. 30 He said to Jacob, "Quick, let me have some of that red stew! I'm famished!" (That is why he was also called Edom. 31 Jacob replied, "First sell me your birthright."33 But Jacob said, "Swear to me first." So he swore an oath to him, selling his birthright to Jacob. 34 Then Jacob gave Esau some bread and some lentil stew. He ate and drank, and then got up and left. So Esau despised his birthright.

ESAU DESPISES AND SELLS HIS BIRTHRIGHT

And so, the plot thickens. A bargain made between Jacob and Esau about a "right", which was Esau's by birth, but Jacob's by promise. It was for a spiritual privilege, and we see Jacob's desire of the birthright, but he sought to obtain it by crooked courses. He was partly right, that he coveted earnestly the best gifts, but he was wrong in that he took advantage of his brother's need of food.

The inheritance of their father's worldly goods, did not descend to Jacob, and was not meant in this proposal. It included the future possession of the land of Canaan by his children's children, and the covenant made with Abraham as to Christ the promised seed. The believing Jacob valued these above all things, the unbelieving Esau despised them.

Jacob's pottage pleased Esau's eye. Gratifying the sensual appetite can ruin thousands of precious souls. When hearts walk after their own eyes, and when they serve their own bellies, they are sure to be punished. Just ask the presidential candidate Mitt Romney.

It is the greatest folly to part with our invested interest in God, Christ, and heaven, for the riches, honors, and pleasures of this world. It is a bad bargain to do what Esau did, who sold his birthright for a dish of pottage. Esau ate and drank, pleased his palate, satisfied his appetite, and then carelessly rose up and went along his way, without any serious thought, or any regret about the bad bargain that he had made. Esau despised his birthright. His neglect and contempt afterwards, and in justifying himself in what he had done, put the bargain past recall.

People are ruined, not so much by doing what is wrong or incorrect, but by doing it and not repenting of it. (Repeat)

CONCLUSION

In New Testament times, inheritance practices were influenced by Greek and Roman regulations, which focused less on the elder son. The Greeks relied on wills to pass on their property. However, if no will existed, property was divided equally among sons in good standing. Under Roman law, the property of a man who died without a will went to his wife and children.

Like that old commercial saying, *"You can learn a lot from a dummy"*, for God's sake make a will! Do not leave what God has blessed you with up to the *Commonwealth of Virginia*.

The Apostle Paul made it plain in (Col. 1:15), when he described Jesus as the "firstborn over all creation" and emphasized the spiritual birthright of all Christians as "heirs of God and joint heirs with Christ, if indeed we suffer with Him" (Rom. 8:17). And so, a willingness to share in the sufferings of Christ is the condition for the blessings we receive as His spiritual heirs.

My brothers and sisters, remember that "Christ died that we may have the right to the tree of life, and may enter through the gates into that fair city of God." I proclaim this day, there is absolutely no way on this side of heaven that I'm going to give up my God given rights! You're looking at me kind of funny. What are my rights, you ask?

- I'm a child of the King!
- I am God's child, for I am born again of the incorruptible seed of the Word of God, which lives and abides forever!
- I am forgiven of all my sins and I am washed in the blood of the Lamb!
- I'm more than a conqueror!
- I am firmly rooted, I am built up.
- I'm strengthened in the faith, overflowing with joy and thanksgiving!
- I'm the apple of my Father's eye.

The songwriter said it best...

HYMN # 450 BLESSED ASSURANCE, JESUS IS MINE!

Blessed assurance, Jesus is mine! O what a foretaste of glory divine!
Heir of salvation, purchase of God,
Born of His spirit, washed in His blood.
This is my story, this is my song, Praising my Savior all the day long;
This is my story, this is my song, Praising my Savior all the day long!

Will You Be Ready When Jesus Comes?

SCRIPTURE: Matthew 25:1-13
SUBJECT: Will you be ready when Jesus comes?

INTRODUCTION:

In this parable (an earthly story with a heavenly meaning), Jesus communicates the significance of accepting or rejecting His offer of salvation.

The words in this text of the scriptures are aimed at those who are not ready to accept the Lord and the terrible judgment that will fall upon them. Christ also forewarns us that in His second coming, He comes as Judge and Lord of the entire earth.

My beloved, the hands of time are winding down. The tick of the clock is more profound. You can see clearly the handwriting on the wall of time. Jesus is coming back! Will you be ready when He comes?

MATTHEW 25:1-13 (PARABLE OF THE WISE AND FOOLISH VIRGINS)

"1 Then the kingdom of heaven shall be likened to ten virgins who took their lamps and went out to meet the bridegroom. 2 Now five of them were wise, and five were foolish. 3 Those who were foolish took their lamps and took no oil with them, 4 but the wise took oil in their vessels with their lamps. 5 But while the bridegroom was delayed, they all slumbered and slept.6 "And at midnight a cry was heard: 'Behold, the bridegroom is coming; go out to meet him!' 7 Then all those virgins arose and trimmed their lamps.

8   And the foolish said to the wise, 'Give us some of your oil, for our lamps are going out.' 9 But the wise answered, saying, 'No, lest there should not be enough for us and you; but go rather to those who sell, and buy for yourselves.' 10 And while they went to buy, the bridegroom came, and those who were ready went in with him to the wedding; and the door was shut.11 "Afterward the other virgins came also, saying, 'Lord, Lord, open to us!' 12 But he answered and said, 'Assuredly, I say to you, I do not know you.'13 "Watch therefore, for you know neither the day nor the hour in which the Son of Man is coming.

Sermon

MATTHEW 22:1-4

"Then the kingdom of heaven shall be likened to ten virgins who took their lamps and went out to meet the bridegroom. Now five of them were wise, and five of them were foolish. Those who were foolish took their lamps and took no oil with them, but the wise took oil in their vessels with their lamps."

The term virgin, represents that which is pure and good. How many of you know that just being good is not going to get you into the kingdom of God?

To be foolish is to be stupid and unwise. The Bible says in Psalm 14:1, a fool is one who believes "There is no God".

I don't know about you, but until I met Jesus, I made some really stupid, silly, idiotic, and unwise choices in my life! (Smile)

Since I met this blessed Savior, since He washed and made me whole, I will never cease to praise Him. I'll shout it while eternity rolls, that He touched me. Oh He touched me, and Oh the joy that fills my soul! Something happened, and now I know, He touched me and made me whole!

Now what does the oil represent? Well I'm not talking about Crisco oil. I'm not talking about the oil out back for heating the church, although this anointing oil can also set you on fire!

The oil in this parable represents the "Holy Spirit". God Himself dwelling within you and me! Jeremiah said, "it feels like fire shut up in my bones".

Those five wise virgins who took oil in their vessels with their lamps were ready, saved, sanctified, and being filled with the Holy Spirit.

MATTHEW 22: 5, 6

> "But while the bridegroom was delayed, they all slumbered and slept. And at midnight a cry was heard: Behold the bridegroom is coming; go out to meet him.

There's something about midnight. It's the darkest hour of the night. I'm not talking about the break of day, nor am I talking about the noonday. Midnight, is the darkest hour of one's life.

1. No two midnights will be quite the same:
2. For some, midnight could mean to be diagnosed with cancer.
3. For another, midnight could be the AIDS Virus.
4. To another, midnight could be a head on collision by a drunk driver.
5. Young people, midnight for you could be, while you're just sitting in your classroom, a gunman enters your school with a AR-15 machine gun and starts shooting towards you.

Midnight, is the darkest hour and the time that you least expect Jesus to come.

I'm here to tell you that Jesus is coming back!

He could come while you slumber and sleep, or while you sit in the midst of being apathetic and complacent. God is preparing the way for His son's return. Ready or not, Jesus is coming back.

He will come individually (for you), He will come collectively (Sandy Hook School kids), and I'm a living witness that He will come infinitely. For in the book of Hebrews, the word of God says, "He that will come, shall come and he will not tarry."

MATTHEW 22: 7-9

> Then all those virgins arose and trimmed their lamps. And the foolish said to the wise, give us some of your oil, for our lamps are going out. But the wise answered, saying, No, lest there should not be enough for us and you; but go rather to those who sell, and buy for yourselves.

When you hold a lamp up in the darkness of the night, it casts a shadow, a reflection of you. A lot of you have been hiding behind the shadows of your mother and the shadows of your father. Maybe you've even been hiding in the shadow of your brother or sister. You must let your own light shine before men, women, boys, and girls, that they may see your good works and glorify the Father who sits in heaven.

The lyrics to the song "God Bless the Child That Has is Own" are so powerful. Am I not right?

I want to make one thing perfectly clear; you can't buy this thing. Salvation nor the Holy Spirit is for sale. They are both free.

The only way you can have it, is to do these simple things: Romans 10:9

1. Confess with your mouth the Lord Jesus
2. Believe in your heart that God has raised Him from the dead

At this point you are born again and the Holy Spirit himself bears witness with our spirit that we are children of God. (Romans 8:16)

MATTHEW 22:10-13

> And when they went to buy the bridegroom came, and those who were ready went in with him to the wedding; and the door was shut. Afterward the other virgins came also, saying, Lord, Lord, open unto us! But he said, Assuredly, I say to you, I do not know you. Watch therefore, for you know neither the day nor the hour in which the Son of Man is coming."

My beloved the scriptures says, "You will know them by their fruits." (Matthew 7:16) Those five wise virgins, who were ready, saved, sanctified and being filled with the Holy Spirit went in with the bridegroom (Jesus).

They had in their possession the fruits of the Holy Spirit: love, joy, peace, longsuffering, kindness, goodness, faithfulness, gentleness, and self-control.

The other five foolish virgins did not. And then the door was shut, and those virgins cried to no avail, "Lord, Lord, open to us".

Because Jesus sternly said in Matthew 7:21

> "Not everyone who says to Me, Lord, Lord, shall enter into the kingdom of heaven, but he who does the will of My Father in heaven."

My brothers and my sisters, will you really be ready when Jesus comes?

Are you doing the will of the Father or are you doing your own thing?

CONCLUSION

This year, we have abused power and called it politics. We have neglected to discipline our children and called it self-esteem. We have coveted our neighbor's possessions and called it ambition. We have polluted the air with profanity and pornography and called it freedom of speech. We have ridiculed the values of our forefathers and called it the Generation X. We have sent our children to a Holy War and called it a war against terrorism.

This year we must cry out! Search us oh, God, and know our hearts. Cleanse and forgive us from every sin and set us free.

Like your servant David, create in us a clean heart, renew a steadfast spirit within us. Do not cast us away from your presence. Please Lord, do not take your Holy Spirit from us.

Lord, we want to be ready, saved, sanctified, and filled with your Holy Spirit when you come for us.

Saints, I never worry about what time it is, because yeah, though I walk through the valley of the shadow of death; I will fear no evil for the Lord God Almighty will be with me. Thy Word and thy Holy Spirit will comfort me. My God continually prepares a table before me in the presence of my enemy. My head is anointed with His precious oil, my cup is running over!

I don't have to worry about backbiters or backstabbers because Your Goodness and Your Mercy, Lord, shall follow me all the days of my life, and I will dwell in the house of the Lord forever and ever!

The Question is Will You Be Ready When Jesus Comes?

SONG: I Want to Be Ready,
I Want to be Ready, I want to be Ready,
Walk in Jerusalem just like John!

You Don't Love God? What's Wrong With You? I Love God!

SCRIPTURES: Deuteronomy 6:1-9
Malachi: 2:10
Matthew 3:17 Romans 8:15
SUBJECT: Understanding God's Being

INTRODUCTION:
No man or woman has ever seen God, but the Bible reveals that the nature of God is spirit, unity and trinity. He is a spirit, a personal, infinite being. He is one in substance or nature and incapable of being divided into separate parts. He is three, eternally existing in three coequal persons as God the Father, God the Son and God the Holy Spirit.

Some of the attributes we use to describe who God is and how He acts toward us are: loving, holy, constant, righteous judge, eternal, omniscience (all-knowing), omnipresence (all-present), and omnipotence (all-powerful).

While great mystery surrounds God's nature, it is reassuring to know that our God is truly real!

Today we will discuss three facets of God, which I pray will bring us much closer to Him. My young people can say it best, You Don't Love God? What's Wrong With You? I Love God!

1. God the Father of All
2. God the Father of Jesus Christ
3. God the Father of Believers

DEUTERONOMY 6:1-9
NEW KING JAMES VERSION

THE GREATEST COMMANDMENT

1 "Now this is the commandment, and these are the statutes and judgments which the Lord your God has commanded to teach you, that you may observe them in the land which you are crossing over to possess, 2 that you may fear the Lord your God, to keep all His statutes and His commandments which I command you, you and your son and your grandson, all the days of your life, and that your days may be prolonged. 3 Therefore hear, O Israel, and be careful to observe it, that it may be well with you, and that you may multiply greatly as the Lord God of your fathers has promised you—'a land flowing with milk and honey.' 4 "Hear, O Israel: The Lord our God, the Lord is one! 5 You shall love the Lord your God with all your heart, with all your soul, and with all your strength. 6 "And these words which I command you today shall be in your heart. 7 You shall teach them diligently to your children, and shall talk of them when you sit in your house, when you walk by the way, when you lie down, and when

you rise up. 8 You shall bind them as a sign on your hand, and they shall be as frontlets between your eyes. 9 You shall write them on the doorposts of your house and on your gates.

Sermon

1. GOD THE FATHER OF ALL:

MALACHI: 2:10

"Have we not all one Father? Has not one God created us? Why do you deal treacherously with one another by profaning the covenant of the fathers?"

My brothers and my sisters, we all were created by God. He is our Father and we are His offspring. God is the Father of all because He is the sustainer of life. Every person, living being, is an object of His fatherly care and a candidate for His heavenly kingdom.

But not everyone will have eternal life. Only those who confess with their mouths of the Lord Jesus and believe in their hearts that God raised Him from the dead.

God is not willing that anyone should perish. Even when men and women reject Him, He still provides for them just like the believers with His sunshine, rain, fruitful seasons, food, and goodness and mercy! You Don't Love God? What's Wrong With You? I Love God!

2. GOD THE FATHER OF JESUS CHRIST:

MATTHEW 3:17

"And suddenly a voice came from heaven, saying, "This is my beloved Son, in whom I am well pleased."

Everyone eventually wonders in what sense God may be called the Father of Jesus Christ and Jesus Christ the Son of God. The answer to this question is not a simple one.

First, we must recognize that the title Son of God does not speak of a physical nature. Remember God is a spirit. Jesus Christ was the Son of God before He ever assumed a humane body in Bethlehem. Galatians says, "But when the fullness of time had come, God sent forth His Son, born of a woman."

Second, the title Son of God, expresses a unique relationship. He is the begotten of God in a sense that no one can ever claim. Some call it "eternal generation" signifying the timelessness of this God- from God relationship. Jesus said this in John 3:16, 17, and 18;

> "For God so loved the world that He gave His only begotten Son, that whoever believes in Him should not perish but have everlasting life. For God did not send His Son into the world to condemn the world, but that the world through Him might be saved.
>
> He who believes in Him is not condemned; but he who does not believe is condemned already,

> because he has not believed in the name of the only begotten Son of God."

These scriptures will stand the test of time! You Don't Love God? What's Wrong With You? I Love God!

3. GOD THE FATHER OF BELIEVERS:

ROMANS 8:15

> "For you did not receive the spirit of bondage again to fear, but you received the Spirit of adoption by whom we cry out, Abba, Father."

To obtain God as Father is not a result of our own merit, but the result of Jesus Christ. God is the special Father of all who believe in His beloved Son Jesus Christ.

To the Christians, God is called our Father, because we have a new standing before Him. Unbelievers are the offspring of God, only because He created them. They do not have this special Father/child position that we as Christians do. Their standing is rather as condemned sinners before God the righteous Judge.

Thanks be to God, when a person believes in Christ as their personal Savior, his or her estate is wonderfully changed from grim condemnation to privileged sons and daughters! We become "heirs of God and joint heirs with Christ." Romans 8:17

The uniqueness of this Father/child relationship is that we become family and take on some of the same realities that exist between our earthly families. We have a new birth.

This means that we are born again and that we partake of the Father's' nature. We must start sounding and acting like the Father, and when we act up we are then disciplined by the Father. I know I'm right! What I really like about this Father/child relationship is that it carries with it new brothers and sisters. I'm talking about you and you and you! You Don't Love God? What's Wrong With You? I Love God!

CONCLUSION

My beloved brothers and sisters, my family, young people, I conclude with these words:

"You should love the Lord your God with all your heart, with all your soul, and with all your might.

And these words which I command you today shall be in your heart. You shall teach them diligently to your children, and shall talk of them when you sit in your house, when you walk by the way, when you lie down, and when you rise up. You shall bind them as a sign on your hand, and they shall be as frontlets between your eyes. You shall write them on the doorposts of your house and your gates."

YOU DON'T LOVE GOD? WHAT'S WRONG WITH YOU? I LOVE GOD!

Tithes, Offerings, Alms God's Plan For Blessing You!

SCRIPTURES: Malachi 3: 8-12
Luke 6:38 Proverbs 19:17
SUBJECT: Tithes, Offerings, and Alms

INTRODUCTION:

Are you sick and tired of going in circles when it comes to your finances? Many Christians are slow to learn the basic principles of giving and receiving and never seem to rise above their circumstances.

As a Christian, we have a source of financial abundance that knows no limits. God has promised to meet our every need, spiritually, physically, and materially. The spiritual cornerstone of giving states that it is more blessed to give than to receive (Acts 20:35); if you increase your giving, you'll increase your blessing (Matthew 6: 19, 20); and last but not least, the kingdom of God must take priority in your life (Matthew 6:33).

In order to receive financially from God, He says that there are certain responsibilities that we must fulfill. If we do our part, God will do His part and meet all our needs according to His riches in glory by Christ Jesus.

Today, I will share with you some spiritual laws that will set you on the right track and help you to receive financial abundance from God.

Tithes, Offerings and Alms; God's Plan for Blessing you!

MALACHI 3: 6-12 NEW KING JAMES

6   "For I am the Lord, I do not change; therefore you are not consumed, O sons of Jacob. 7 Yet from the days of your fathers you have gone away from My ordinances And have not kept them. Return to Me, and I will return to you," Says the Lord of hosts. "But you said, 'In what way shall we return?'

8   "Will a man rob God? Yet you have robbed Me! But you say, 'In what way have we robbed You?' In tithes and offerings. 9 You are cursed with a curse, for you have robbed Me, Even this whole nation.

10   Bring all the tithes into the storehouse, That there may be food in My house, And try Me now in this," Says the Lord of hosts, " If I will not open for you the windows of heaven and pour out for you such blessing That there will not be room enough to receive it.

11   "And I will rebuke the devourer for your sakes, So that he will not destroy the fruit of your ground, nor shall the vine fail to bear fruit for you in the field," Says the Lord of hosts; 12 and all nations will call you blessed, for you will be a delightful land," Says the Lord of hosts.

1. TITHING AND OPEN WINDOWS

MALACHI 3:10

> "Bring all the tithes into the storehouse, that there may be food in My house, and prove Me now in this says the Lord of host if I will not open for you the windows of heaven and pour out for you such a blessing that there will not be room enough to receive it."

One of your first responsibilities as Christian is to tithe. Many people don't like to hear about tithing. It's one subject that puts them into a state of anxiety and fear. They say, "We can't even make ends meet now, how in the world can we give away ten percent of our income?"

Those who think this way, fail to ever see the blessings that follow tithing. These people are not trusting God to be their unlimited source of supply. You will have no trouble tithing if you are willing to see God as your ultimate provider.

Don't limit yourself to just your paycheck for all your income. Tithing carries some definite blessings. One blessing is that you'll have meat in your house. If you are experiencing a financial pinch to the point of not being able to buy meat at the grocery store, then maybe you should start tithing.

If you tithe, God will also give you spiritual meat from His Word. So enter into His courts with thanksgiving and praise on you lips, expecting to be fed spiritual beef from the Man or Woman of God!

GOD ALSO MADE SOME PROMISES TO THOSE WHO TITHE:

- He will pour out a blessing from the windows of heaven; out from the panes of heaven comes a deluge of good things; so much that you have to share it with someone else.
- God promises to rebuke the devourer. In other words He will rebuke anything or anyone that keeps your money from going as far as it should go. He'll make one dollar seem like ten dollars! Saints I know I'm right about this!

2. OFFERINGS AND MEASURED RETURNS

LUKE 6:38

"Give and it shall be given to you; good measure, pressed down, and shaken together; and running over will be put into your bosom. For with the same measure that you use, it will be measured back to you."

Now let's talk about offerings. The Bible tells us that we are to give offerings. What is an offering? An offering is something that is above the first ten percent.

As Christians, we are obligated to pay tithes—it is something we owe God.

Offerings, on the other hand, should come strictly from what you feel led of the Lord to give. When you give an offering, it moves men to give to you. And your return depends upon the measure that you've given—the more you give, the more He'll give to you!

3. ALMS AND MULTIPLIED BLESSINGS

PROVERBS 19:17

> "He that have pity on the poor lends unto the Lord; and that which he hath given will He pay him again."

Last but not least, we will talk about almsgiving. Almsgiving is not tithing, and it is not an offering. It is a loan which God says He will repay. Technically, we don't pay or give alms. They are something we sow.

The Apostle Paul wrote in 2nd Corinthians 9:6-10:

"But this I say, 'He who sows sparingly will reap sparing, and he who sows bountifully will reap also bountifully. So let each one give as he purposes in his heart, not grudgingly or of necessity; for God loves a cheerful giver.

CONCLUSION

My brothers and my sisters, God is not primarily occupied with the amount of our giving, but with the motive that lies behind our giving. You see all the money in the world belongs to God.

My gift to Him does not make him any richer, it makes me richer spiritually, because in my heart, I finally realized that everything I have is His. I am giving because I love Him and want to give back just a portion of what He's given to me!

Our failure to give tithes, offering, and alms is a serious matter. The person who fails to honor God with his giving, actually robs God. This is not because it impoverishes God, but because it denies the God ordained means for support of the Lord's work and His ministers.

God's plan for blessing us financially is perfect. God said "try me and see".

Saints, I've tried Him and …

Because I tithe, and God is faithful to His Word, there's meat in my house,

Because I tithe, and God is faithful to His Word, He opens up the windows of heaven, pours out blessings upon me, that there is not room enough for me to receive them,

Because I tithe and God is faithful to His Word, He rebukes the devourer (Satan) for my sake,

And Because I Tithe, give an Offering and sow Alms, and God is faithful to His Word,

I'm blessed coming in, I'm blessed going out.

I'm the head and not the tail.

I'm above and not beneath.

I have more than enough.

All my needs are met.

All my bills are paid.

Why? This is because the Lord is my Shepherd and I shall not want for anything!

WE MUST REMEMBER THAT THE MORE YOU GIVE, THE MORE HE GIVES TO YOU.

Why Seek The Living Among The Dead?

SCRIPTURE: Luke 24: 1-7
Matthew 27: 52, 53
SUBJECT: Jesus Lives! Look for Him Among the Living!

INTRODUCTION:

The Gospel writers devoted many pages to the events leading up to the crucifixion of Jesus. The final week of His earthly ministry began with the triumphal entry into Jerusalem. The praises and cheers of "Hosanna" from the crowd soon changed to cries of "Crucify Him" before the week was over. Jesus spent most of the week teaching in the temple area during the day. His evenings were spent in the home of Mary, Martha, and Lazarus in Bethany.

Significant events occurred during this week. The Sanhedrin challenged Jesus' authority. Jesus was betrayed and arrested. He went to three civil trials and was formally sentenced to death by Pontius Pilate. He embarked upon a journey to Golgotha (Calvary's Cross) down the Jerusalem street, known today as Via Dolorosa. Finally, He was crucified.

On the third day, the glory and the foundation of the Christian Church and faith was fulfilled. Jesus conquered the grave, as He had promised, in the historical Resurrection. Thank God Almighty, He is Alive!

After His resurrection, Jesus ministered another forty days before His ascension to the right hand of God the Father. Which brings us to our text today. The angels of the Lord pose a question to you and me, "Why seek the Living among the Dead?"

WE WILL ADDRESS THREE POINTS:

1. Dead Church
2. Dead Faith
3. Dead Spirituality.

LUKE 24:1-7

> "Now on the first day of the week, very early in the morning, they, and certain other women with them, came to the tomb bringing the spices which they had prepared. But they found the stone rolled away from the tomb. Then they went in and did not find the body of the Lord Jesus. And it happened, as they were greatly perplexed about this, that behold, two men stood by them in shining garments. Then as they were afraid and bowed their faces to the earth, they said to them, "Why do you seek the living among the dead? He is not here, but is risen! Remember how He spoke to you when He was still in Galilee, saying, The Son of Man must be delivered into the hands of sinful men, and be crucified, and the third day rise again."

Sermon

1. DEAD CHURCH:
WHY SEEK THE LIVING AMONG THE DEAD?

Have you ever been in a dead church? Jesus spoke of this church condition in Revelations 3. The church of Sardis was considered decadent, self-indulgent, had a famous name, known far and wide. People came from near and far, claiming to be alive, but Jesus said, spiritually you are dead. Why? The people of God were glorifying the building, the walls, the music, the pastor, and had forgotten about the Lord and Savior Jesus Christ!

We don't have that problem here at this church, because we enter into this house with praise on our lips! We praise His name with songs! We praise His name with dance! We praise His name with stringed instruments! We praise His name with drums, clashing cymbals and loud cymbals! We praise His name with the piano and the keyboard! We praise the name of Lord with tambourines! We praise His name through our giving! Yes this church is alive!

Besides, the Word of God said, "Let everything that has breathe praise the Lord!" (Psalm 150:6)

2. DEAD FAITH?
WHY SEEK THE LIVING AMONG THE DEAD?

The book of James Chapter 2 says,

> "What does it profit, my (brothers and sisters) if someone says he has faith but does not have works? Can faith save him/her?

If a brother or sister is naked and destitute of daily food, and one of you says to them, 'Depart in peace, be warmed and filled,' but you do not give them the things which are needed for the body, what does it profit? This is also true of faith by itself. If faith is not accompanied by works, it is dead.

Faith proves itself by works!

I challenge the Missionaries and the entire household of faith, we must do better than last year.

We will continue to visit the sick and the shut-in, but we must be more conscious of the needs of the homeless, the widow, the fatherless, the motherless, those who are incarcerated, and the lost youth of this generation. We must seek them out, and show them faith and love through Christ Jesus by our good works.

> For as the body without the spirit is dead, so faith without works is dead! (JAMES 2:26)

3. DEAD SPIRITUALLY?
WHY SEEK THE LIVING AMONG THE DEAD?

To be spiritually dead, is to not know or accept the Lord Jesus Christ as your personal Savior. We are appointed only once to die in the body. But there is another death for those who have not confessed the Lord and Savior Jesus Christ with their mouths and believe in their hearts that God raised Him from the dead. This second death is eternal and everlasting damnation in the lake that burns with fire and brimstone. (Rev. 21:8)

You have a choice, to follow Christ or to follow Satan. You can choose eternal life or eternal death. The choice is yours.

In Matthew the 27th chapter, verses 52 and 53; after the resurrection of Christ, the dead saints of God rose from their graves and went into the holy city and appeared unto many.

I believe in my sanctified soul, that these dead saints said to their family and loved ones…

"If you are seeking Jesus, you can't find Him in nobody's grave. He is alive! And guess what? He did not forget about us! He did not leave us nor did He forsake us! He came way down and set our captive souls free!

> Oh death where is thy sting? O grave where is thy victory?

CONCLUSION

If you are seeking Jesus Christ, come to a church that is praising Jesus.

If you are looking for a blessing, come to a church that is faithfully doing mission work.

If you are truly seeking Jesus, all you've got to do is reach up toward heaven. He is omnipotent, ever present, alive and waiting with open arms.

BECAUSE HE LIVES, I WE CAN FACE TOMORROW. WHY SEEK THE LIVING AMONG THE DEAD?

Watch Your Tongue

SCRIPTURE: James 3: 1-10
SUBJECT: The Right To Remain Silent

INTRODUCTION:
From our youth, we were taught to dread an unruly tongue. I remember my parents saying *"If you don't have anything good to say don't say nothing"*.

Pious and edifying language is the genuine produce of a sanctified heart, and none of us who are Christians, expect to hear curses, lies, boastings, and reveling from a true believer's mouth.

The Apostle James in our text today does not represent the "taming of the tongue" as impossible, but as extremely difficult without the divine power of the Holy Spirit.

Today we will explore (4) key areas in which we should - "Watch Your Tongue".

JAMES 3:1-10 (NEW KING JAMES VERSION)

1   My brethren, let not many of you become teachers, knowing that we shall receive a stricter judgment. 2 For we all stumble in many things. If anyone does not stumble in word, he is a perfect man, able also to bridle the whole body. 3 Indeed, we put bits in horses' mouths that they may obey us, and we turn their whole

> body. 4 Look also at ships: although they are so large and are driven by fierce winds, they are turned by a very small rudder wherever the pilot desires. 5 Even so the tongue is a little member and boasts great things. See how great a forest a little fire kindles!

6 And the tongue is a fire, a world of iniquity. The tongue is so set among our members that it defiles the whole body, and sets on fire the course of nature; and it is set on fire by hell. 7 For every kind of beast and bird, of reptile and creature of the sea, is tamed and has been tamed by mankind. 8 But no man can tame the tongue. It is an unruly evil, full of deadly poison. 9 With it we bless our God and Father, and with it we curse men, who have been made in the similitude of God. 10 Out of the same mouth proceed blessing and cursing. My brethren, these things ought not to be so.

Sermon

1. BLASPHEMY

Christians use the word blasphemy primarily to mean harsh speech against God or sacred persons or things.

But the Word of God clearly states in Matthew 12:31, 32 NKJV

> "Every sin and blasphemy will be forgiven men, but the blasphemy against the Holy Spirit will not be forgiven men. Anyone who speaks a word against the son of man, it will be forgiven him, but whoever speaks against the Holy

Spirit, it will not be forgiven him, either in this age or the age to come."

Now you will know if you have committed this sin, if you see the desire to be a Christian gone. No spiritual impressions will ever again come to your soul. Your soul will be subject to eternal condemnation. My brothers and my sisters, the soul is a conscious personality endowed with perpetual life. God loves the soul more than all creation, for He fashioned it after His own image and He made it like unto Himself.

To sin against the Holy Spirit is to sin against your own soul. In other words, to blaspheme against the Holy Spirit is to shut yourself off forever from access to God. Those who have committed this sin are completely given over to Satan and have not the slightest interest in spiritual matters.

2. EVIL-SPEAKING

Evil-speaking closely parallels the modern expression to "put someone down". Three times in one verse James uses this word: "Do not speak evil of one another, brethren. He who speaks evil of a brother and judges his brother, speaks evil of the law and judges the law. But if you judge the law, you are not a doer of the law but a judge" (James 4:11).

Other translations of these words "Evil-speaking" include:
- "Backbite" *(to secretly defame)*
- "Revile" *(to insult, scorn, berate)*,
- "Defame" *(to insult, slander, offend)*, and last but not least
- "Slander" *(to smear, defamation, character assignation)*.

James said, "My brethren, these things ought not to be so".

3. COMPLAINING

Simply means to "murmur", "complain", "grumble", or "gripe".

Paul commands Christians to *"do all things without murmuring and disputing"* (Phil. 2:14) and Peter tells us to *"be hospitable to one another without grumbling.* (1 Pet. 4:9).

Apparently these two apostles knew human nature very well.

4. WHISPERERS

In general, whispering is not wrong, unless one whispers gossip, evil or other unsavory things. Paul taught the not so saintly Corinthians that backbiters and whisperers are really the same. Whisperers are secret slanderers and backbiters are more public.

Again, James said, "My brethren, these things ought not to be so".

CONCLUSION

Police officers are required to give Miranda warnings in very specific situations. A person must be in custody of the police. Custody is not necessarily defined as being in jail or handcuffed. A person can be in custody on a street, in his/her home, or in a parking lot, if the person is deprived of his freedom in a significant way. The other requirement is that the police are questioning the person. Without these two requirements, Miranda is not required.

MIRANDA RIGHTS

1. You have the right to remain silent.
2. Anything you say can be used against you in a court of law.
3. You have the right to consult with a lawyer and have the lawyer present during questioning.
4. If you cannot afford a lawyer, one will be appointed if you so desire.

On many occasions individuals would give up these rights. I know of one in particular who chose to remain silent: Jesus Christ.

MATTHEW 26: 62-64

> "And the high priest arose and said to Him, "Do you answer nothing? What is it these men testify against you?" But Jesus kept silent. And the high priest answered and said to Him, "I put you under oath by the living God: Tell us if you are the Christ, the Son of God!"

Our Lord and Savior Jesus Christ illustrated through himself the ability to "bridle the tongue" even under great injustices, ridicule, tribulation, physical and mental pain and suffering. Why didn't Jesus defend himself? Why did Jesus choose to remain silent?

If Jesus would have said just a word, eternity would have stood still, time rolled back into the unthinkable past, the earth and the fullness thereof, and all mankind would have ceased to be no more. He endured so much, simply for our salvation.

- They whipped my Jesus, they whipped him all night long and he remained silent.
- They pressed a crown of thorns on his head and he remained silent.
- They mocked him and spat on him and he remained silent.
- They made him carry an old rugged cross and he remained silent.
- They pierced him in his side and Jesus remained silent.

I'm so glad saints that our Savior chose his words carefully and said, "Father, forgive them, for they do not know what they do." "Father, 'into Your hands I commit My spirit.'" Having said this, He breathed His last. (Luke 23: 34, 46)

Jesus bridled his tongue so that you and I today could have the "right to eternal life".

Remember saints, watch your tongue! You have the "right to remain silent".

Three Wise Decisions

SCRIPTURE: Matthew 2: 1-12
SUBJECT: Wise Men Make Three Wise Decisions

INTRODUCTION:
To have wisdom, is to possess understanding, or insight. The Bible says in Proverbs 9:10, "The fear of the Lord is the beginning of Wisdom and knowledge of the Holy One is understanding."

We will discuss today: Three wise men that made three very wise decisions: (1.) Seek God! (2.) Follow God! (3.) Worship and Obey God!

MATTHEW 2: 1-12

"Then Herod, when he had secretly called the wise men, determined from them what time the star appeared. And he sent them to Bethlehem and said, "Go and search diligently for the young Child, and when you have found Him, bring back word to me, that I may worship Him also. When they heard the king, they departed; and behold, the star which they had seen in the East went before them, till it came and stood over where the young Child was. When they saw the star, they rejoiced with exceedingly great joy. "And when they had come into the house, they saw the young Child with Mary His mother, and fell down and worshipped Him. And when they had opened their treasures, they presented gifts to Him: gold, frankincense, and myrrh. Then, being divinely warned in a dream that they should not return to Herod, they departed for their country another way."

Sermon

MATTHEW 2: 7, 8

"Then Herod, when he had secretly called the wise men, determined from them what time the star appeared. And he sent them to Bethlehem and said, "Go and search diligently for the young Child, and when you have found Him, bring back word to me, that I may worship Him also."

The Old Testament prophets predicted and longed for the coming of the Anointed One, who would bring redemption and deliverance to God's people. In Matthew, the first canon of the New Testament, we find that not everyone was all that excited about Jesus' coming, especially King Herod.

Do we have any supervisors in the church? You can understand, in a way how King Herod felt. Imagine that you've been working in a position of authority and all of a sudden, a new kid on the block shows up on the scene. Imagine how you would feel if your boss and all your subordinates begin bragging and boasting about how great the new guy is.

Like King Herod, you would suddenly become troubled and concerned about your status and your position.

If you're not wrapped up and tangled up in the Lord, you might start plotting, scheming, befriending your co-workers, and trying to find some dirt on the new guy. You might really want this person gone, like yesterday! Am I not right? I know I'm right about it!

Nevertheless, King Herod told the Three Wise Men to do one significant thing:

"GO AND SEARCH DILIGENTLY FOR THE YOUNG CHILD"

1. The first decision that the Wise Men made was to seek after the Lord and Savior.

Isaiah the prophet said, "Seek the Lord while He may be found, Call upon Him while He is near." (Isaiah 55:6)

Our Lord and Savior said, "Ask and it will be given to you; seek and you will find; knock and it will be opened unto you." (Matthew 7:7)

MATTHEW 2: 9, 10

> "When they heard the king, they departed; and behold, the star which they had seen in the East went before them, till it came and stood over where the young Child was. When they saw the star, they rejoiced with exceedingly great joy."

With pillars of cloud and fire, God led Moses and the Israelites out of bondage and through the wilderness.

And so again, God led these Three Wise Men by another amazing manifestation, a star, to Mary's baby and our Savior, Jesus.

2. The second decision the Three Wise Men made was to follow God and rejoice in His divine guidance.

I am reminded of a song that speaks of being led. If we are willing to go with him all the way, we too can travel a righteous path and be blessed.

MATTHEW 2:11, 12

"And when they had come into the house, they saw the young Child with Mary His mother, and fell down and worshipped Him.
And when they had opened their treasures, they presented gifts to Him: gold, frankincense, and myrrh.

Then, being divinely warned in a dream that they should not return to Herod, they departed for their country another way."

This brings us to third decision the wise men made:

3. Obey and Worship God! (Repeat)

Jesus, being the descendant of David made Him more than earthly qualified to be King of Israel. King Herod knew this all too well and so He used the Three Wise Men to find baby Jesus, so that he could destroy Him.

But how many of you know that God always gives us a warning before impending doom?

It could be in a friend who simply asks you come and fellowship with them at church instead of going to the shopping mall or that club. It could be that co-worker during a Christmas party who said, "I'll take you home man, I think you've had too much to drink."

It could be the Spirit of the Lord speaking to you as to the Three Wise Men. "Don't return to Herod, go another way."

Obedience, is better than sacrifice!

CONCLUSION

Mary and Joseph were grateful and happy to receive the gifts from the Three Wise Men, for they were of great value. The greatest gift that the Three Wise Men really gave was an example of how to worship and be obedient to the Spirit of God!

Jesus gave us a wonderful gift before He ascended back to the Father. The Holy Spirit. This gift from the Lord is our helper, guide, and teacher, and will keep us safe in this very present age.

If you don't get anything under the tree this Christmas, remember the precious gift that Jesus left us upon His departure, the Holy Spirit. Through this gift many other wonderful presents manifest:

1. Holy Spirit Empowers-"But truly I am full of power by the Spirit of the Lord" *(Micah 3:8)*

2   Holy Spirit Bears Witnesses- "The Spirit Himself bears witness with our spirit that we are children of God" *(Romans 8:16))*

3   Holy Spirit Gives Joy-"For the kingdom of God is not food and drink, but righteousness and peace and joy in the Holy Spirit" (Romans 14:17)

4   Holy Spirit Sanctifies-"God from the beginning chose you for salvation through sanctification by the Holy Spirit and belief in truth *(2nd Thessalonians 2:13)*

5   Holy Spirit Bears Fruits-"Love, Joy, Peace, Longsuffering, Kindness, Goodness, Faithfulness, Gentleness, and Self-control," *(Gal. 5:22,23)*

6   Holy Spirit Gives Gifts-"Wisdom, Knowledge, Faith, Healings, Miracles, Prophecy, Discerning of Spirits, Tongues, Interpretation of Tongues" *(1st Corinthians 12:3-11)*

If I were you, the most important gift that I would want is the Holy Spirit!

My brothers and sisters, like the Three Wise Men, in the quiet of the night, we too can still hear the Spirit of God speaking to us and compelling us to make these three wise decisions:

(1.) SEEK GOD! (2.) FOLLOW GOD! (3.) WORSHIP AND OBEY GOD!

You Can Lead A Horse To Water But You Can't Make Him Drink

SCRIPTURE: Acts 8:26-39
SUBJECT: The Holy Spirit, A Witness of Jesus Christ

INTRODUCTION:
Jesus last recorded words, known as the Great Commission are as follows: "You shall be witnesses to Me in Jerusalem, and in all Judea and Samaria, and to the end of the earth".

The great book of Acts, written by Luke, is the story of men and women who took the "Great Commission" seriously and began to spread the news of a risen Savior to the most remote corners of the known world.

In our text today, Philip, whose name means "lover of horses", was one of the original apostles of Jesus. He was also one of the first to preach the gospel of Jesus Christ throughout Palestine in the cities around Jerusalem.

This same Philip was among a small group of fearful men after the death of Christ who became empowered with the Holy Spirit on the day of Pentecost and began to transform into one of the greatest witnesses for the church of God.

Philip learned through the preaching and teaching of the gospel that, "You can lead a horse to water but you can't make him drink."

ACTS 8:26-39 NEW KING JAMES VERSION

26 Now an angel of the Lord spoke to Philip, saying, "Arise and go toward the south along the road which goes down from Jerusalem to Gaza." This is desert. 27 So he arose and went. And behold, a man of Ethiopia, a eunuch of great authority under Candace the queen of the Ethiopians, who had charge of all her treasury, and had come to Jerusalem to worship, 28 was returning. And sitting in his chariot, he was reading Isaiah the prophet. 29 Then the Spirit said to Philip, "Go near and overtake this chariot." 30 So Philip ran to him, and heard him reading the prophet Isaiah, and said, "Do you understand what you are reading?" 31 And he said, "How can I, unless someone guides me?" And he asked Philip to come up and sit with him. 32 The place in the Scripture which he read was this: " He was led as a sheep to the slaughter; And as a lamb before its shearer is silent, So He opened not His mouth 33 In His humiliation His justice was taken away, And who will declare His generation? For His life is taken from the earth." 34 So the eunuch answered Philip and said, "I ask you, of whom does the prophet say this, of himself or of some other man?" 35 Then Philip opened his mouth, and beginning at this Scripture, preached Jesus to him. 36 Now as they went down the road, they came to some water. And the eunuch said, "See, here is water. What

hinders me from being baptized?" 37 Then
Philip said, "If you believe with all your heart,
you may." And he answered and said, "I believe
that Jesus Christ is the Son of God." 38 So
he commanded the chariot to stand still. And
both Philip and the eunuch went down into the
water, and he baptized him. 39 Now when they
came up out of the water, the Spirit of the Lord
caught Philip away, so that the eunuch saw him
no more; and he went on his way rejoicing.

26 Now an angel of the Lord spoke to Philip,
saying, "Arise and go toward the south along
the road which goes down from Jerusalem to
Gaza." This is desert. 27 So he arose and went.

There are some golden nuggets in these verses…

1 First of all, the place where the Lord sent Philip
was the desert. It was a dry wasteland, and a
desolate and barren region. Has the Lord ever
told you to go some place that was like that?
Has God ever requested your presence in a
dry, boring, dead place, with no one praising
God, no one thirsting for or seeking after
righteousness. Did you go any way?

Or just maybe it was your life, at one point, that was like this desert, desolate, empty, and depressing. Have you ever felt like you needed someone or something to quench your soul's thirst?

The Lord will bring two people together to be a witness to His Word. He said, "For where two or three are gathered together in my name, I am there in the midst of them." (Matthew 18: 20)

2   The Ethiopian was a eunuch, a male who was deprived of his testes or external genitals. This meant that he was not able to produce children. Isaiah the prophet spoke of the eunuch from a vision, describing them as a "dry tree".

But the Lord said in Isaiah 56:4,5, "To the eunuchs who keep My Sabbaths, and choose to please Me, and hold fast My covenant, even to them I will give in my house and walls a place and name better than that of sons and daughters; an everlasting name that shall not be cut off."

God is speaking today to the men and women, who can not have children. You have a work and a place in the house of the Lord. You have the quality time to minister to the fatherless and the motherless. You can do this powerful ministry without distractions and without obligations. I tell you God will not forget your labor of love in ministering to his children!

30 So Philip ran to him, and heard him reading the prophet Isaiah, and said, "Do you understand what you are reading?" And he said, "How can I, unless someone guides me?" And he asked Philip to come up and sit with him.

3   Philip asked the Ethiopian a very serious question, "Do you understand what you are reading? And the Ethiopian responded with

the truth, "How can I, unless someone guides me."

Saints we need to be taught the Word of God at an early age. This is why I compel you to bring your children to Church School. They will have instructions in the Word of God. They will learn about Jesus. They will begin to know the work of the Holy Spirit, who is the teacher and discerner of the Word of God.

4. My essential job as a pastor is to preach the Gospel. What is the Gospel of Jesus Christ?

God so loved the world that He gave His only begotten Son and whosoever believeth in him should not perish but have life eternal. This same Jesus came down Forty and Two generations, He was conceived by the Holy Spirit, born of the Virgin Mary, suffered under Pontius Pilate, was crucified, was dead, was buried, but on the third day he rose from the dead with all power in his hand and as I speak he sits on the right hand of God the Father Almighty. And guess what he will come again, and judge the living and the dead!

This is the Gospel of Jesus Christ! If we confess with our mouths the Lord Jesus and believe these words in our heart, we are saved!

The Ethiopian knew that he needed someone to help interpret or explain the scriptures, someone to lead him to Christ.

Both Philip and I may "preach the horns off a bull", but it is up to an individual to make a conscious decision to accept Jesus as his/her Lord and Savior. In other words, you can lead a horse to the water but you can't make him drink.

CONCLUSION

ACTS 8:36-40

> "Now as they went down the road, they came to some water. And the eunuch said, See, here is some water. What hinders me from being baptized? Then Philip said, "If you believe with all your heart, you may." And he answered and said, "I believe that Jesus Christ is the Son of God." So he commanded that the chariot to stand still. And both Philip and the eunuch went down into the water, and he baptized him. Now when they came up out of the water, the *Spirit of the Lord caught Philip away, so that the eunuch saw him no more; and he went on his way rejoicing."

Now there are some diamonds and pearls in these verses...

First, were they not in the desert? How did they find water in such a dry place? Why did the eunuch see the water first before Philip?

Jesus said this, "If anyone thirsts, let him come to Me and drink. He who believes in Me, as the Scriptures has said, out of his heart will flow rivers of living water. But this he spoke concerning the Spirit, whom those believing in Him would receive" (John 7:37-39)

The eunuch saw the water first. Do you know why? It was because he was the one in need of the quenching! Philip was already filled with the Holy Spirit.

Saints, when the Holy Spirit comes, He moves upon the heart of every man woman, boy and girl, and compels them to come to Christ. The Ethiopian was thirsting after righteousness and began seeking the Lord; "I believe that Jesus Christ is the Son of God."

THESE ARE THE FIRST STEPS TO CHRISTIAN DISCIPLESHIP:

Now after acknowledging the Lord Jesus as your personal Savior your next steps are to 1. Join a church, 2. Be baptized, 3. Fellowship with the saints of God, and last but not least, continue to 4. Learn and Study God's infallible Word.

I can lead you to Christ, but it is you that must drink of the water of life freely!

I am reminded of a song that speaks of the blood from Emmanuel's veins. We must all desire for our blood to lose every guilty stain. We can only do this with God.

At 9 year's old I gave my life to Christ, and I said, "Where He leads me I will follow, where He leads me I will follow, wherever the Lord leads me I will follow, I'll go with Him, with Him, all the way!

"YOU CAN LEAD A HORSE TO WATER BUT ONLY CHRIST CAN MAKE HIM DRINK."

Too Blessed to Be Stressed! Too Anointed To Be Disappointed!

SCRIPTURE: Psalm 1:1-6
SUBJECT: The Blessings of being a Christian

INTRODUCTION:
The book of Psalm is the largest and perhaps the most widely used book in the Bible. It explores the full range of humane experiences in a very personal and practical way. The book of Psalm was set to the accompaniment of stringed instruments and served as the temple hymnbook and devotional guide for the Jewish people.

The book of Psalms was originally called the "Book of Praises" because almost every psalm contains some note of praise to God. Almost half of the 150 Psalms were written by David.

Our text for today, Psalm 1, is a reflection of the experiences of King David, who was a good shepherd, great minister of music, fearless warrior, and one of God's most beloved Kings. David reminds me a little of President William Clinton. He had some relationship problems, but he was a man who truly cared for the people of this United States and trusted and feared God.

Today, through these scriptures, I pray we will come to know this: We, Christians, are too blessed to be stressed and too anointed to be disappointed!

PSALM 1:1-6

Blessed is the man Who walks not in the counsel of the ungodly,
Nor stands in the path of sinners,   Nor sits in the seat of the scornful; 2 But his delight is in the law of the Lord,   And in His law he meditates day and night. 3 He shall be like a tree   Planted by the rivers of water,   That brings forth its fruit in its season,
Whose leaf also shall not wither; And whatever he does shall prosper. 4 The ungodly are not so, But are like the chaff which the wind drives away.

5   Therefore the ungodly shall not stand in the judgment, Nor sinners in the congregation of the righteous. 6 For the Lord knows the way of the righteous, But the way of the ungodly shall perish.

Sermon

PSALM 1:1, 2:

"Blessed is the man who walks not in the counsel of the ungodly, nor stands in the path of the sinners, nor sits in the seat of the scornful;

*WALKS NOT IN THE COUNSEL OF THE UNGODLY:

1. Saints, don't seek counsel from anyone who does not know the Lord.
2. Two wrongs don't make it right!
3. Seek out wise counsel, someone who cares for your spiritual well being.
4. Find someone who will tell you the righteous way to do things.

*NOR STANDS IN THE PATH OF SINNERS:

If you have a friend or even a family member who is unsaved, and you have continually encouraged them to turn from their wicked ways, then let me give you some wise counsel from David. Let them go!

I've personally experienced this from my heroin addicted sibling. I told her, "There is no way on this side of heaven you are going to disrespect my parents and drag them into that pit of hell with you. Get out of my parent's holy house! I informed her that she had to make a decision. She could either choose to go into a rehabilitation center or to jail. "The choice is yours", I said. I think you all know which one she chose.

Saints, don't continue to stand in the doorway of a sinner's lifestyle. Get out of their way. Let them go and fall into that pit or into the muck and mire, and into that hog pin. Get out of their pathway, and believe me after they dwell in that mess for awhile, you'd better believe that they will come running back to the ark of safety!

Our main goals and objectives as Disciples of Christ are:

FOLLOW THE EXAMPLES OF CHRIST

- Compel them to come.
- Tell them the truth (Word of God).

We can not hogtie and drag anyone into the kingdom of God. We are saints not saviors!

*NO ONE SITS IN THE SEAT OF THE SCORNFUL

The scornful, means the disrespectful. These are individuals who go against the will and law of God. These people could also be saved but not quite filled with the Holy Spirit.

Galatians 5th Chapter speaks of these characteristics:

- Adulterer
- Fornicator
- Hater
- Jealous
- Envious
- Drunkenness
- Dissensions (always stirring up trouble)

These are just to name a few.

Do not sit in their seats. Paul reminds us that those who continue to do these things will not inherit the kingdom of God. The things they do are unclean. It's like sitting behind someone on a dirty toilet seat. I know I'm right about this thing.

PSALM 1:2, 3

> "But his delight is in the Law of the Lord, and
> in His law he meditates day and night."

Saints, like David, we are too blessed to be stressed and too anointed to be disappointed!

As a saint of the Most High God, we have fighting words from God.

We can use them day and night.

When we rise up, we must learn to say,

> "This is the day that the Lord has made I will rejoice and be glad in it."

And during the day when the enemy thinks he has caught you off guard, I dare you to say:

> "The Lord is my keeper; the Lord is my shade upon my right hand. The sun shall not smite me by day, nor the moon by night. The Lord shall preserve me from all evil, He shall preserve my soul.
> (PSALM 121)

Then when you lay down at night, place these words in your spirit:

> "I will both lie down in peace, and sleep; for you alone, O Lord, make me dwell in safety."

(PSALM 4:8)

Like David, we have more than a slingshot and a rock. We have a greater weapon, that sixty-six shooter called The Holy Bible. Meditate on it both day and night!

CONCLUSION

Nelson Mandela said, "There is no easy walk to freedom anywhere, and many of us will have to pass through the shadow of death again and again before we reach the mountaintop of our desires."

As Christians, we do not walk blindly down this path of righteousness. We are assured that there is a bright light at the end of the tunnel of life. The bright and morning star, and His name is Jesus Christ. We have the root and offspring of David, who has given us freely the water of life. If we stay planted and rooted in Jesus Christ, we will be blessed and prosperous.

As a people of God, we have a great hope, for we believe that Jesus died and rose from the dead. If we die in Him we also will rise up with Him. For the Word of God says, that we who are alive and remain until the coming of the Lord, will by no means precede those who died in Christ Jesus.

The Bible tells me, the Lord Himself will descend from heaven with a shout, with the voice of an archangel, and with the trumpet of God. And the dead in Christ will rise first. Then those who are alive and remain shall be caught up together with them in the clouds to meet the Lord in the air! (1st Thessalonians 4:13-18)

You are too blessed to be stressed, too anointed to be disappointed! You are a child of the King! You are God's child, born again of the incorruptible seed of the Word of God, which lives and abides forever!

You are too blessed to be stressed, too anointed to be disappointed!

You are firmly rooted, built up, and strengthened in the faith, overflowing with joy and thanksgiving!

MY BELOVED BROTHERS AND SISTERS, I'M TOO BLESSED TO BE STRESSED, TOO ANOINTED TO BE DISAPPOINTED!

Who Let The Dogs Out?

SCRIPTURE: Isaiah 56:9-12
Rev. 22:10-17
SUBJECT: Who is responsible for the language/culture of youth today?

INTRODUCTION:

This sermon is dedicated to the youth and their parents/guardians. Through the Word of God and the help of the Holy Spirit, I will address some critical issues that our youth are facing. Parents you will hear some things you probably have heard before. Just holler "Amen"! Youth, I will discuss derogatory language, disrespectful words, undisciplined lifestyles, profanity, laziness, and last but not least, death. Subjects we never want to really talk about but are a prerequisite in this present age.

Why? The Lord has clearly shown us through the news media that we are losing our children. The question is whose fault is it? Are our children going crazy? As parents or guardians, have we done all that we can do to instruct them in the ways that they should be going?

Saints, the question for today is, Who Let the Dogs Out?

AS GOD LOVES ME

ISAIAH 56:9-12 NKJ

"All the beast of the field, come to devour, all you beast in the forest. His watchmen are blind. They are all ignorant; they are all dumb dogs, they cannot bark; Sleeping, lying down, loving to slumber. Yes, they are greedy dogs, which never have enough. And they are shepherds who can not understand; they all look to their own way, everyone for his own gain, from his own territory. Come one says, I will bring wine, and we will fill ourselves with intoxicating drink; tomorrow will be as today, and much more abundant."

WHO LET THE DOGS OUT?

The word dog, in our text today is used over 40 times in the Bible. And guess what? It almost always means the same thing; a descriptive term of that which is evil or wicked.

Young people, one of the worst words in the world to call anyone, especially a black brother is a "dog".

The Bible gives these characteristics of a dog:

1. Devouring beast
2. Blind
3. Ignorant
4. Dumb
5. Cannot bark (talking loud saying nothing)
6. Sleeping, Lying down, Loving to slumber
7. Greedy, never have enough

8. Bad shepherds who cannot understand, selfish financial gain
9. Partying, drinking and living for today

Those characteristics remind me of the enemy.

> 1st Peter 5:8 says, "Be sober be vigilant; because your adversary the devil walks about like a roaring lion, seeking whom he may devour."

THE QUESTION REMAINS: WHO LET THE DOGS OUT?

Young people, the Lord sent me here to this house of prayer to talk to you. I am the angel of the Lord for this church. I stand behind this sacred desk to tell you the truth, the Word of God. I refuse to sugar coat this word. I'm not here just to make you feel good. I have to answer to a higher calling. God sent me to be a standard bearer, to hold up His standards and commandments.

Don't get me wrong, I'm not perfect for all have sinned and fall short of the glory of God. We sin daily by, thought, word or deed. But God has chosen me to be the good shepherd, to feed His sheep. I'm not just seeking money, I'm truly concerned about your souls.

God will forgive you for your sins, but to continue to do the same transgression over and over again is like tempting God. (Luke 4:9-12)

Satin tried to tempt Jesus in the wilderness…

"Why don't you jump from this cliff, the angels will break your fall, you won't even hurt your feet against the rocks." Jesus said, "Thou shall not tempt the Lord thy God."

WHAT ARE SOME OF THE WAYS WE TEMPT GOD?

- Disobedience to His Commandments

THE TEN COMMANDMENTS:

1. Trust God only (Ex. 20:3,4)
2. Worship God only (Ex. 20:5,6)
3. Use God's name in ways that honor Him (Ex.20:7)
4. Rest on the Sabbath day and think about God (Ex. 20:8-11)
5. Respect and obey your parents (Ex.20:12)
6. Protect and respect human life (Ex.20:13)
7. Be true to your husband or wife (Ex.20:14)
8. Do not take what belongs to others (Ex, 20: 15)
9. Do not lie about others (Ex.20:16)
10. Be satisfied with what you have (Ex.20:17)

OTHER WAYS WE TEMPT GOD:

- Disobedience to the State Laws
- Drunkenness
- Drugs (friends say try it "you want get hooked")

- Smoking
- Sex before marriage

CONCLUSION

The answer to today's question is: we all let the dogs out. We continue to let society dictate who and what we should say, who and what we should wear, and whom we should hook-up with.

We let the dogs out, when we neglect to discipline and raise our children. We let the dogs out when we allow networks to pollute our minds with profanity and TV with pornography.

Saints, God has already given us the master plan through his divine word.

That's why He said in Revelations 22:11-17 NKJV:

"He who is unjust, let him be unjust still; he who is filthy, let him be filthy still; he who is righteous, let him be righteous still; he who is holy let him be holy still. And behold, I am coming quickly, and my reward is with me, to give to every one according to his work. I am Alpha and Omega, the Beginning and the End, the First and the Last.

Blessed are those who do His commandments that they may have the right to the tree of life, and may enter through the gates into the city.

But outside are dogs and sorcerers and sexually immoral and murderers and idolaters, and whoever loves and practices a lie.

I Jesus have sent my angel to testify to the churches. I am the Root and the Offspring of David, the Bright and

Morning Star. And the Spirit and the bride say, Come! And let him who hears say Come! And let him who thirsts, Come! And whoever desires let him take of the water of life freely."

WHO LET THE DOGS OUT?

He Saw The Best In Me!

SCRIPTURE: 1st Corinthians 15: 1-11
KEY VERSE: 15: 9
SUBJECT: Least of the Apostles became one of the Best!

INTRODUCTION:

How many of you know that you don't have to be what people call you? If they say you're "good for nothing", you don't have to be "good for nothing".

There could be no better example of someone who almost the entire early Christian church thought was going to be "good for nothing" than the Apostle Paul. Before his encounter with our Lord and Savior Jesus Christ, Paul would systematically seek out, and persecute those who even thought they were Christians. In fact, if Paul were here today he would be placed on the "Most Wanted" list as a terrorist.

Thanks, be to God, this same tenacious Paul on the road to Damascus, encountered a savior, and a redeemer in Jesus Christ. If Paul was here today, he would boldly proclaim, "He saw the best in me, when everyone else around could only see the worst in me!"

1 CORINTHIANS 15:1-11
(NEW KING JAMES VERSION)

1   Moreover, brethren, I declare to you the gospel which I preached to you, which also you received and in which you stand, 2 by which also you are saved, if you hold fast that word which I preached to you—unless you believed in vain. 3 For I delivered to you first of all that which I also received: that Christ died for our sins according to the Scriptures, 4 and that He was buried, and that He rose again the third day according to the Scriptures, 5 and that He was seen by Cephas, then by the twelve. 6 After that He was seen by over five hundred brethren at once, of whom the greater part remain to the present, but some have fallen asleep.

7   After that He was seen by James, then by all the apostles. 8 Then last of all He was seen by me also, as by one born out of due time. 9 For I am the least of the apostles, who am not worthy to be called an apostle, because I persecuted the church of God. 10 But by the grace of God I am what I am, and His grace toward me was not in vain; but I labored more abundantly than they all, yet not I, but the grace of God which was with me. 11 Therefore, whether it was I or they, so we preach and so you believed.

Sermon

9   For I am the least of the apostles, who am not worthy to be called an apostle, because I persecuted the church of God.

The Apostle Paul knew that his past was a detrimental way to start a ministry, yet he used the same vigor he had seeking and persecuting the saved, to encourage the unsaved. His mentality became "follow me as I follow Christ".

Some looked at Paul like he had lost his mind. Yet Paul continued to preach about Jesus Christ, his crucifixion, his death and resurrection.

Saints, Paul never forgot who saved him: Jesus Christ! Paul never forgot what redeemed him: The Blood of Christ! We should never get so sophisticated, so educated, or "so progressive" that we forget that it was Jesus and His blood shed on Calvary's cross that set us free!

You see saints, something happens when you meet Jesus. He can touch us in a way that overwhelming joy touches our souls. Paul's mind, body and soul were changed on that old dusty road to Damascus. The risen Christ became his faith, his hope and his life!

How many of you know that you don't have to be perfect to be used by God? The Apostle Paul was once the "chief of sinners". Can I really tell Paul's story? While traveling on a road to Damascus, to arrest Jewish people who had accepted Jesus as the Messiah, a startling bright light from heaven forced Paul to the ground. Then Jesus asked Paul, "Why persecutest thou me?"

Then Paul was struck blind and was led into the city. Ananias met Paul and told him that he had been chosen by God as a messenger for the Gentiles (Acts 9:17). Soon after Paul received his sight, like other believers he was then baptized.

Paul knew for himself that life will sometimes "knock you off course" but that you can get back up and keep going in Christ Jesus!

But Paul also realized that being "knocked off course" wasn't necessarily a bad thing, some of us are like Paul "hard headed" and need a few spiritual knocks up side the head, by the good Lord. I know I'm right!

> 10　But by the grace of God I am what I am, and His grace toward me was not in vain; but I labored more abundantly than they all, yet not I, but the grace of God which was with me.

What Paul was trying to say in this passage of scripture was that he was a true witness to the awesome changing power of Christ in our lives and that out of all the apostles he had the most to prove.

The Apostle Paul may have been the least of the apostles, but he knew if he "kept his eyes on the prize", one day he would be one of the best laborers in the vineyard for Christ Jesus.

Paul's radical change and "call" challenged and encouraged him and us, to forget the things which were behind and to not worry about what they say you used to be or do. This teaches us to reach forth, and to stretch ourselves forward, towards the finish line. The Apostle Paul pressed on toward perfection as an example to all believers.

Like Paul, I'm just a nobody, trying to tell everybody, about somebody who can save your soul!

> 11　Therefore, whether it was I or they, so we preach and so you believed.

The doctrine of Christ's death and resurrection is the foundation of Christianity. Remove this, and all our hopes for eternity sink at once. The Apostle Paul was highly favored, but he always had a low opinion of himself, and expressed it.

When sinners are, by divine grace, turned into saints, God causes the remembrance of their former sins to make them humble, diligent, and faithful. God by divine grace sees only the best and all that is valuable in us. If you give your life to Jesus, I guarantee He will bring out the best in you!

I really admired the Apostle Paul's willingness to do or suffer any thing, so that others could be saved. This hope and prospect carried him through all the difficulties of his work and labor for the Lord.

Saints, maybe to you it seems that we, preachers are repetitious, for we preach Sunday in and Sunday out the same gospel that Paul taught: "That Christ died for our sins according to the Scriptures, and that He was buried, and that He rose again the third day according to the Scriptures."

This is the engrafted word of God that saves our souls!

CONCLUSION

My brothers and sisters, "God demonstrated His own love toward us, in that while we were still sinners, Christ died for us. Much more then, having been justified by His blood, we shall be saved from wrath through Him. For if when we were enemies we reconciled to God through the death of His Son, much more, having been reconciled, we shall be saved by His life. (Romans 5: 8, 9, 10)

We preach these declarations of God so that you may know and believe. When God now looks at us, He sees the blessed blood of His beloved Son, Jesus Christ. I'm so thankful that through the blood of Christ, God Saw the Best in Me!

One Nation Under God

SCRIPTURE: 2nd Kings 20: 1-11
SUBJECT: A Great Leader and Nation That Fears God

INTRODUCTION:
The prophets of God played a prominent role in the books of First and Second Kings. God used them to remind the kings of their covenant responsibilities as His theocratic administrators. In other words, when the king keeps the covenant/laws, he and the nation are richly blessed.

Unfortunately, today judgment consistently falls upon those who refuse to obey God's law. May of whom are concerned more with their own plans and rejecting the righteous plans of God.

The book of Second Kings was written from a prophetic viewpoint, teaching that the decline and collapse of both Israel and Judah occurred because of failure on the part of the rulers and people to heed the warnings of God's messengers. The spiritual climate of a nation determines its political and economic conditions.

Six years before the overthrow of Israel's capital of Samaria, Hezekiah became king of Judah. Hezekiah's exemplary faith and reform, can also encourage us to fly flags high during moments to honor those in service such as Labor Day. These moments remind us that we are and should remain "One Nation Under God".

2 KINGS 20:1-11 (NEW KING JAMES VERSION) HEZEKIAH'S LIFE EXTENDED

1   In those days Hezekiah was sick and near death. And Isaiah the prophet, the son of Amoz, went to him and said to him, "Thus says the LORD: 'Set your house in order, for you shall die, and not live.'" 2 Then he turned his face toward the wall, and prayed to the LORD, saying, 3 "Remember now, O LORD, I pray, how I have walked before You in truth and with a loyal heart, and have done what was good in Your sight." And Hezekiah wept bitterly.

4   And it happened, before Isaiah had gone out into the middle court, that the word of the LORD came to him, saying, 5 "Return and tell Hezekiah the leader of My people, 'Thus says the LORD, the God of David your father: "I have heard your prayer, I have seen your tears; surely I will heal you. On the third day you shall go up to the house of the LORD. 6 And I will add to your days fifteen years. I will deliver you and this city from the hand of the king of Assyria; and I will defend this city for My own sake, and for the sake of My servant David."'"

Sermon

Hezekiah, whose name means *whom Jehovah has strengthened*, is the Son of Ahaz; whom he succeeded on the throne of the kingdom of Judah. He reigned twenty-nine years. He is spoken of as a great and good king. In public life, he followed the example of his great grandfather Uzziah.

He abolished idolatry from his kingdom, and among other things he destroyed the "brazen serpent" which had been removed to Jerusalem, and had become an object of idolatrous worship.

Hezekiah refused to pay the tribute which his father had paid, and "rebelled against the king of Assyria, and served him not". This led to the invasion of Judah by Sen-na-cherib (2 Kings 18:13-16), who took forty cities, and besieged Jerusalem with mounds.

And so, Hezekiah yielded to the demands of the Assyrian king, and agreed to pay him three hundred talents of silver and thirty of gold.

But Sen-na-cherib dealt treacherously with Hezekiah, and a second time within two years invaded his kingdom. This invasion issued in the destruction of Sennacherib's army. Hezekiah prayed to God, and "that night the angel of the Lord went out, and smote in the camp of the Assyrians 185,000 men."

HEZEKIAH'S SICKNESS AND HIS RECOVERY IN ANSWER TO PRAYER

2   Then he turned his face toward the wall, and prayed to the LORD, saying, 3 "Remember now, O LORD, I pray, how I have walked before You in truth and with a loyal heart, and have done what was good in Your sight." And Hezekiah wept bitterly. 4 And it happened,

> before Isaiah had gone out into the middle court, that the word of the LORD came to him, saying, 5 "Return and tell Hezekiah the leader of My people, 'Thus says the LORD, the God of David your father: "I have heard your prayer, I have seen your tears; surely I will heal you. On the third day you shall go up to the house of the LORD. 6 And I will add to your days fifteen years. I will deliver you and this city from the hand of the king of Assyria; and I will defend this city for My own sake, and for the sake of My servant David."'"

Hezekiah was sick unto death, in the same year in which the king of Assyria besieged Jerusalem. A warning to prepare for death was brought to Hezekiah by Isaiah.

Prayer is one of the best preparations for death, because by it we fetch in strength and grace from God, to enable us to finish our course in life and rest in peace with the Lord.

Hezekiah *wept bitterly*: some gather from this action that he was unwilling to die, but it is in the nature of man to dread the separation of the soul and the body. To rest in peace with thee is a feeling that not one of us can describe until we reach that moment.

Yet Hezekiah does not pray, Lord, spare me, but, *Lord, remember me*. God always hears the prayers of the broken hearted, and will give health, length of days, and temporal deliverances, as much and as long as it is truly good, for "we know that all things work together for good to them that love God, to them who are the called according to his purpose" Romans 8: 28 .

Hezekiah was not perfect, he made some mistakes. One in particular was after he was given the miracle of 15 more years to live, Hezekiah showed his treasures and armor, and other proofs of his wealth and power to the Chaldean ambassadors from Babylon.

This was the effect of pride and ostentation, Hezekiah began to depart from his simple reliance on God. He also missed the opportunity of speaking to the Chaldeans, about how God had truly blessed him by extending his life, and of pointing out to them the absurdity and evil of idolatry.

It is common to show our friends our houses and possessions, but sometimes our possessions take possession of us. (Repeat)

These earthly toys give us a false sense of security, and a false sense of inspiration and happiness that makes us think that everything we have, revolves around materialistic items. If we do this in the pride of our hearts, to gain applause from men, not giving praise to God, it becomes sin in us, as it did in Hezekiah.

I remind folks that, "I make money but money don't make me".

CONCLUSION

"If my people, which are called by my name, shall humble themselves, and pray, and seek my face, and turn from their wicked ways; then will I hear from heaven, and will forgive their sin, and will heal their land." 2 Chronicles 7:14 (King James Version)

My brothers and my sisters we must continually pray for our political and spiritual leaders. There are some difficult days ahead but Hezekiah has shown us by faith, humility, obedience, and the power of prayer that we will make it through these tough times.

God has graciously allowed us to witness a (modern day king) in 44th President Barack Obama. His presence reigned over us and has shown what genuine concern for the people of God looks like. In the midst of his presidency, initiatives such as the *Health Care Law (Obama Care)* and *Finance Reform* were recorded in history as two of the top initiatives of his presidency.

We must also recognize that the President needs our prayers, so that he can continue to make godly decisions for this nation and the world.

America is a great nation that fears God and holds dear to his Commandments which sets us apart from other nations. We have a national oath of solidarity and patriotism called the *Pledge of Allegiance*, originally composed by Francis Bellamy in 1892.

The phrase *"under God"* was incorporated into the Pledge of Allegiance by a Joint Resolution of Congress - amending of the Flag Code enacted in 1942. President Eisenhower signed the bill into law on Flag Day, June 14, 1954.

They have taken everything that is faith-based out of the schools (prayer/scriptures) but this sacred oath:

THE PLEDGE OF ALLEGIANCE

"I pledge allegiance to the flag of the United States of America, and to the republic for

which it stands, one nation under God,
indivisible, with liberty and justice for all."

My brothers and my sisters we are and should remain "One Nation Under God".

I am reminded of a song that encourages us to have faith in the grace that was shed for each of us. That same grace can be found in leadership and service. We must remain prayerful for those who give their lives to be a soldier in the army of all that is good.

I'd Rather Have Jesus Than Silver or Gold!

SCRIPTURE: Acts 3: 1-10
KEY VERSE: Acts 3: 6
SUBJECT: The Lame Man Healed!

INTRODUCTION:

Saints I have a saying, "I make money but money doesn't make me." In other words, having a whole lot of money doesn't mean a hill of beans if you do not have good health, peace of mind, joy or happiness. The text today, by the examples of the apostles Peter and John encourages us to say boldly: "I'd rather have Jesus than silver or gold".

ACTS 3: 1-10 (NEW KING JAMES VERSION)

1   Now Peter and John went up together to the temple at the hour of prayer, the ninth hour. 2 And a certain man lame from his mother's womb was carried, whom they laid daily at the gate of the temple which is called Beautiful, to ask alms from those who entered the temple; 3 who, seeing Peter and John about to go into the temple, asked for alms. 4 And fixing his eyes on him, with John, Peter said, "Look at us." 5 So he gave them his attention, expecting to receive something from them. 6 Then Peter

said, "Silver and gold I do not have, but what I do have I give you: In the name of Jesus Christ of Nazareth, rise up and walk." 7 And he took him by the right hand and lifted him up, and immediately his feet and ankle bones received strength. 8 So he, leaping up, stood and walked and entered the temple with them—walking, leaping, and praising God. 9 And all the people saw him walking and praising God. 10 Then they knew that it was he who sat begging alms at the Beautiful Gate of the temple; and they were filled with wonder and amazement at what had happened to him.

Sermon

The apostles and the first believers attended the temple worship at the hours of prayer. Peter and John seemed to have been led by a divine direction, to work a miracle on a man above forty years old, who had been a cripple from his birth.

> Acts 3: 4, 5 "And fixing his eyes on him, with John, Peter said, "Look at us." 5 So he gave them his attention, expecting to receive something from them."

"LOOK AT US"

It is imperative when you come into the house of God and into the presence of the Lord, that you pay strict attention to the entire worship experience. Have you ever noticed sometimes folk try to distract you during the prayer, song of praise, reading of the scripture or even while the pastor is preaching the Word of God?

During the worship service, the Lord should have your undivided attention, for the Holy Spirit is at work teaching, convicting, convincing, converting, healing, and increasing our faith. "So then faith cometh by hearing, and hearing by the word of God" Romans 10: 17 .

Every time we enter into this sanctuary, we should be expecting a blessing, expecting a miracle and expecting to hear from the Lord!

ACTS 3: 6

> "Then Peter said, "Silver and gold I do not have, but what I do have I give you:"

"BUT WHAT I DO HAVE"

What did Peter and John have that was worth more than silver or gold? They had Jesus and power from the Holy Spirit.

Jesus made this promise in Acts 1: 8 "But you shall receive power when the Holy Spirit has come upon you; and you shall be witnesses to Me in Jerusalem, and in all Judea and Samaria, and to the end of the earth."

He also gave these instructions to the twelve disciples in Matthew 10: 8-10 "Heal the sick, cleanse the lepers, raise the dead, cast out demons. Freely you have received, freely give. Provide neither gold nor silver nor copper in your money belts, nor bag for your journey, nor two tunics, nor sandals, nor staffs; for a worker is worthy of his food."

There was no way on this side of heaven that Peter and John could just walk past this lame man as others did. They had to do something for him. And guess what? They were equipped to do something amazing by the power of the Holy Spirit!

Acts 3: 6, 7 "In the name of Jesus Christ of Nazareth, rise up and walk." And he took him by the right hand and lifted him up, and immediately his feet and ankle bones received strength.

Peter, in the name of Jesus of Nazareth, bid the lame man to rise up and walk. Yes, Jesus Christ of Nazareth can make us whole!

How many of you know that there is power in the name of Jesus!

James 5: 13-16 "Is anyone among you suffering? Let him pray. Is anyone cheerful? Let him sing psalms. Is anyone among you sick? Let him call for the elders of the church, and let them pray over him, anointing him with oil in the name of the Lord. And the prayer of faith will save the sick, and the Lord will raise him up. And if he has committed sins, he will be forgiven. Confess your trespasses to one another, and pray for one another, that you may be healed. The effective, fervent prayer of a righteous man avails much.

> Acts 3: 8 "So he, leaping up, stood and walked and entered the temple with them—walking, leaping, and praising God."

"ENTERED THE TEMPLE WITH THEM"

Did you ever wonder why the lame man was outside of the temple?

During my studies the scriptures revealed that Moses was instructed by God to not allow any man who has a defect to approach the altar.

READ-LEVITICUS 21:16-23

> "He shall not go near the veil or approach the altar, because he has a defect, lest he profane My sanctuaries; for I the LORD sanctify them."

This is probably why the lame man was placed outside the temple. But I believe the songwriter said it best, *"Now behold the Lamb, the precious Lamb of God, who was born into sin that I may live again, the Precious Lamb of God"*. "But he was wounded for our transgressions, he was bruised for our iniquities: the chastisement of our peace was upon him; and with his stripes we are healed" (Isaiah 53:5).

Jesus proclaimed this, "The Spirit of the LORD is upon Me, Because He has anointed Me To preach the gospel to the poor; He has sent Me to heal the brokenhearted, To proclaim liberty to the captives And recovery of sight to the blind, To set at liberty those who are oppressed; To proclaim the acceptable year of the LORD." Luke 4:18, 19

Saints I don't know about you but, I'd rather have Jesus than silver or gold.

CONCLUSION

This miracle of the lame man was done to show Jesus Christ to be the controller and conqueror of Satan, and a healer of all diseases. Whenever Christ gives a new life, in recovery from sickness, it should be a new life, spent more than ever in his service and to his glory.

Once the good Lord has saved us and made us whole, our business should be to spread Christ's name every place we go, and to use our influence in bringing sinners to him, that his hands may be laid upon them for their healing. We were not sent into this world to live to ourselves only, but to glorify God, and to do good works in this generation.

The apostles Peter and John referred all to their Lord, and refused to receive any honor for the miracle of the lame man, except as the Lord's undeserving instruments. The apostles knew that they were poor, weak, sinful men, and depended on Jesus for everything. "Silver and gold I do not have, but what I do have I give you."

Respect Yourself!

SCRIPTURE: Romans 12:1-16
KEY VERSE: Romans 12:1
SUBJECT: Making Your Body a Living Sacrifice to God!

INTRODUCTION:

The Apostle Paul entreated the Romans, as his brethren in Christ, by the mercies of God, to present their bodies as a living sacrifice unto God. This is a powerful appeal. We receive from the Lord every day the fruits of his mercy. So why shouldn't we render ourselves unto Him? All we are, all we have, and all we can do in reasonable service is acceptable to our God. We must desire to become a yielded instrument for God's service.

The text today gives us instructions on how we must first honor and respect ourselves. Do you wonder why this is so important? The Staples Singers said it best *"How in the world you gonna respect someone else if you don't respect yourself?"* Today we will explore three (3) key points:

1. Your Body as a Living Sacrifice to God
2. Serving God with Your Spiritual Gifts
3. Behaving Like a Christian!

DR. JACQUELINE HARDY HARRIS

ROMANS 12:1-16 (NEW KING JAMES VERSION)

1 I beseech you therefore, brethren, by the mercies of God, that you present your bodies a living sacrifice, holy, acceptable to God, which is your reasonable service. (2) And do not be conformed to this world, but be transformed by the renewing of your mind, that you may prove what is that good and acceptable and perfect will of God. (3) For I say, through the grace given to me, to everyone who is among you, not to think of himself more highly than he ought to think, but to think soberly, as God has dealt to each one a measure of faith. (4) For as we have many members in one body, but all the members do not have the same function, (5) so we, being many, are one body in Christ, and individually members of one another. (6) Having then gifts differing according to the grace that is given to us, let us use them: if prophecy, let us prophesy in proportion to our faith; (7) or ministry, let us use it in our ministering; he who teaches, in teaching; (8) he who exhorts, in exhortation; he who gives, with liberality; he who leads, with diligence; he who shows mercy, with cheerfulness. (9) Let love be without hypocrisy. Abhor what is evil. Cling to what is good. (10) Be kindly affectionate to one another with brotherly love, in honor giving preference to one another; (11) not lagging in diligence, fervent in spirit, serving the Lord; (12) rejoicing in hope, patient in tribulation, continuing steadfastly in prayer; (13) distributing to the needs of the saints, given to hospitality. (14) Bless those

who persecute you; bless and do not curse.
(15) Rejoice with those who rejoice, and weep with those who weep. (16) Be of the same mind toward one another.

Sermon

ROMANS 12:1-2
(NEW KING JAMES VERSION)

1. I beseech you therefore, brethren, by the mercies of God, that you present your bodies a living sacrifice, holy, acceptable to God, which is your reasonable service. (2) And do not be conformed to this world, but be transformed by the renewing of your mind, that you may prove what is that good and acceptable and perfect will of God.

YOUR BODY-LIVING SACRIFICE TO GOD

The work of the Holy Ghost first begins in the yielding of your body and mind to God. Your will, affections, and conversations change into the likeness of God. Your body and mind become transformed by the knowledge of the Word of God and you begin to walk in the Spirit. In other words, you embrace the mind of Christ Jesus! You simply desire to do whatever God commands you to do.

Fortunately, this yielding to the Holy Spirit leads not only to dedication but can also result in separation. The scripture says, "do not be conformed to the world" (Romans

12:2). You can not revel in the lust of this world and do the will of God at the same time.

Young people, you can not be a part of a gang, use drugs, or be sexually active and continue to do the will of God. *For your body is the temple of the Holy Spirit* and the Holy Spirit will not dwell in an unclean place.

Have you ever noticed that some people stop coming to church when they are in the world? Or what about those who slip into the church late and sit on the back pew thinking no one will see them? Your mind becomes darkened by sin. Sin can blind you and cause you to turn a blind eye in the presence of the gifts that God has prepared for you.

1. SERVING GOD WITH SPIRITUAL GIFTS

ROMANS 12:3-8
(NEW KING JAMES VERSION)

3   For I say, through the grace given to me, to everyone who is among you, not to think of himself more highly than he ought to think, but to think soberly, as God has dealt to each one a measure of faith. (4) For as we have many members in one body, but all the members do not have the same function, (5) so we, being many, are one body in Christ, and individually members of one another. (6) Having then gifts differing according to the grace that is given to us, let us use them: if prophecy, let us prophesy in proportion to our faith; (7) or ministry, let us use it in our ministering; he who teaches, in teaching; (8) he who exhorts, in exhortation; he who gives, with liberality; he who leads,

with diligence; he who shows mercy, with cheerfulness.

Pride is also a sin in us by nature. We need to be cautioned and armed against it. All the saints make up one body in Christ, and Christ is the Head of the body. In the spiritual body, some are fitted for and called to different works and positions: such as prophets, ministers, teachers, exhorters, liberal givers, musicians, singers and diligent leaders.

Whatever our gifts or positions may be, let us try to employ ourselves humbly, diligently, cheerfully, and in simplicity, not seeking our own credit or profit. I must warn you, that which you don't use you will lose! Christians who submit to the lordship of Christ in reverence and service will always grow in their spiritual lives.

2. BEHAVING LIKE A CHRISTIAN!

ROMANS 12:9-16
(NEW KING JAMES VERSION)

9   Let love be without hypocrisy. Abhor what is evil. Cling to what is good. (10) Be kindly affectionate to one another with brotherly love, in honor giving preference to one another; (11) not lagging in diligence, fervent in spirit, serving the Lord; (12) rejoicing in hope, patient in tribulation, continuing steadfastly in prayer; (13) distributing to the needs of the saints, given to hospitality. (14) Bless those who persecute you; bless and do not curse.

(15) Rejoice with those who rejoice, and weep with those who weep. (16) Be of the same mind toward one another.

Christians must not only do that which is good, but we must cleave to it. All our duty towards one another is summed up in one word, "Love". Sunday in and Sunday out, we the ministers of God compassionately proclaim:

The Summary of the Decalogue

"Hear what Christ Our Savior saith, thou shalt love the Lord thy God with all thy heart, and with all thy soul, and with all thy mind. This is the first and great commandment. And the second is like unto it; thou shalt love thy neighbor as thyself. On these two commandments hang all the Law and the Prophets."

CONCLUSION

My Brothers and Sisters, God must be served in the Spirit, under the influence of the Holy Spirit. The Lord is honored by our hope and trust in Him. He is served, not only by working for him, but by sitting still, quietly and patiently, when he calls us to suffer. Patience for God's sake is true piety (holiness). Saints, I've learned that those who rejoice in hope are more likely to be patient in tribulation.

We should not be coldhearted in the duty of prayer, the Word of God says, "pray without ceasing". Not only must there be kindness to friends, and brethren, but Christians must not harbor anger against their enemies. Bless, and curse not! This means do not bless them while you pray, and curse them when you come up off your knees, but bless them always, and curse not at all!

My beloved, Christian love will make us take part in the sorrows and joys of each other. For it is written, "Vengeance is Mine, I will repay," says the Lord. " If your enemy is hungry, feed him. If he is thirsty, give him a drink. In doing so, you will heap coals of fire on his head." In others words they will be ashamed that they have treated you unrighteous in the sight of God.

We as a people of color have a rich and blessed spiritual heritage that came from the struggles and prayers of a righteous slave and holy forerunner Bishop Richard Allen, Founder of the African Methodist Episcopal Church (1787); who proclaimed...

'We were stolen from our mother country, and brought here. We have tilled the ground and made fortunes for thousands... This land which we have watered with our tears and blood, is now our mother country'.

A true Christian knows that nothing is below us, except sin. We should never find in our hearts to look down on a brother or sister except to reach down and lift them up!

But remember, "How in the world you gonna respect someone else, if you don't Respect Yourself?"

Many Are Called, But Few Are Chosen

SCRIPTURE: Matthew 20: 1-16
Matthew 9: 35-38
SUBJECT: Called and Chosen Laborers of God's Vineyard

INTRODUCTION:

This parable, an earthly story with a heavenly meaning, was written to prepare Jesus' called and chosen disciples for the great leadership roles that they would provide in the church after Christ's ascension.

After praying all night, (Luke 6:12-16), Jesus chose these twelve disciples:

1. Simon Peter (Cephas) Leader of the apostles
2. Andrew, brother of Simon
3. James, son of Zebedee and brother of John
4. John, the beloved apostle
5. Philip, from Bethsaida
6. Bartholomew
7. Mathew, from Cana of Galilee
8. Thomas, (Didymus, which means "Twin")

9. Simon, the Canaanite
10. James, the son of Alphaeus
11. Lebbaeus, or Thaddeus
12. Judas Iscariot, who betrayed Jesus

The Twelve include two sets of fishermen brothers, a tax collector, and a traitor. The terms disciple and apostle are often used interchangeably in referring to these men. A disciple, is a learner or follower, while an apostle generally refers to a person who is chosen for a special message or commission (John 13:16). The Twelve were definitely apostles because Jesus chose them for a specific mission; to carry on His work after He ended His earthly ministry.

The text today, Matthew 20:1-16, clearly speaks to the faithful laborers of this church: "Many are called but few are Chosen".

MATTHEW 20: 1-16
(NEW KING JAMES VERSION)

1 "For the kingdom of heaven is like a landowner who went out early in the morning to hire laborers for his vineyard. 2 Now when he had agreed with the laborers for a denarius a day, he sent them into his vineyard. 3 And he went out about the third hour and saw others standing idle in the marketplace, 4 and said to them, 'You also go into the vineyard, and whatever is right I will give you.' So they went. 5 Again he went out about the sixth and the ninth hour, and did likewise. 6 And about the eleventh hour he went out and found others standing idle,

and said to them, 'Why have you been standing here idle all day?' 7 They said to him, 'Because no one hired us.' He said to them, 'You also go into the vineyard, and whatever is right you will receive.' 8 "So when evening had come, the owner of the vineyard said to his steward, 'Call the laborers and give them their wages, beginning with the last to the first.'
9 And when those came who were hired about the eleventh hour, they each received a denarius. 10 But when the first came, they supposed that they would receive more; and they likewise received each a denarius. 11 And when they had received it, they complained against the landowner, 12 saying, 'These last men have worked only one hour, and you made them equal to us who have borne the burden and the heat of the day.'
13 But he answered one of them and said, 'Friend, I am doing you no wrong. Did you not agree with me for a denarius? 14 Take what is yours and go your way. I wish to give to this last man the same as to you. 15 Is it not lawful for me to do what I wish with my own things? Or is your eye evil because I am good?' 16 So the last will be first, and the first last. For many are called, but few chosen."

Sermon

MATTHEW 20: 1-6

"For the kingdom of heaven is like a landlord, who went out early in the morning to hire laborers for his vineyard. Now when he had

> agreed with the laborers for a penny a day, he sent them into his vineyard. And he went out about the third hour and saw others standing idle in the marketplace, and said to them, 'You also go into the vineyard, and whatever is right I will give you.' And they went. Again he went about the sixth and ninth hour, and likewise.

The landlord made an agreement with the laborers for a penny (Roman currency one denarius) for a day's work. That would be, about $3.65 cents for a whole year of work. Not very much is it?

In Matthew the 10th Chapter, Jesus sent out His disciples and commanded them saying,

> "Provide neither gold nor silver nor copper in your money belts, nor bag for your journey, nor two tunics, nor sandals, nor staffs; for a worker is worthy of his food."

When you make a vow to do a work for the Lord, do not be too overly concerned about being paid. At least not on this side of heaven.

Those of you who are called to positions in the church, such as Trustees, Stewards, Missionaries, Ushers, Ministers of Music, Singers, Dancers, Administrative Secretaries, Superintendents, Teachers, Custodian, Pastor's Aides, Prayer Warriors, Deaconesses, and Ministers, I say to you that your labor will not be in vain.

The work you have done will speak for you!

God will make it right sometimes before the end of the road. I know I'm right!

MATTHEW 20: 6-7

> And about the eleventh hour he went out and found others standing idle, and said to them, 'Why have you been standing here idle all the day? They said to him, 'Because no one hired us.' He said to them 'You also go into the vineyard, and whatever is right you will receive."

There is an old cliché that states that an idle mind is the devil's advocate.

Jesus also said,

> "But I say to you that every idle word men may speak, they will give account of it in the Day of Judgment."

In other words, my brothers and my sisters, you better stop standing on that corner talking loud and saying nothing.

"Girl, I can't find no job with all these babies."

"Man, I don't care what nobody says, I ain't working at no Burger King."

The Bible says,

> "If anyone will not work, neither shall he eat."
> 2ND THESSALONIANS 3:10

Saints, I just feel in my sanctified soul that God doesn't want nor does he need any lazy people! I am reminded of a song that speaks about a coward soldier. There is not a need for one in the midst of God's work.

GOD DON'T WANT AND HE DON'T NEED NO COWARD SOLDIER!

There is a task, job, or work He has for each one of us to do.

I truly believe that we must do that work while it is yet day, for when night (death) comes, no man, woman boy or girl can work!

> "The harvest truly is plentiful, but the laborers are few. Therefore pray the Lord of harvest to send out laborers into His harvest."
> MATTHEW 9: 37, 38

CONCLUSION

MATTHEW 20:8-16

> "So the last shall be first, and the first shall be last. For many are called, but few are chosen."

Fortunately, this would not occur in this day and age. The Labor Union representatives and lawyers would jump all over this. The landowners would be on national news, and probably beaten by one or more of the laborers.

But the prophet Isaiah said it best,

"My thoughts are not your thoughts, neither are your ways my ways," says the Lord. (Isaiah 55:8)

If we look at this passage of scripture in the natural and not in the spirit we will never understand what God is saying.

Saints, the Lord wants all of us to enter into the Kingdom of God but unfortunately some will not. You see many are called to repentance and salvation, but all will not hear or answer. The Lord is not preferential. He has "no respect of person." Just because I'm a preacher and I have been saved since I was 9 years old, does not mean that my reward is greater than yours, or that I'll enter into the Kingdom of God before you.

In God's eye, it does not matter how long you labor for Him, but that you decided to do something for Him.

Is this fair? Is this right?

I can only say this, "I'd rather be a doorkeeper in the house of the Lord, than to dwell in the tents of the wicked."

I'm also reminded of the thief on the cross, who was slipping into to darkness, and the very pit of hell, had but a few hours. He made a profound decision, to accept Jesus as his Lord and Savior.

And Jesus promised this Thief, "Assuredly I say to you, today you will be with Me in Paradise" (Luke 23:43)

I don't know about you but whatever the Lord wants me to do, I'm going to do it! I may get tired, I may get weary and might get a little worn, but I know that I was not just called but chosen to do this work for the Lord. I'm not concerned about financial gain, for you see God will make it right at the end of the road. When the enemy comes up against you, just stand flat footed, hold your head up and say…

AS GOD LOVES ME

A charge to keep I have, a God to glorify
A never dying soul that fitted for the sky
To serve the present age my calling to fulfill
Oh may in all my power engage to do my Master's will

If that's not good enough you tell them...

I'm a soldier in the army of the Lord
I'm a sanctified soldier in the army of the Lord
And if I die, let me die, in the army of the Lord

If that's not good enough you tell them...

MANY ARE CALLED, BUT FEW ARE CHOSEN!

Christmas, It's Not About Us, It's About Jesus!

SCRIPTURE: Isaiah 9:6, 7
SUBJECT: The Reason for the Season

INTRODUCTION:

Isaiah, who was one of God's most resolute and persistent prophets today through the scriptures tells us of the Messiah, Jesus Christ, boldly prophesying of Christ's Birth, Christ's Mission, Christ's Death and His Gospel Invitation of Salvation.

Isaiah, whose name means "Yahweh is Salvation", reminds us through these Holy Scriptures the true reason for the season: Christmas, It's Not about Us, It's About Jesus!

Sermon

ISAIAH 9:6, 7

"For unto us a Child is born, unto us a Son given; and the government will be upon His shoulder. And His name will be called Wonderful, Counselor, Mighty God, Everlasting Father, Prince of Peace. Of the increase of His government and peace there

will be no end, upon the throne of David and
over His kingdom, to order it and establish
it with judgment and justice from that time
forward, even forever. The zeal of the Lord of
host will perform this.

It is crucial that we remember that the very existence of the Son of God did not commence with His birth in Bethlehem. Jesus was spoken of as the "Son" before He was even a man.

1. The Prophet Micah said He would be born in Bethlehem.
2. Daniel spoke of what time and season He would be born.
3. Jeremiah told of the slaughter of children by King Herod.
4. Hosea spoke of His escape from Egypt.
5. Zechariah prophesied of His triumphal entry on a donkey and the piercing of His side.
6. Even John said, He existed "in the beginning" before anything was created.

JOHN 1:1-3

"In the beginning was the Word, and the Word was with God, and the Word was God, He was in the beginning with God. All things were made through Him, and without Him nothing was made that was made."

While Christ was indeed preexistent and appeared occasionally to men as the "Angel of the Lord" in the Old Testament. He took on a body permanently when He was conceived in Mary's womb.

This incomparable event of God becoming man in Jesus Christ is called The Incarnation. This miracle was prophesied hundreds of years ago and was fulfilled historically in the Virgin Mary, whose blessed womb, by the power of the Holy Spirit, conceived a child.

Now Mary, even though she would be ostracized for being pregnant out of wedlock, realized that it wasn't all about her; it was about the child that she was carrying. Having been born of a woman, Jesus Christ was fully man, apart from sin, therefore more than qualified to become our Redeemer.

The Apostle Paul said, "For He made Him who knew no sin to be sin for us, that we might become the righteousness of God in Him." (2nd Corinthians 5:21)

CHRISTMAS, IT'S NOT ABOUT US, IT'S ABOUT JESUS!

Jesus, the Son of a Living God, Mary's baby, wrapped in swaddling cloths, and laid in a manger, because there was no room for them at the inn. This same Jesus would later take on the weight and the sins of the whole world upon His shoulder.

He was fully God and fully man united in one person. This allowed him to be compassionate toward us. He knew just what we felt spiritually, physically, mentally, and socially.

Christ even suffered the same pain, hunger, thirst, fatigue, temptation and humiliation as you and I.

Jesus remained focused. He was constantly in touch with "God the Father" and He knew what His mission was:

(LUKE 4:18, 19)

> "The Spirit of the Lord is upon Me, because He anointed Me to preach the gospel to the poor. He has sent Me to heal the brokenhearted, to preach deliverance to the captives and recovery of sight to the blind, to set at liberty those who are oppressed, to preach the acceptable year of the Lord."

Jesus made it more plain and simple in John 10:10...

"I have come that you may have life, and that they have it more abundantly."

CHRISTMAS, IT'S NOT ABOUT US,
IT'S ABOUT JESUS!

CONCLUSION

My beloved Brothers, Sisters, Daughters and Sons, as you rush through these last few weeks trying to buy that last-minute gift, we must be reminded that Christmas is not about us, it's about Jesus and what He is to us! It's about Jesus and what He has done for us!

1. We call Him Wonderful because of His miraculous birth, death and resurrection. (ISAIAH 7:14), (MARK 16:6,7), (1ST CORINTHIANS 15:4)

2. We call Him Counselor because He knows our most secret thoughts and sits on the right hand of God the Father interceding for us. (HEBREW 7:25)

3. We call Him Mighty God because no one can do what He has done except He is God. "I lay down My life that I may take it again- No one takes it from Me, but I lay it down of Myself. I have power to lay it down, and I have power to take it again. This command I have received from My Father." (JOHN 10:17, 18)

4. We call Him Everlasting Father because he cares for us and promised us, "Most assuredly, I say to you, he who hears my words and believes in Him who sent Me has everlasting life, and shall not come into judgment, but has passed from death into life." (JOHN 5:24)

5. We call Him Prince of Peace because He is the perfect model of humility and self-giving love; "These things I have spoken to you that in Me you will have peace. In the world you will have tribulation; but be of good cheer I have overcome the world." (JOHN 16:33)

CHRISTMAS, IT'S NOT ABOUT US, IT'S ABOUT JESUS!

CHRISTMAS PRAYER

Heavenly Father, we do not pray that you will come and be among us, for we know that you are already here. You are always with us. So, we ask today that our eyes be open to your presence, that we will see you at work in us, in our denomination, in our congregation, in our communities and in our homes.

And certainly, Father we do not ask that another Advent of your Son break upon us as the dawn of a new day, but rather that we will understand his Advent in the person of Jesus Christ, who came to make His dwelling place with us forever. We are here not just because you live in our places of worship, but rather through the symbols of worship and the very act of worship and praise. The Holy Spirit makes us mindful of how you are with us always, and how we can open our hearts to your love and power in every experience in life.

Lord God, I pause to ask that you forgive us for our unfaithfulness and continue to bless our every effort to advance your Kingdom. This is thine humble servant's prayer, in the precious name of Jesus I do pray. Amen.

SONG: #172 AMEN, AMEN

Amen, Amen, Amen, Amen!
See the little baby, lying in the manger, on Christmas morning...
Amen, Amen, Amen!
See Him in the temple, talking to the elders, how they all marveled...
Amen, Amen, Amen!
See Him in the garden praying to the Father, in deepest sorrow...
Amen, Amen, Amen!

DR. JACQUELINE HARDY HARRIS

See Him on the cross, bearing all my sins, in bitter agony...
Amen, Amen, Amen!
(sing slow) Talking about Jesus, Mary's baby, Savior of the whole world!
Amen, Amen, Amen!

CHRISTMAS, IT'S NOT ABOUT US, IT'S ABOUT JESUS

The Blood Of Jesus

SCRIPTURE: Matthew 26:26-30
KEY VERSE: Matthew 26:28
SUBJECT: The Blood of Jesus: The Ultimate Sacrifice for All

INTRODUCTION:
God permitted His beloved Son, full of grace and truth, to come from a world of indescribable glory, to a world marred and darkened with sin. He permitted Him to leave the bosom of His love and the adoration of angels, to suffer shame, insult, humiliation, hatred, degradation, and ultimately death.

"The chastisement of our peace was upon Him; and with His stripes we are healed." (Isaiah 53:5)

God so loved the world that He gave His only-begotten Son. This was the ultimate sacrifice of great propitiation and reconciliation of the sins of the world. The spotless Son of God took upon Himself the very burden of sin (separation from God). That's why on the cross He cried in anguish, "My God My God, why hast Thou forsaken Me? (Matthew 27:46)

On the first Sunday of each month, we commemorate this sacrament of the church called "Holy Communion".

We do this in memory of the sacrifice and shed blood of our Lord and Savior Jesus Christ. Do we really understand the significance of the Blood of Jesus? Are we aware of the price Jesus paid for our redemption?

I pray, through the scriptures, we will come to know the ultimate sacrifice that Jesus made, "For this is My blood of the new covenant, which is shed for many for the remission of sins." Matthew 26:28

JESUS INSTITUTES THE LORD'S SUPPER

26 And as they were eating, Jesus took bread, blessed and broke it, and gave it to the disciples and said, "Take, eat; this is My body." 27 Then He took the cup, and gave thanks, and gave it to them, saying, "Drink from it, all of you. 28 For this is My blood of the new covenant, which is shed for many for the remission of sins. 29 But I say to you, I will not drink of this fruit of the vine from now on until that day when I drink it new with you in My Father's kingdom." 30 And when they had sung a hymn, they went out to the Mount of Olives.

Sermon

During the Old Testament times, sacrifice was a ritual by which the Hebrew people offered the blood or flesh of an animal to God in payment for their sins, and presented offerings by which they gave another life in place of their own.

Sacrifice originated in the Garden of Eden, when God killed animals and made tunics for Adam and Eve. God provided them with the skin of animals as a covering symbolizing that sinful man could come before God without fear of death.

Mankind continued this sacrificial system as they fell deeper into sin. In the Mosaic Law, sacrifice had three central principles:

1. CONSECRATION - sanctification
2. EXPIATION - the covering-up of sin
3. PROPITIATION - satisfaction of divine anger through the sin offering, where guilt from a worshiper's sin would symbolically be transferred by the laying of hands on the animal to be sacrificed.

God soon became weary from the stench of these sacrifices and sent His only begotten Son, Jesus Christ, the ultimate sacrifice, who laid down His life for the sins of all people.

Hebrews 9:12 clearly states,

> "Not the blood of goats and calves, but with
> His own blood He entered the most Holy
> place once and for all, having obtained eternal
> redemption."

What has the sacrifice of the Blood of Jesus given us?

4. PEACE WITH GOD

> "Therefore, having been justified by faith we have peace with God through our Lord Jesus Christ"
>
> (ROMANS 5:1)

Now when God looks at us, He sees only the blood of His beloved Son. We are hidden in Christ Jesus and sealed by His Holy Spirit!

What else has the sacrifice of the Blood of Jesus given us?

5. JUSTIFICATION AND SALVATION

> "But God demonstrates His own love toward us, in that while we were still sinners, Christ died for us. Much more than, having been justified by His blood, we shall be saved from wrath through Him. For if when we were enemies we reconciled to God through the death of His Son, much more, having been reconciled, we shall be saved by His life.
>
> (ROMANS 5: 8, 9, 10)

This declaration of God, credits His Son Jesus Christ's perfect righteousness to our spiritual account, putting our sins on His account and stamping the balance "Paid in Full". Somebody needs to say Amen! Thank You Jesus!

Finally, what has the sacrifice of the Blood of Jesus done us?

6. SET US FREE FROM SIN AND GIVEN US ETERNAL LIFE

> "Knowing that Christ, having been raised from the dead, dies no more. Death no longer has dominion over Him. For the death He died, He died to sin once for all; but the life that He lives, He lives to God. Likewise you also, reckon yourselves to be dead indeed to sin, but alive to God in Christ Jesus our Lord.
>
> (ROMANS 6:9-11)

> But now having been set free from sin, and having become slaves to God, you have your first fruit to holiness, and the end, everlasting life. For the wages of sin is death, but the gift of God is eternal life in Christ Jesus our Lord.
>
> (ROMANS 6:22, 23)

LET US ALL REJOICE IN KNOWING THAT WE HAVE BEEN SAVED BY THE BLOOD OF JESUS.

The Power of Prayer

SCRIPTURE: Matthew 6: 5 -17
SUBJECT: More prayer more power;
Little prayer little power

INTRODUCTION:
The Lord's Prayer, or the Model Prayer, is cherished by all Christians because of the Author (Jesus Christ), and for its simplicity and instructive value. Jesus drew great strength from His Heavenly Father through prayer and it was only natural that He should teach His followers about the significance and meaning of prayer.

The Scribes and Pharisees were guilty of two great faults in prayer, vain-glory and vain repetitions. Our text today is Matthew's account of the Lord's Prayer which comes from a portion of Jesus' sermon on the Mount which warned against this hypocrisy in prayer.

Prayer is a major tool in the Christian warfare. It is a privilege to take everything to God in prayer. In this lesson, we will discuss: 1. How to prepare for prayer, 2. Principles of answered prayers, and 3. Obstacles that could hinder your prayers. More prayer more power. Little prayer little power.

MATTHEW 6: 5-15
KING JAMES VERSIONS

5   And when thou prayest, thou shalt not be as the hypocrites are: for they love to pray standing in the synagogues and in the corners of the streets, that they may be seen of men. Verily I say unto you, They have their reward. 6 But thou, when thou prayest, enter into thy closet, and when thou hast shut thy door, pray to thy Father which is in secret; and thy Father which seeth in secret shall reward thee openly. 7 But when ye pray, use not vain repetitions, as the heathen do: for they think that they shall be heard for their much speaking. 8 Be not ye therefore like unto them: for your Father knoweth what things ye have need of, before ye ask him. 9 After this manner therefore pray ye: Our Father which art in heaven, Hallowed be thy name. 10 Thy kingdom come, Thy will be done in earth, as it is in heaven. 11 Give us this day our daily bread. 12And forgive us our debts, as we forgive our debtors. 13And lead us not into temptation, but deliver us from evil: For thine is the kingdom, and the power, and the glory, for ever. Amen. 14 For if ye forgive men their trespasses, your heavenly Father will also forgive you: 15 But if ye forgive not men their trespasses, neither will your Father forgive your trespasses.

WHAT IS PRAYER?

Simply put, prayer is communicating with God. Real prayer is expressing our devotion to our heavenly Father, inviting Him to talk to us as we talk to Him.

PRAYER PREPARATION:

1. Acknowledge Him
2. Worship Him
3. Call on Him

PROVERBS 3:5-6

"Trust in the Lord with all thine heart; and lean not unto thine own understanding. In all thy ways acknowledge him, and he will direct thy paths."

MATTHEW 6:9

"After this manner therefore pray: Our father which art in heaven, Hallowed be thy name."

JEREMIAH 33:3

"Call unto me, and I will answer thee, and show thee great and mighty things, which thou knowest not."

MATTHEW 7:7-8

"Ask and it will be given you; seek, and ye shall find; knock, and it shall be opened unto you." For everyone that asketh receiveth; and he that seeketh findeth; and him that knocketh it shall be opened."

MATTHEW 6:33

"But seek ye first the kingdom of God, and his righteousness; and all these things shall be added unto you."

GOD ANSWERS PRAYERS ACCORDING TO THE FOLLOWING PRINCIPLES:

1. Obedience
2. In The Name of Jesus

3. According to His Will
4. With Faith

1ST JOHN 3:22

"And whatsoever we ask, we receive of him, because we keep his commandments, and do those things that are pleasing in his sight."

JOHN 15:16

"That whatsoever ye shall ask of the Father in my name, he may give it you"

1JOHN 5:14-15

"And this is the confidence that we have in him, that, if we ask anything according to his will, he heareth us: And if we know that he hears us whatsoever we ask, we know that we have the petitions that we desired of him."

MARK 11:22-24

"And Jesus answering saith unto them, Have faith in God. For Verily I say unto you, That whosoever shall say unto this mountain, Be thou removed, and be cast into the sea; and shall not doubt in his heart, but shall believe that those things which he saith shall come to pass; he shall have whatsoever he saith. Therefore I say unto you, what things soever ye desire, when ye pray, believe that ye receive them, and ye shall have them."

JAMES 1:5-6

"If any of you lack wisdom, let him ask of God, that giveth to all men liberally, and upbraideth not; and it shall be given him. But let him ask in faith, nothing wavering. For he that wavereth is like a wave of the sea driven with the wind and tossed."

1. With Persistence
2. In Fellowship with God
3. With Thanksgiving

LUKE 18:1

"That men ought to always pray and not faint"

JOHN 15:7

"If ye abide in me, and my words abide in you, ye shall ask what ye will, and it shall be done unto you."

PSALM 66:18

"If I regard iniquity in my heart, the Lord will not hear me."

PHILIPPIANS 4:6-7

"Be careful for nothing; but in everything by prayer and supplication with thanksgiving let your requests be known unto God. And the peace of God, which passeth all understanding, shall keep your hearts and minds through Christ Jesus."

FOR YOUR NOTES

WHAT ARE SOME THINGS THAT HINDER YOUR PRAYERS?

1. Selfish Purposes
2. Iniquities

3. Idols In The Heart
4. Lack of Charity

1ST JOHN 2: 15-17

"Love not the world, neither the things that are in the World. If any man love the world, the love of the Father is not in him. For all that is in the world, the lust of the flesh, and the lust of the eyes, and the pride of life, is not of the Father, but is of the world. And the world passeth away, and the lust thereof: but he that doeth the will of God abideth for ever."

ISAIAH 59:1, 2

"Behold the Lord's hand is not shortened, that it cannot save; neither his ear heavy that he cannot hear: But your iniquities have separated between you and your God, and your sins have hid his face from you, that he will not hear."

EZEKIEL 14:3

"Son of, these men have set up their idols in their heart, and put the stumbling block of their iniquity before their face: should I be inquired of at ail by them?"

LUKE 6:38

"Give and it shall be given unto you; good measure, pressed down, and shaken together, and running over, shall men give unto your bosom. For with the same measure that ye mete withal it shall be measured to you again."

LACK OF FORGIVENESS & RESTORATION

MATTHEW 6: 14, 15

"For if ye forgive men their trespasses, your heavenly Father will also forgive you: 15 But if ye forgive not men their trespasses, neither will your Father forgive your trespasses."

MARK 11:25

"And when you stand praying, forgive, if ye have ought against any: that your Father also which is in heaven may forgive you your trespasses."

WRONG FAMILY RELATIONSHIP

1 PETER 3:7

"Likewise, ye husbands, dwell with them according to knowledge, giving honor unto the wife, as unto the weaker vessel, and as being heirs together of the grace of life; that your prayers be not hindered."

DOUBT

(JAMES 1:6-8)

"But let him ask in faith, nothing wavering. For he that wavereth is like a wave of the sea driven with the wind and tossed. For let not that man think that he shall receive any thing of the Lord. A double minded man is unstable in all his ways."

CONCLUSION

The Lord's Prayer begins with *"Our Father which art in heaven, Hallowed be thy name"*, indicating the spirit of adoration and reverence in which the heavenly Father should be approached by His children. *"Thy kingdom come, Thy will be done in earth, as it is in heaven"* expresses the longing for a society on earth where God's will is perfectly done as it is in heaven. *"Give us this day our daily bread"* addresses a loving Father who is concerned for our physical welfare, and it also expresses our dependence on Him to supply our needs. *"And forgive us our debts, as we forgive our debtors"* is a petition for pardon as we approach God in a spirit of forgiveness toward others. *"And lead us not into temptation, but deliver us from evil"* is a request for continual protection from the snares of Satan and all evil forces. *"For thine is the kingdom, and the power, and the glory, forever"* appropriately attributes all power and glory to God for all eternity.

Father in the name of Jesus, we thank you for this prayer. Amen!

SONG: Somebody prayed for me!

What Must I Do To Get Eternal Life?

SCRIPTURE: Matthew 19: 16-22
SUBJECT: What Good Thing Must I Do To Get Eternal Life?

INTRODUCTION:
Many of us are so busy making a living we don't take the time out to live. We are so busy in the hustle and bustle of daily living that we fail to realize that Life is not so much in what we get but Life is what we give. The great Benjamin Elijah Mays said it best, "If you really want to be rich then give yourself away".

In our text today we have a young man who had some difficulties, because he was seeking happiness but he could not find it. He had a lot of money but it didn't give him peace, he had a lot of money but it didn't give him joy, he had a lot of money but it didn't give him happiness. Happiness, my beloved is nothing that you and I can pursue after; happiness is a result of a bi-product.

You looking at me kind of funny let me see can I put it another way, when those BP workers drill for oil offshore, from that same oil they make stuff called asphalt that we drive our cars on. They don't drill oil for asphalt; no asphalt is a bi-product of oil.

Yes, I think Jesus said it best in Matthew 6:33, "Seek ye first his kingdom and his righteousness and all these things will be given to you as well."

Through this text we will try to answer the one Question of Life; "What good thing must I do to get Eternal life?"

MATTHEW 19: 16-22
NEW KING JAMES VERSION

16 Now behold, one came and said to Him, "Good Teacher, what good thing shall I do that I may have eternal life?" 17 So He said to him, "Why do you call Me good? No one is good but One, that is, God. But if you want to enter into life, keep the commandments." 18 He said to Him, "Which ones?" Jesus said, "'You shall not murder,' 'You shall not commit adultery,' 'You shall not steal,' 'You shall not bear false witness,' 19 'Honor your father and your mother,' and, 'You shall love your neighbor as yourself.'" 20 The young man said to Him, "All these things I have kept from my youth. What do I still lack?" 21 Jesus said to him, "If you want to be perfect, go, sell what you have and give to the poor, and you will have treasure in heaven; and come, follow Me." 22 But when the young man heard that saying, he went away sorrowful, for he had great possessions.

MATTHEW 19: 16 NIV

"Now a young man came to Jesus and asked, "Good teacher what good thing must I do to get eternal life?"

AS GOD LOVES ME

WHAT MUST I DO?

Christianity is not a matter of doing but Christianity is a matter of being. We don't do tricks to be a Christian; all we have to do is believe God and accept what God has given us.

And what has God given us? God has given Grace, unmerited mercy in the person of his beloved son, Jesus, and all we have to do is reach out, except him and say thank you!

GOOD THINGS?

I can't sing enough
I can't preach enough
I can't pray enough

In fact, no amount of anything can earn us eternal life. We just have to reach up to heaven and say thank you!

SAINTS, THAT'S WHY WE COME BEHIND THESE SACRED WALLS, JUST TO SAY THANK YOU!

Thank you for saving me!
Thank you for guiding me!
Thank you for protecting me!
Thank you for directing me!
Thank you for keeping me!
Thank you Lord for holding me and placing your loving arms around me.

Missionaries, we go out there to serve God. We come in here, this tabernacle of praise just to say Lord I thank you!

DR. JACQUELINE HARDY HARRIS

WHAT MUST I DO TO "GET" ETERNAL LIFE?

You know why he asked Jesus this question, because he had money.

Sometimes our possessions take possession of us. (Repeat)

It gives us a false sense of security, a false sense of inspiration and happiness that has us thinking that everything we have revolves around what we have.

I remind folks that, "I make money but money don't make me".

"Good Teacher"

I almost forgot, this is the good part; when some one wants to butter you up, when someone wants to set you up, when someone thinks they have you in the palm of their hands, they say those flowery, flaunting words …

The lovely, vivacious and beautiful… First Lady:

_____

The emanate, debonair, illustrious… Pastor:

_____

Yes, those flowery words…

But Jesus said to this young man, why are you calling me good?

1. You don't even trust me, why are you calling me good?
2. You don't even believe in me, why are you calling me good?

3. You don't even follow me, why are you calling me good?
4. You don't even know me, why are you calling me good?

So, Jesus redirects this young man and says, "There is only one Who is good, that is the Father."

Matthew 19: 17, 18, 19 "Obey the Commandments"

This young man had a lot of money but he didn't have joy, didn't have peace, and didn't have happiness. So Jesus had compassion on the young man and said, I know what you want son, you want happiness.

Well if you really want happiness then do what God says, "Obey the commandments". This young man then said, "Which ones?"

Which Ones?

You know the Lord always amazes me. When the young man said 'which one of the commandments', Jesus said the 6, 7, 8, 9, 10 and 5th Commandments. Why didn't he say 5, 6, 7, 8, 9, and 10th Commandments, look like Jesus couldn't count or something?

I've found out if you go to God he will deal with you where you are.

Let me see can I put it another way; I dare you to try to pray for someone you don't like. What God will do is start working on you first!

You see the 6, 7, 8, 9, 10, 5th Commandments are the second tables of the Decalogue. These commandments deal with relationships.

I finally realized that what God is doing to me is far more important than what God is doing through me.

Saints you know where we all fall short, not in serving, not in giving, but in relationships. Before Jesus left he said to the disciple, you'll love one another, take care of one another. In other words, you'll get along now! It grieves God's heart when we don't get along. We share the same pulpit but we don't get alone, we sing in the same choir but we don't get alone, we're all missionaries but we don't get along. God wants us to get alone!

MATTHEW 19:20

> "All these I have kept, the young man said,
> "What do I lack?"

What do I lack? I believe The Apostle Paul said it best in the 3rd Chapter of Romans; "we all have sinned and fall short of the glory of God". In other words we all have missed the mark.

So Jesus told this young man you're missing something son. You have a good bow and you are aiming your arrow right but you've missed the mark.

Like a lot of people, they come to church every Sunday but they're missing something, some are church leaders but their missing something. In fact some stand behind this sacred desk and can still miss the mark.

Why? Because they just don't trust God. They don't obey God. They don't reach out and say, Thank you Lord! You don't hear me.

Matthew 19: 21, 22 "Go, Sell, and Give"

So this self-righteous young man looks Jesus in his eyes and said,

"I've done all that what else do I lack."

Then Jesus told him these profound words: Go, Sell and Give.

But this young man wasn't ready to give up anything. In fact history behind this text revealed that this young man did not love and care for his parents or siblings. He did not share all his wealth with them. That's why Jesus told him to keep the commandments that dealt with relationships. "Honor your Mother and your Father".

During our Missionary Offering we quote this familiar passage of scripture:

Charge them that are rich in this world that they be not high-minded nor trust in uncertain riches, but in the living God who giveth us richly all things to enjoy; that they do good; that they be rich in good works, ready to distribute, willing to communicate, laying up in store for themselves a good foundation against the time to come that they may lay hold on eternal life. (Timothy 6:17, 18, 19)

Saints, if you really want to know where God's heart is, give to the poor, someone who can't give back to you.

CONCLUSION:

My beloved, we are indeed in trying times; some of you might say, "I don't have a lot of money". Well if you don't have any money then you can Go and tell somebody about Jesus.

If you don't have anything to sell then Sell Jesus Christ. Tell them that Jesus is a way out of no way. Tell them Jesus is a mighty good Lawyer. Tell them Jesus is a mighty good

Doctor. Tell them Jesus is the Lily of the valley. Tell them Jesus is the Bright and Morning Star. Tell them Jesus is Alpha and Omega, the Beginning and the End! Yes if you don't have anything to give then Give them Jesus Christ!

My brothers and my· sisters the last words Jesus said to this young man were "Come and Follow Me". Jesus extended The Invitation to Christian Discipleship, but this young man just walked away. Please, I compel you to don't walk away today. Please accept Christ!

I was only (9) years old when I gave my life to Jesus...

I heard the voice of Jesus say come unto me and rest, lay down thy weary one lay down, thy head upon my breast. I came to Jesus just as I was weary, worn, and sad, I found in Him a resting place and He has made me glad!

Yes, at nine years old I made a conscious decision to accept Jesus as my personal Savior. And deep down in my heart I said...

All to Jesus I surrender, all to Him I freely give;

I will ever love and trust Him, In His presence daily live

When I started to accumulate stuff, good paying job, cars, houses, I still said...

All to Jesus I surrender, humbly at His feet I bow,

Worldly treasures all forsaken Take me Jesus, take me now!

I surrender all! I surrender all!

All to Thee, my blessed Savior, I surrender all!

THIS SERMON WAS INSPIRED BY REVEREND DR. B. J. VIRGIL-WHAT MUST I DO TO GET ETERNAL LIFE

The Bible Is Right, Somebody's Wrong

SCRIPTURE: 2nd Timothy 3: 1-17
2nd Timothy 4: 1-4
SUBJECT: The Bible/Word of God, is Essential in Life

2 TIMOTHY 3:1-17
(NEW KING JAMES VERSION)

1 But know this, that in the last days perilous times will come: 2 For men will be lovers of themselves, lovers of money, boasters, proud, blasphemers, disobedient to parents, unthankful, unholy, 3 unloving, unforgiving, slanderers, without self-control, brutal, despisers of good, 4 traitors, headstrong, haughty, lovers of pleasure rather than lovers of God, 5 having a form of godliness but denying its power. And from such people turn away! 6 For of this sort are those who creep into households and make captives of gullible women loaded down with sins, led away by various lusts, 7 always learning and never able to come to the knowledge of the truth. 8 Now as Jannes and Jambres resisted Moses, so do these also resist the truth: men of corrupt minds, disapproved concerning the faith; 9

but they will progress no further, for their folly will be manifest to all, as theirs also was. 10 But you have carefully followed my doctrine, manner of life, purpose, faith, longsuffering, love, perseverance, 11 persecutions, afflictions, which happened to me at Antioch, at Iconium, at Lystra—what persecutions I endured. And out of them all the Lord delivered me. 12 Yes, and all who desire to live godly in Christ Jesus will suffer persecution. 13 But evil men and impostors will grow worse and worse, deceiving and being deceived. 14 But you must continue in the things which you have learned and been assured of, knowing from whom you have learned them, 15 and that from childhood you have known the Holy Scriptures, which are able to make you wise for salvation through faith which is in Christ Jesus. 16 All Scripture is given by inspiration of God, and is profitable for doctrine, for reproof, for correction, for instruction in righteousness, 17 that the man of God may be complete, thoroughly equipped for every good work.

Sermon

The Bible is the greatest book ever written. In it, God Himself speaks to mankind. It is a book of divine instruction. It offers comfort in sorrow, guidance in perplexity, advice for our problems, rebuke for our sins, and daily inspiration for our every need.

The Bible is not simply one book. It is an entire library of books covering the whole range of literature. It includes history, poetry, drama, biography, prophecy, philosophy, science, and inspirational reading. Little wonder, then, that all or part of the Bible has been translated into more than 1,200 languages, and every year, more copies of the Bible are sold than any other single book.

The Bible alone truly answers the greatest questions that men of all ages have asked: "Where have I come from?" "Where am I going?" "Why am I here?" "How can I know the truth?" For the Bible reveals the truth about God, explains the origin of man, points out the only way to salvation and eternal life, and explains the age-old problem of sin and suffering.

The great theme of the Bible is the Lord Jesus Christ and His work of redemption for mankind. The person and work of Jesus Christ are promised, prophesied, and pictured in the types and symbols of the Old Testament. In all of His truth and beauty, the Lord Jesus Christ is revealed in the gospels. The full meanings of His life, His death, and His resurrection are explained in the epistles. His glorious coming again to earth in the future is unmistakably foretold in the book of Revelations. The great purpose of the written Word of God, the Bible, is to reveal the living Word of God, the Lord Jesus Christ (JOHN 1:1-18).

THE BIBLE IS RIGHT, SOMEBODY'S WRONG!

Dr. Wilbur M. Smith, a great theologian relates seven great things that the study of the Bible will do for us:

1. The Bible discovers sin and convicts us.

    ### 1ST JOHN 5:17

    "All unrighteousness is sin"

2. The Bible helps cleanse us from the pollutions of sin.

    ### 1ST JOHN 1:9

    "If we confess our sins, He is faithful and just to forgive us *our* sins and to cleanse us from all unrighteousness."

3. The Bible imparts strength.

    ### ISAIAH 40:29

    "He gives power to the weak, And to *those who have* no might He increases strength."

4. The Bible instructs us in what we are to do.

    ### MATTHEW 22:37

    'Jesus said to him, "'You shall love the Lord your God with all your heart, with all your soul, and with all your mind.'

5. The Bible provides us with a sword for victory over sin.

    ### 1ST JOHN 5:1-5

"Whoever believes that Jesus is the Christ is born of God, and everyone who loves Him who begot also loves him who is begotten of Him. 2 By this we know that we love the children of God, when we love God and keep His commandments. 3 For this is the love of God, that we keep His commandments. And His commandments are not burdensome. 4 For whatever is born of God overcomes the world. And this is the victory that has overcome the world—our faith. 5 Who is he who overcomes the world, but he who believes that Jesus is the Son of God?"

6. The Bible makes our lives fruitful.

GALATIANS 5:22, 23

"But the fruit of the Spirit is love, joy, peace, longsuffering, kindness, goodness, faithfulness, gentleness, self-control. Against such there is no law. "

7. The Bible gives us power to pray.

JAMES 5:13-16

"13 Is anyone among you suffering? Let him pray. Is anyone cheerful? Let him sing psalms. 14 Is anyone among you sick? Let him call for the elders of the church, and let them pray over him, anointing him with oil in the name of the Lord. 15 And the prayer of faith will save the sick, and the Lord will raise him up. And if he has committed sins, he will be forgiven.

> 16 Confess your trespasses to one another, and pray for one another, that you may be healed. The effective, fervent prayer of a righteous man avails much."

You do not need a whole library of books to study the Bible. The Bible is its own best commentator and interpreter. With all of the instructive help of a good Bible, you have a whole lifetime of Bible study. The Bible is Right, Somebody's Wrong!

The more fully we know the doctrine of Christ, as taught by the apostles, the more closely we shall cleave to it. As good men, by the grace of God, grow better, so bad men, through the craft of Satan, and the power of their own corruptions, grow worse. The way of sin is downhill, such go on from bad to worse, deceiving and being deceived. Those who deceive others, deceive themselves, as they will find at the last and great Day of Lord, to their own cost. The Bible is Right, Somebody's Wrong!

Saints, some will turn away from the truth. They will grow weary of the plain gospel of Christ. They will be greedy of fables, and take pleasure in them. Ministers of God must continue to give the people of God sound doctrine, preaching that which is certain, plain, and to the purpose. The Bible is Right, Somebody's Wrong!

CONCLUSION

When every man/woman is eager for what he/she can get, and anxious to keep what he/she has, this makes them dangerous to one another. When men/women do not fear

God, they will not regard mankind. When children are disobedient to their parents, that makes the times perilous. The Bible is Right, Somebody's Wrong!

The love of this world is often the cause of turning back from the truths and ways of Jesus Christ. False doctrine is very destructive; Cults have always had various ways to attract new members. These cults make use of the Bible by twisting its message, and Christians who are not well grounded in the faith can be taken in by an atmosphere of solidarity (form of godliness). But it is a trap; the victim is set to wandering off course, farther and farther into uncharted waters; sinking deeper and deeper into sin. The Bible is Right, Somebody's Wrong!

The Apostle Paul was guided by Divine inspiration and he encourages us today, as long as we live, we must still learn from this great inspirational book, the Bible. We should thank God and the Holy Spirit in having given us so many writings of wise and pious men such as Paul; who said at the close of his great ministry these profound words:

2 TIMOTHY 4: 1-4
(NEW KING JAMES VERSION)

1. I charge you therefore before God and the Lord Jesus Christ, who will judge the living and the dead at His appearing and His kingdom: 2 Preach the word! Be ready in season and out of season. Convince, rebuke, exhort, with all longsuffering and teaching. 3 For the time will come when they will not endure sound doctrine, but according to their own desires, because they have itching ears, they will heap

up for themselves teachers 4 and they will turn their ears away from the truth, and be turned aside to fables. 5 But you be watchful in all things, endure afflictions, do the work of an evangelist, fulfill your ministry.

IN OTHER WORDS, THE BIBLE IS RIGHT, SOMEBODY'S WRONG!

Servant Of God's Gospel Doing God's Work God's Way!

SCRIPTURE: 1st Thessalonians 2:1-12 verses

SUBJECT: Servant of the Gospel, Doing God's Work God's Way!

INTRODUCTION:

During The Apostle Paul's 2nd missionary journey, he along with Silas and Timothy started a church in Thessalonica. Many Jews and pagan worshipers were convinced and converted by Paul's teachings.

Some Jewish leaders were jealous of Paul's success and charged him with sedition. He was thought to be stirring up trouble, implementing unorthodox teachings, and always talking about this man named "Jesus".

One night Paul's friends in Christ ushered him out to Berea. The enemy was in pursuit, so Paul left Berea and went to Athens, and from Athens to Corinth.

While Paul was in Athens, he became concerned for the church he had started in Thessalonica. He had only been there for three Sabbaths. This is approximately one month. Paul knew that they were only babes in Christ, so he sent Timothy back to check on their spiritual welfare. Timothy returned with good news! The church in Thessalonica had been faithful to all of Paul's teachings and was growing gracefully in Christ Jesus!

Chapter 2, the text for this day, Paul defends his ministry and his integrity, conduct and motives, in answer to his enemies who challenged his character and message. By doing this, Paul gives us a glimpse of the qualities of a Servant of God's Gospel, Doing God's Work, God's Way!

Who are Servants of the Gospel?

Pastor, Evangelist, Preacher, Prophet, Steward, Deacon, Deaconess, Missionary, Teacher, Minister of Music, Trustee, just to name a few...

1ST THESSALONIANS 2:1-12
NEW KING JAMES VERSION

1 For you yourselves know, brethren, that our coming to you was not in vain. 2 But even after we had suffered before and were spitefully treated at Philippi, as you know, we were bold in our God to speak to you the gospel of God in much conflict. 3 For our exhortation did not come from error or uncleanness, or was it in deceit. 4 But as we have been approved by God to be entrusted with the gospel, even so we speak, not as pleasing men, but God who tests our hearts. 5 For neither at any time did we use flattering words, as you know, nor a cloak for covetousness—God is witness. 6 Nor did we seek glory from men, either from you or from others, when we might have made demands as

apostles of Christ. 7 But we were gentle among you, just as a nursing mother cherishes her own children. 8 So, affectionately longing for you, we were well pleased to impart to you not only the gospel of God, but also our own lives, because you had become dear to us. 9 For you remember, brethren, our labor and toil; for laboring night and day, that we might not be a burden to any of you, we preached to you the gospel of God. 10 You are witnesses, and God also, how devoutly and justly and blamelessly we behaved ourselves among you who believe; 11 as you know how we exhorted, and comforted, and charged every one of you, as a father does his own children, 12 that you would walk worthy of God who calls you into His own kingdom and glory.

Sermon

VERSE #2:

"But even after we had suffered before and were spitefully treated at Philippi, as you know, we were bold in our God to speak to you the gospel of God in much conflict."

A servant of the gospel, preaches or teaches boldly even in the face of opposition and controversy or shamefully entreated. While Paul and Silas were in Philippi, Paul rebuked a spirit of divination from a young slave girl. Her masters were angry with Paul because this young woman gave them great financial gain with her ability to foretell events (remember Miss Cleo, some gifts come without repentance). In response, they beat Paul and Silas and had them jailed without a trial.

Paul was a Roman citizen and should not have been treated in such a manner by law. Nevertheless he was, but the hand of God gave Paul and Silas their freedom.

Possibly, you could understand how Paul felt, if you've been in a relationship and were treated badly. You can remember how reluctant you were to start all over again with someone else.

What Paul is saying here, is that no matter how bad we were treated in Philippi, we still came boldly to you in Thessalonica to preach the Gospel again!

VERSE #3:

> For our exhortation did not come from error
> or uncleanness, or was it in deceit.

A servant of God's Gospel Doing God's Work, God's Way, preaches or teaches the true doctrine. He or she does not try to dress up the word, or turn it around to suit his purpose. Nor will they sugar coat the word to make you feel better ...

Example: I recently read about a very popular t.v. Evangelist, who did not believe in the Holy Trinity (God the Father, The Son and The Holy Spirit). It is certain that there is one true God, who eternally exists as three distinct persons and that the three are co-equal, co-eternal, and one in essence. This great orator also did not practice the giving of open Holy Communion. As a pastor and servant of God's gospel in the African Methodist Episcopal Church, I am compelled to protect the flock from these erroneous teachings. When you look at our church program, you will see the "Apostle's Creed" which serves as our affirmation of faith. This is what we believe as Christians, and followers of Jesus Christ. This t. v. Evangelist is faithfully committed to his theology. My brothers and sister, we need to be faithful to what we believe: The Holy Trinity.

VERSE#4:

> But as we have been approved by God to be entrusted with the gospel, even so we speak, not as pleasing men, but God who tests our hearts.

A servant of God's Gospel Doing God's Work God's Way, is a steward of the Gospel. This Gospel does not belong to us, it belongs to God!

Speaking of ownership, I'd like to interject this verse parenthetically: "The Earth is the Lord's and the fullness thereof and they that dwell therein". In other words you don't even belong to yourself, you belong to God! Yet we sometime complain about giving 10% to God, forgetting that he owns 100% of what we have. I tell my church if you give God 10% He'll help you take care of that 90% you have left. Besides one day, you will have to stand before God and give an account of your time, talent, tithing, and gifts of grace. A servant of the Gospel is a great Steward of his Gospel.

VERSE#5, 6:

> For neither at any time did we use flattering words, as you know, nor a cloak for covetousness—God is witness. Nor did we seek glory from men, either from you or from others...

A servant of God's Gospel does not resort to manipulative tactics, gimmicks, or acts of putting on a show, trying to impress you with our oratorical skills, or how well we can scream and holler. It is about being of service for God's work.

Most importantly, we must all remember to keep our motives pure and righteous. We are here all here to follow the Word of God. There should be no other hidden agendas. Amen!

VERSE#7, 8:

> Just as a nursing mother cherishes her own children...

A servant of God's Gospel, Doing God's Work God's Way, cares for the children of God as a mother cares for her child.

Moms, you can understand what Paul is saying here. A mother gives her child nourishing food from her breast. This same mother would also give her very life for her child. Mothers give up having some things so that their children can have better than what they might have had. Mothers teach their children the right way to go. Even when children appear to go astray, mothers in the midst of disappointment still say, "That's my baby, I don't care what he's done! I'm going to keep on praying and fasting, I ain't going to give in, I ain't going to give out, and I ain't going to give up on God! That's my flesh and blood, that's my child!

A servant of God's Gospel is like this also. Sunday in and Sunday out he or she teaches you the right way to go. When we see you going the wrong way, we become concerned. I say we are like post signs on the highway of life, giving directions, instructions and information.

A servant of the Gospel cares for the soul of every man, woman, boy and girl!

VERSE #9:

> For laboring night and day, that we might not be a burden…

Now Paul is not saying the preacher should not be paid. That would negate the other letters he wrote:

- 1st Tim 5: 17 "An elder that rules well deserves double honor"
- 1st Tim 5: 18 "Muzzle not the ox that treads the corn"
- Gal 5: 6 "Let him who is taught the word share in all good things with him who teaches"

What Paul is saying, "I'm not worried about you paying me, I already have a job as a tent maker. Working both night and day! I came here to preach the Gospel, whether you pay me or not!

VERSE# 10, 11, 12:

There are some golden nuggets in these verses: Devoutly, Justly, Blamelessly, Exhorted, Comforted, Walk-worthy...

In others words:

- I have no right telling you to be holy, if I'm not holy!
- You must walk the walk, before you can talk the talk!
- You must dwell with God, before you can tell of God!
- You must know before you can show!

Now we are not perfect, Romans 3:23 says, "All have sinned and come short of the glory of God". And if you back up a few verses it says, "There's none righteous no not one". But, this is a daily walk with God, seeking perfection. And in that great Day, our hope and desire is to hear God say, well done my good and faithful servant well done!

CONCLUSION

A servant of God's Gospel doing God's work God's way, preaches, teaches, prays, sings, and even plays musical instruments boldly! They tell you the truth, true doctrine, and are great stewards of God's Gospel. He or she is not concerned about financial gain, for God will make it right at the in the road.

They care for the soul of mankind, therefore he or she preaches the right message for the right reasons.

AND WHAT IS THE RIGHT MESSAGE?

God so loved the world that he gave his only begotten Son and whosoever believes in him should not perish but have life eternal. This same Jesus came down forty and two generations, he was conceived by the Holy Spirit, born of the virgin Mary, suffered under Pontius Pilate, was crucified, was dead, and was buried, but on the third day he rose from the dead with all power in his hand and as I speak he sits on right hand of God the Father Almighty! And guess what? He shall come again and judge the living and the dead!

That's the right-message, but what are the right-reasons?

1. So that Sinners may be Sanctified!
2. So that Saints may be Edified!
3. And last but not least, so that God may be Glorified!

My brothers and my sisters, it will not be easy doing this great work of God. Before your time, they persecuted the prophets, but when the enemy comes up against you, hold your head up and stick your chest out, and stand boldly to tell them these words:

A charge to keep I have, a God to glorify. A never dying soul to save that fitted for the sky.

Young people, if that's not good enough, you tell them…

To serve the present age my calling to fulfill. Oh may in all my power engage to do my master's will.

Pastors (Dad), if that's not good enough, you tell them…

I'm a soldier in the army of the Lord! I'm a sanctified soldier in the army of the Lord! And if I die, let me die in the army of the Lord…

A SERVANT OF GOD'S GOSPEL,
DOING GOD'S WORK, GOD'S WAY!

New Year, New Attitude

SCRIPTURE: Luke 23:32-43
Romans 8: 38, 39

INTRODUCTION:
A great scholar (Dr. Charles Swindoll) once said, "The longer I live, the more I realize the Impact of Attitude on Life".

Attitude, to me is more important than facts. Attitude is more important than the past, education, money, success, what other people think or say or do. Attitude is more important than appearance, giftedness or skill.

I've come to the conclusion that attitude will make or break a company.

Attitude will make or break up a church.

I'm a living witness that attitude will make or break up a home.

The most remarkable thing to remember is that we have a choice regarding the attitude we will embrace each day.

We cannot change our past.

We cannot change the fact that people will act in a certain way.

We certainly cannot change the inevitable, that is death.

We can adjust our attitudes.

I am convinced that life is 10% of what happens to me and 90% how I react to what happens to me!

And so this day we will embrace two (2) very distinct attitudes.

LUKE 23:32-43 (NEW KING JAMES VERSION)

32 There were also two others, criminals, led with Him to be put to death. 33 And when they had come to the place called Calvary, there they crucified Him, and the criminals, one on the right hand and the other on the left. 34 Then Jesus said, "Father, forgive them, for they do not know what they do." And they divided His garments and cast lots. 35 And the people stood looking on. But even the rulers with them sneered, saying, "He saved others; let Him save Himself if He is the Christ, the chosen of God." 36 The soldiers also mocked Him, coming and offering Him sour wine, 37 and saying, "If You are the King of the Jews, save Yourself." 38 And an inscription also was written over Him in letters of Greek, Latin, and Hebrew: THIS IS THE KING OF THE JEWS. 39 Then one of the criminals who were hanged blasphemed Him, saying, "If You are the Christ, save Yourself and us." 40 But the other, answering, rebuked him, saying, "Do you not even fear God, seeing you are under the same condemnation? 41 And we indeed justly, for we receive the due reward of our deeds; but this Man has done nothing wrong." 42 Then he said to Jesus, "Lord, remember me when You come into Your kingdom." 43 And

Jesus said to him, "Assuredly, I say to you, today you will be with Me in Paradise."

Sermon

ATTITUDE #1: (LUKE 23:39 NKJV)

"Then one of the criminals who were hanged blasphemed him saying; 'If thou be Christ save thyself and us.'"

Blasphemy against the Holy Spirit: Blasphemy is the unpardonable sin. It is unforgivable. Jesus died and ascended unto Heaven. On the cross, He represented God the Father, God the Son, but also God the Holy Spirit. And so it is written: "Every sin and blasphemy will be forgiven men, but the blasphemy against the Holy Spirit will not be forgiven men. Anyone who speaks a word against the son of man, it will be forgiven him, but whoever speaks against the Holy Spirit, it will not be forgiven him, either in this age or the age to come." (Matthew 12:31, 32 NKJV)

Now you will know if you have committed this sin, it would appear that the desire to be a Christian will have forever past. No spiritual impressions will ever again come to your soul. For your soul will be subject to eternal condemnation. My brothers and my sister the soul is a conscious personality, endowed with perpetual life. God loves the soul more than all creation, for He fashioned it after His own image and He made it like unto Himself.

To sin against the Holy Spirit is to sin against your own soul. In other words to blaspheme against the Holy Spirit is to shut yourself off forever from access to God. Those who have committed this sin are completely given over to Satan and have not the slightest interest in spiritual matters. Like the other thief on the cross saying, "Save yourself and us". He never realized that Jesus was there not just for his sake but also for all mankind!

Now check this out...

Murder: Is not an unpardonable sin. David had Bathsheba's husband killed, and confessed his sins to God and was forgiven.

Adultery: Is not an unpardonable sin. The Samaritan woman had so many men, she didn't know what to do. Christ forgave her.

Theft: Being a thief is not an unpardonable sin Resisting the awesome convicting power of the Holy Spirit, is an unpardonable sin.

My sports fans you can relate to this. The Holy Spirit is like those football cleats the players wear, that keep them from slipping and sliding. The Holy Spirit does the same thing - it holds you in place.

The enemy thought he had you but by the power of the Holy Spirit, you stood your ground. Yes, you might have gotten hit but you didn't fall down. Amen!

ATTITUDE #2: (LUKE 23:40, 41, 42 NKJV)

> "But the other, answering, rebuked him saying, Do you not even fear God, seeing you are

under the same condemnation? And we indeed justly, for we receive the due rewards of our deeds; but this man have done nothing wrong. Then he said to Jesus, Lord, remember me when you come into your kingdom."

Examples of some Attitudes:

1. One young man said to me, "My Papa was a rollin stone wherever he laid his hat was his home.... I've got a lot of ladies too, who don't know who their children's father is.

2. One young lady said, "My Mama had a lot of babies, I got a lot of babies too. I can't find no job with all these babies."

3. One brother said to me, "My Daddy sold drugs, and his Daddy sold drugs ... What do you expect? I sell drugs. How else am I gonna make it?

4. A beautiful sister said to me, "My Mama sold her body, her mama did too. She flipped her long blonde hair and put her hand on her "baby's got back" and she said these words, "I can get anything I want with this body!"

Attitudes! There comes a point in one's life when you must come into the realization that you are in that situation or particular circumstance not because of your parents, peers, the principal of your school, the police department and not even because of your pastor.

You're where you are in life, sometimes because of you! You!

You make choices in your life. You can choose to do good, or you can choose to do evil. You can choose to follow Christ or you can choose to follow Satan. If you choose to follow Satan, you will end up where God has prepared for Satan; the Lake which burns with fire and brimstone.

But if you choose to follow Christ and His Commandments, you will be blessed to the right of the tree of life, and enter through the gates of that fair city of God!

I want you to really listen because this is very important. Confession is not only good for the soul, it saves the soul.

One thief confessed his sins, and he believed in his heart that the man who hanged to his side was indeed the "Son of a Living God".

Then he looked at his friend and realized that the reason he was hanging on that old rugged cross was because he hung out with the wrong crowd.

I could imagine this remorseful thief said to his running partner, "We were wrong man, we stole and robbed people for years. That's why we're hanging on this cross. I've made up my mind. I'm not going to hang with you no more! I want to hang with this guy now, Jesus Christ. He ain't done nothing wrong. He just wants to save our souls."

Now, even though this thief had but a few hours and life was slipping away, he uttered these profound words, "Lord remember me". In other words, "Jesus, don't leave me here, please take me with you".

Jesus remembering what he had just told his Disciples earlier, "Also I say to you whoever confesses me before men, him the Son of man also will confess before the angels of God. But he who denies me before men will be denied before the angels of God."

And so Jesus not only being The Word, but also a man of His Word, said to the thief; "Assuredly, I say to you, today, not tomorrow, today you will be with me in Paradise." (Luke 23:43)

CONCLUSION

Saints, the hands of time are winding down. The tick of the clock is more profound. Yesterday is dead and gone, and tomorrow is promised to no one. You can see clearly the handwriting on the wall of time. Jesus is coming back! You must have a made up mind and thoroughly be convinced whom you're going to serve!

I don't know about you but I've made up my mind and like the Apostle Paul: "I am truly persuaded that neither death, nor life, nor angels, nor principalities, nor powers, nor things present, nor things to come, nor height, nor depth, nor any other creature, absolutely nothing, absolutely no-one, shall be able to separate me from the love of God, which is in Christ Jesus our Lord and Savior!" (Romans 8:38, 39)

And with this new attitude I've come to this conclusion...

- That, Jesus must not bear the cross alone and all the world go free,

- No there's a cross for everyone and there's a cross for me.
- This consecrated cross I'll bear till death shall set me free,
- Then I'll go home, a crown I'll wear, for there's a cross just for me!
- New Year, New Attitude!

WHAT'S YOUR ATTITUDE?

I Shall Not Be Moved

SCRIPTURE: Psalm 62:1-12
KEY VERSES: Psalm 62:1-6
SUBJECT: In Commemoration of Rosa Parks (1913-2005) 'The Mother of the Civil Rights Movement'

INTRODUCTION:
On December 1, 1955, a 42 year old lady with rimless glasses and a petite frame got off from her job at the Fair Department Store, where she had been working since early morning as a seamstress. She spent most of her days, taking up hemlines and letting out waistlines for the white patrons of the Fair Department Store.

She walked to Cleveland Avenue in the heart of downtown Montgomery, Ala., boarded a city bus in the front door, paid the same dime as all other riders paid, got off the bus and hurried and re-entered through the back door, because sometimes the bus driver would drive away in the midst of this humiliating process.

Once on the bus, everyone knew that the first four rows were for whites patrons only, and could not be used, under any circumstances, by black patrons. If no white patrons needed a seat, blacks patrons could sit there. If one white patron wanted a seat, every black patron in the middle section. had to get up and stand at the back of the bus.

On December 1, 1955, Rosa Parks, impeccably dressed, sat in the middle section of a 1948 General Motors bus. A white male patron got on, and every black male patron, black woman patron and black child patron in that section got up to make way. Everyone, except Mother Rosa Parks. The bus driver, J. F. Blake, asked her to stand up. She said a single word, "No". The driver then put the bus in park, and told Mother Rosa Parks that he would have her arrested if she did not follow his directions. Mother Parks responded: "You may do that." With those soft-spoken words, the rest of the story is history.

The life and legacy of Rosa Parks, 'The Mother of the Civil Rights Movement' resounds clearly today in this powerful 62nd Psalm of David: I Shall Not Be Moved!

PSALM 62: 1-12 (NEW KING JAMES VERSION)

1 Truly my soul silently waits for God; From Him comes my salvation. 2 He only is my rock and my salvation; He is my defense; I shall not be greatly moved. 3 How long will you attack a man? You shall be slain, all of you, like a leaning wall and a tottering fence. 4 They only consult to cast him down from his high position; they delight in lies; they bless with their mouth, but they curse inwardly.

5 My soul, wait silently for God alone, for my expectation is from Him. 6 He only is my rock

and my salvation; He is my defense; I shall not be moved.

7   In God is my salvation and my glory; The rock of my strength, And my refuge, is in God. 8 Trust in Him at all times, you people; Pour out your heart before Him; God is a refuge for us. 9 Surely men of low degree are a vapor, Men of high degree are a lie; if they are weighed on the scales, they are altogether lighter than vapor. 10 Do not trust in oppression, nor vainly hope in robbery; if riches increase, do not set your heart on them. 11 God has spoken once, twice I have heard this: That power belongs to God. 12 Also to You, O Lord, belongs mercy; for You render to each one according to his work.

Sermon

Why would an individual suffer such humiliation and unimaginable degradation? Why? Mother Rosa Parks explained her actions in these soft-spoken words.

> *"I was not tired physically, or no more tired than I usually was at the end of a working day. I was not old... I was only 42. No, the only tired I was, was tired of giving in."*

Dr. Martin Luther King Jr., at the first Montgomery Improvement Association meeting said these words about Mother Parks,

> *"Just the other day, one of the finest citizens in Montgomery was taken from a bus and carried to jail because she refused to give her seat to a white person. I'm happy it happened to a person like Mrs. Parks, for nobody can doubt the boundless outreach of her integrity, the height of her character, the depth of her Christian commitment."*

For the next 381 days, black citizens of Montgomery organized a piecemeal transportation system, consisting of privately owned cars that carted some 30,000 black citizens around town. They had made up their minds that they weren't going to get back on the bus until "Jim Crow" got off.

Somebody needs to say Amen!

King David's defiant spirit resonated in this fair city of Montgomery...

PSALM 62:1-3

1 Truly my soul silently waits for God; From Him comes my salvation. 2 He only is my rock and my salvation; He is my defense; I shall not be greatly moved. 3 How long will you attack a man? You shall be slain, all of you, Like a leaning wall and a tottering fence.

Mother Rosa Parks, like King David, trusted only in God. She remained humble, meek, and pure in character. If someone like Mother Rosa Parks could be thrown into jail, then no one was safe.

After her arrest, there were mass demonstrations that eventually changed every aspect of life in America for Blacks. From schools, to work, to housing and education, discriminatory laws began to fall like a *"tottering fence"*; with the passing of the Civil Rights Acts of 1964 and 1965.

President Barack Obama said this about the famous photograph of Mother Rosa Parks being fingerprinted at the jail;

> *"Parks' gaze in this photograph is one of a woman who was not looking for trouble the day she refused to give up her seat; one who was not planning to get arrested... In her eyes, you see a woman who was ready for the choice she made. One who, when confronted with a decision that could have meant physical harm and certainly meant the loss of her own freedom, was prepared to accept all consequences in the name of what was right... of what was true."*

Mother Rosa Parks, a Consecrated Deaconess of the African Methodist Episcopal Church expressed dismay that the younger generation seemed to be taking their hard won rights for granted and that parents were to blame.

Saints, we should not shield young people from the past, or what our grandparents suffered during segregation. When we do that, they become complacent and began to think life is a bed of roses. We know that the school system will not tell the true story of the suffering of this great woman, who simply tried to make life better for generations to come.

It is up to you and me to continue the legacy.

CONCLUSION

My brothers and my sisters, during the legendary life of Mother Rosa Parks, she proved how one person can make a lasting difference with determination. One person can make a monumental difference with commitment. One person can make an everlasting historical difference with patience, and deep faith in God!

And like King David, Mother Rosa Parks trusted the Lord until her death in 2005 at the blessed age of 92.

Mother Rosa Parks, was eulogized by the Bishop Adam J. Richardson of the AME Church. Mother Parks sat down for the last time, at the feet of our Lord and Savior Jesus Christ, whom she loved so much. In His arms she found rest from the labor and toils of this old earth. She has done all that the good Lord has asked of her and more, and we thank God Almighty for her display of courage and righteousness!

Saints, there was one word not in Mother Parks' righteous mind and that was the word "fear"; because she was assured of this ...

PSALM 62: 5, 6

> "My soul, wait thou only upon God; for my expectation is from Him. He is my rock and my salvation: He is my defense, I shall not be moved."

SERMON DEDICATED to Dr. Leeomia Kelly, Mother-in-Ministry

The Dream Will Never Die!

SCRIPTURE: Genesis 37: 18-20   Joel 2: 28
Habakkuk 2: 2, 3
SUBJECT: Keeping the Dream Alive

INTRODUCTION:

Commemoration of Dr. Martin Luther King, Jr.

> Words are capable of great good and evil. Words can deeply injure or revive!
> Words can have a widespread influence;
> Words from the wicked are like a fire-spreading torch. But words from the good Prophet of God bring forth good fruits!
>
> GENESIS 37:18-20
> (NEW KING JAMES VERSION)

> "Now when they saw him afar off, even before he came near them, they conspired against him to kill him. Then they said to one another, "Look, this dreamer is coming! Come therefore, let us now kill him and cast him into some pit; and we shall say, 'Some wild beast has devoured him.' We shall see what will become of his dreams!"
>
> JOEL 2:28
> (NEW KING JAMES VERSION)

"And it shall come to pass afterward That I will pour out My Spirit on all flesh; Your sons and your daughters shall prophesy, Your old men shall dream dreams, Your young men shall see visions."

HABAKKUK 2:2, 3
(NEW INTERNATIONAL VERSION)

"And the Lord answered me and said, Write the vision, and make it plain on tablets, that he may run that reads it. For the vision is yet for an appointed time; but at the end it will speak, and it will not lie. Though it tarry, wait for it; because it will surely come, it will not tarry"

Sermon

Prophet: A person who speaks with divine inspiration and foretells future events.

Prophetic Word: The "Word of the Lord" is a phrase referring to communication made by God to His people. This prophetic word was addressed to mankind and demanded a response.

Vision/Dream: Unusual foresight, an image or ideal of spiritual nature, seen or obtained under the influence of the divine inspiration of God.

Dr. Martin Luther King Jr., a great Prophet of God, was born on January 15, 1929, in the fair city of Atlanta, Georgia. As the son and grandson of Baptist preachers, he was reared in the black church tradition. To this heritage, he added a thorough academic preparation, earning the degrees of B. A., B. D., and Ph. D. in Systematic Theology from Boston University.

In 1954, Dr. King became pastor of a church in Montgomery, Alabama. Like the Prophet Habakkuk, Dr. King was a freethinking prophet who was not afraid to wrestle with issues that tested his faith. In Alabama, Dr. King saw man fragrantly violate God's law and distort justice on every level, without fear of divine intervention.

Black indignation and inhumane treatment on segregated buses culminated in December 1955, in the arrest of Sister Rosa Parks for refusing to give up her seat to a white passenger. Dr. King was catapulted into national prominence as the leader of the "Montgomery Bus Boycott". He became increasingly the articulate prophet, who could not only rally black masses, but could also move the consciences of white citizens!

Dr. King founded the "Southern Christian Leadership Conference" to spearhead non violent mass demonstrations against racism. His nonviolent campaigns were instrumental to the passage of the Civil Rights Act of 1964 and the Voting Rights Act of 1965.

Like most of God's prophets, Dr. King lived in constant danger. Hiis home was violated with dynamite, he was almost fatally stabbed to death, and he was constantly harassed by death threats. He was even jailed, 30 times. Through it all, like the Prophet Habakkuk, he was sustained by his deep faith in God.

In 1957, Dr. King received a viscous telephone threat, late at night. Alone in his kitchen, he wept and prayed to

God. He related that he heard the Lord speaking to him and saying, "Martin Luther, stand up for righteousness, stand up for truth". And God promised Dr. King that he would never leave him alone. Dr. King referred to this vision as his "Mountaintop Experience".

Also the Prophet Habakkuk, after two rounds of dialogue with the Lord about the wickedness of Judah, had his mountaintop experience. This moment increased his understanding of not only the person of God, but also the power and plan of God. "My thoughts are not your thoughts neither are your ways my ways," says the Lord. (Isaiah 55: 8 NIV)

After preaching at the Washington Cathedral, Dr. King went to Memphis in support of the sanitation workers in their struggle for better wages. There, he proclaimed that he had been "to the mountaintop" and had seen "The Promised Land" and that he knew that one day he and his people would be "Free at last", "Thank God Almighty, I am free at last".

On the very next day, April 4, 1968, Dr. Martin Luther King Jr. was cut down by an assassin's bullet. How many of you know that the Word of God had already gone out from the Prophet of God? I believe that the prophet Isaiah said it best, "so is my word that goes out from my mouth: it will not return to me empty, but will accomplish what I desire and achieve the purpose for which I sent it." (ISAIAH. 55:11 NIV)

CONCLUSION

The prophets Habakkuk, Joel, and Dr. Martin Luther King Jr. chose to cling firmly to God and trust Him, even in the worst of circumstances. For you see God's plan is perfect, and nothing is big enough to stand in the way of its ultimate fulfillment.

In spite of appearances, God is still on the throne as Lord of history and ruler of all nations. God may be slow to wrath, but all iniquity will be punished eventually. We may never fully understand God's ways but the more we know "God the Planner" the more we can trust His plans.

No matter what comes to past, remember this one thing: "the righteous shall live by his faith". (Habakkuk 2: 4NIV)

The Lord gave Dr. King many visions and prophetic words and because of those divine inspirational words he was also killed. But the patriarch Joseph reminded us that they may try to kill the Dreamer but The Dream Will Never Die!

One of Dr. King's most memorable speeches, "I Have A Dream" will stand the test of time! I was very young but I'll always remember these words…

"I have a dream that my four young children will someday be judged by the content of their character and not by the color of their skin, I have a dream today…I have a dream that one day every valley shall be exalted and every hill and every mountain shall be made low, the rough places will be made straight, and the glory of the Lord shall be revealed and all flesh shall see it together. This is our Hope, this is our Faith! And with this faith we will be able to work together, to pray together, to struggle together, knowing that we will be free one day. This will be the day when all of God's children will be able to sing with new meaning, "My country 'tis of thee, sweet land of liberty, of thee I sing, land where my fathers died, land of the Pilgrim's pride, from every mountainside, let freedom ring!" And if America is to be a great nation this must come true."

Therefore, on Tuesday, November 4th, 2008 the cry of freedom rang in every voting precinct across this United States of America. From the hilltops of New Hampshire, the mighty mountains of New York, the Stone Mountain of Georgia, and from every hill and molehill of Mississippi, every tenement and every hamlet, from every state, and every city cried freedom! Black men and women, white men and women, old and young, Jews and Gentiles, Protestants and Catholics, Muslims and Arabs, every nationality and social status, rich and poor came to one conclusion: we must have Change and Hope that we can believe in.

The prophetic words "Yes, We Can" became "Yes, We Did!" Senator Barack Obama was elected – "by the content of his character and not by the color of his skin". Somebody say, The Dream Will Never Die!

Dr. Martin Luther King, Jr. wrote his vision down. He made it plain so that you and I could read it and that generations to come may run and tell others.

Dr. King's vision hastened toward the goal and it did not fail.

Although your dreams and your visions may tarry, I encourage you to wait on them. The Word of God says, "It will surely come".

My brothers and sisters, Dr. Martin Luther King, Jr. had a dream, and on January 20th, in the year of our Lord 2009, the dream came true! We were blessed to witness the 56th Inauguration of the 44th President of the United States of America: The first African American President Barack Obama.

A true sign of a Prophet of God is what he prophesied comes to past and proves that The Dream Will Never Die!

Song: Lord I done, done what you told me, I have done, I have done!

This Original Sermon Is Recorded in the Library of Congress

Don't Hate, Participate!

SCRIPTURE: Luke 19: 28-40
KEY VERSE: Luke 19: 40
SUBJECT: Jesus rebukes the Pharisees reference Praise!

INTRODUCTION:
Today we have another blessed opportunity to celebrate Palm Sunday, which occurred in the final week of the Lord's earthly ministry, symbolizing Jesus' triumphal entrance into Jerusalem.

JOHN 12:13 IT STATES:

> "They took branches of palm trees and went forth to meet him and cried, Hosanna: Blessed is the King of Israel that cometh in the name of the Lord".

How many of you know that everyone was not elated about Jesus' coming to Jerusalem? The Pharisees were among those who were unhappy. They literally hated Jesus because He had gained so much popularity for the miracles He had done. When the crowd of disciples began to praise Jesus with much vigor, the Pharisees called to Him and said, *"Teacher rebuke your disciples"*.

Jesus answered and said to them, *"I tell you that if these should keep silent, the stones would immediately cry out."* In other words, Jesus was simply telling the Pharisees, Don't Hate, Just Participate!

Today we will discuss (2) points:

1. The significance of Praise
2. Participation in Praise

LUKE 19: 28-40: THE TRIUMPHAL ENTRY

(28) When He had said this, He went on ahead, going up to Jerusalem. (29) And it came to pass, when He drew near to Bethphage and Bethany, at the mountain called Olivet, that He sent two of His disciples, (30) saying, "Go into the village opposite you, where as you enter you will find a colt tied, on which no one has ever sat. Loose it and bring it here. (31) And if anyone asks you, 'Why are you loosing it?' thus you shall say to him, 'Because the Lord has need of it.'"
(32) So those who were sent went their way and found it just as He had said to them. (33) But as they were loosing the colt, the owners of it said to them, "Why are you loosing the colt?" (34) And they said, "The Lord has need of him." (35) Then they brought him to Jesus. And they threw their own clothes on the colt, and they set Jesus on him. (36) And as He went, many spread their clothes on the road. (37) Then, as He was now drawing near the descent of the Mount of Olives, the whole

multitude of the disciples began to rejoice and praise God with a loud voice for all the mighty works they had seen, (38) saying: "'Blessed is the King who comes in the name of the LORD!' Peace in heaven and glory in the highest!" (39) And some of the Pharisees called to Him from the crowd, "Teacher, rebuke Your disciples." (40) But He answered and said to them, "I tell you that if these should keep silent, the stones would immediately cry out."

Sermon

1. THE SIGNIFICANCE OF PRAISE:

Have you ever been in a church and the people tried to stop you from praising God? Has anyone ever looked at you like you are out of your mind because you started shouting and dancing in the spirit? Have you ever been ushered to a backroom because you just lifted up the name of Jesus? Did you feel uncomfortable in that church? Well, you should have.

The praise of God is very important. It should be a delight to His people and not a chore. In fact, the word of God in Psalms 148:1- 13 proclaims that "all of creation" should join in His praise.

> 1 Praise the LORD! Praise the LORD from the heavens; Praise Him in the heights! (2) Praise Him, all His angels; Praise Him, all His hosts! (3) Praise Him, sun and moon; Praise Him, all you stars of light! (4) Praise Him, you heavens of heavens, And you waters above the heavens! (5) Let them praise the name of

the LORD, for He commanded and they were created. (6) He also established them forever and ever; He made a decree which shall not pass away. (7) Praise the LORD from the earth, You great sea creatures and all the depths; (8) Fire and hail, snow and clouds; Stormy wind, fulfilling His word; (9) Mountains and all hills; Fruitful trees and all cedars; (10) Beasts and all cattle; Creeping things and flying fowl; (11) Kings of the earth and all peoples; Princes and all judges of the earth; (12) Both young men and maidens; Old men and children. (13) Let them praise the name of the LORD, For His name alone is exalted; His glory is above the earth and heaven.

Saints, that's why Jesus proclaimed, "I tell you that if these should keep silent, the stones would immediately cry out."

Have you ever wondered why Jesus said *the stones would immediately cry out*? I too wondered, until I remembered that even a stone has the capability to breathe and it also has life. If you go to a high mountain and yell out a word like "hello", you will hear that word echo back to you three folds, "Hello, Hello, Hello". Are your words bouncing off the stones of the mountain or are the stones interpreting your language and answering back to you? Think about it the next time you yell at that big stony mountain created by God. The stones might be saying, "Don't Hate, Just Participate"!

2. WHY SHOULD WE PARTICIPATE IN PRAISE?

The Apostle Paul explained the necessity of participating in praise clearly in Hebrews 13:15, 16:

> "(15) Therefore by Him let us continually offer the sacrifice of praise to God, that is, the fruit of our lips, giving thanks to His name. (16) But do not forget to do good and to share, for with such sacrifices God is well pleased."

Praise is an expression of worship. Worship means giving reverence and love to God. Worship encompasses several things: thought, feeling and deed, and there are many expressions of it. Our expressions of praise may include thanksgiving, which can be expressed privately and publicly.

EXAMPLES OF PRAISE:

- Smiling jubilantly in the spirit like David!
- Weeping and Shouting like the prophet Jeremiah weeps when hearing the Word of God!
- Singing songs of praises to our Lord!
- Beating soulful praises on the drums and cymbals!
- Playing melodious tunes of praise on those ebony and ivory keys!
- Giving financially until it hurts!

These are all sacrifices of praise/worship and are pleasing in the sight of God!

CONCLUSION:

LUKE 19: 37, 38

> (37) Then, as He was now drawing near the descent of the Mount of Olives, the whole multitude of the disciples began to rejoice and praise God with a loud voice for all the mighty works they had seen, (38) saying: "'Blessed is the King who comes in the name of the LORD!' Peace in heaven and glory in the highest!"

God inhabits the praises of His people! He comes near to you when you hold up holy hands to Him. As the praises go up, the blessings from God come down. I don't know about you, but I just want to please God. If all He really wants us to do is give Him some praise, I think we should just do it!

Praise to God is the single most important act of worship. Praise is one way to show our love, obedience and dedication to God. This act of praise involves the mind, body and soul.

We should also praise with the mind. Our minds control and coordinate our bodies. If you have your mind focused on Jesus, your body can not help but praise Him! The renowned gospel singer *Lee Williams* said, "I tried to hold my feet but my hands started to move; the prophet Jeremiah said, *"It feels like fire shut up in my bones"*.

My Brothers and my Sisters, you will always clash with individuals who do not desire to express themselves in praise and worship like you do. Jesus was always in conflict with the Pharisees, because He was sensitive to the needs and hurts of individuals. The Pharisees placed too much emphasis on minor details while ignoring the "weightier matters of the law", such as "Justice, Mercy, and Faith" (Matthew 23:23).

The Pharisees of today still can not understand why we as Christians insist upon participating in the very act of praise. They say things like, do you really have to carry on like that? Our church is too sophisticated for all that commotion and ruckus. We're on t.v. we can't have you interfering with the service. Sounds familiar, doesn't it?

If you were one of the members of the noisy crew like the disciples, who saw their Savior coming, or the ones in the crowd who were once lame, blind, mute, maimed, demon possessed and made whole again by Jesus the Christ, I tell you they could not help but shout His praises!

I'm not ashamed to say, *"I'm from that noisy crew"* too. I've got so much to praise God for:

- For waking me up this morning, starting me on my way,
- Letting me see the sunshine of a brand-new day,
- For new mercies each and every day,
- Jehovah-Jireh – my provider,

- For every mountain, He brought me over and for every trial He safely seen me through!
- For every heartache, sleepless night, and disappointment, Lord I still praise you!
- Why? If I didn't have a problem, I would not know that God could solve them!

Saints, when I think of the goodness of the Lord, my soul cries out Hallelujah, Thank You Jesus, Glory to God!

I just wish I had somebody who's not ashamed of the Gospel of Jesus Christ. I wish I had a saint of the Most High God, who is willing to open up their mouths and give Him praise today!

AND IF THEY KEEP LOOKING AT YOU LIKE YOU'RE CRAZY, JUST BOLDLY TELL THEM, DON'T HATE, JUST PARTICIPATE!

Church Folk Involved In a Killing!

SCRIPTURE: Luke 23: 13-24
SUBJECT: The Accusers and the Crucifixion of Christ

INTRODUCTION:
Christ's entrance into Jerusalem was triumphant. How ironic it is just a week later after his entrance, the same jubilant crowd now shouts, *"Crucify him! Crucify him!* Saints, this crowd was not filled with strangers but they were followers of Christ. They were what I refer to as "Church Folk Involved in a Killing".

LUKE 23:13-24 (KING JAMES VERSION)

13 And Pilate, when he had called together the chief priests and the rulers and the people, 14 Said unto them, Ye have brought this man unto me, as one that perverteth the people: and, behold, I, having examined him before you, have found no fault in this man touching those things whereof ye accuse him: 15No, nor yet Herod: for I sent you to him; and, lo, nothing worthy of death is done unto him. 16I will therefore chastise him, and release him. 17 (For of necessity he must release one unto them at the feast.) 18 And they cried out all at once,

saying, Away with this man, and release unto us Barabbas: 19(Who for a certain sedition made in the city, and for murder, was cast into prison.) 20 Pilate therefore, willing to release Jesus, spake again to them. 21 But they cried, saying, Crucify him, crucify him. 22And he said unto them the third time, Why, what evil hath he done? I have found no cause of death in him: I will therefore chastise him, and let him go. 23And they were instant with loud voices, requiring that he might be crucified. And the voices of them and of the chief priests prevailed. 24And Pilate gave sentence that it should be as they required.

Sermon

The fear of man brings many into its deadly snare. In today's text, Pilate declares Jesus innocent, and has a mind to release him. To please the people, he punishes Jesus as an evil doer. If no fault be found in Jesus, why chastise him? Pilate yielded at length, he had not the courage or fortitude to go against the crowd.

And so, he delivered Jesus to their will, to be crucified. How many of you know that all this was predestined? The prophets in the Old Testament Scriptures foretold of Jesus' destiny with death

ZECHARIAH 9: 9

"Rejoice greatly, O Daughter of Zion! Shout, Daughter of Jerusalem! See, your king comes to you, righteous and having salvation, gentle and riding on a donkey, on a colt, the foal of a donkey."

PSALM 41: 9 (DAVID)

"Even my close friend, whom I trusted, he who shared my bread, has lifted up his heel against me."

ISAIAH 53: 7

"He was oppressed and He was afflicted, Yet He opened not His mouth; He was led as a lamb to the slaughter, And as a sheep before its shearers is silent, So He opened not His mouth."

ISAIAH 53:5

"But He was wounded for our transgressions, He was bruised for our iniquities; The chastisement for our peace was upon Him, and by His stripes we are healed."

Jesus knew so very well his destiny with death. It had been written in the Holy Scriptures and so it was to be! For Jesus said, in Matthew 5:18: *"For assuredly, I say to you, till heaven and earth pass away, one jot or one tittle will by no means pass from the law till all is fulfilled."*

Now saints, you can understand how Jesus must have felt.
- Have your friends or running partners ever said: "I'm with you man, through the thick and thin? Has anyone ever told you that if you needed them, all you had to do was call? Jesus had been told the same. Have you ever found your-

- self in dire straights and you could not find a friend to call your own? This is how Jesus felt.
- Ladies, you can empathize with Jesus, as domestic violence is prevalent. When someone tells you that they love you and that they worship the ground that you walk on, but that same person beats up on you.

We all can identify with Jesus. Maybe it wouldn't hurt so much if the accusers were strangers. Maybe it would not feel so bad if they were his enemies. They were indeed his followers and followers of Christ. They were *"Church Folk"*.

One week proclaiming, *"Hosanna: Blessed is the King of Israel that cometh in the name of the Lord"* and the very next week shouting, *"Crucify him, crucify him"*.

Which brings me to this point; I've come to this conclusion that words can kill you! Yes, what you say-to and say-about a person can kill them mentally and physically.

The severity of cyberbullying was brought to my attention. The lives and future of nine young people from Massachusetts were placed in jeopardy because they were just living for the moment. These same individuals decided to utilize a social media platform called My Space to bully and degrade another classmate to the point that she hung herself.

Young people and parents, this must not be tolerated! This is a sin before God! Talk to your children and if this type of negative social activity is going on, you must end it immediately!

Parents check out their social media sites and usage. If there is anything derogatory or just not suitable for a Christian, please have your child remove it promptly.

I'm not telling you anything I would not do myself. Please, young people, report these incidents of bullying to your teachers, guidance counselors, and principals and of course to your parents and the police department.

Some states are attempting to make it a law to ban cyberbullying. Unfortunately, those nine young people were charged with serious crimes involving suicide and murder. The Ten Commandments clearly states, "Thou shall not kill". The guilty will reap what they have sown.

Now back to "Church Folk Involved in a Killing" ...

Our Lord and Savior had prepared forty days and forty nights in the wilderness for his journey to Calvary's cross. Jesus was ready, physically and spiritually for the challenge. He knew that our salvation was in his righteous hands. This man called Jesus had become our friend and was soon to be our Savior. He was indeed ready for the Cross but I really wonder if he was ready for the *"Church Folk"*.

Some "Church Folk", are those who proclaim that they are saved, sanctified, filled with the Holy Ghost on one week and turn around and stab you in the back the next week. Some *"Church Folk"*, don't add up. Instead of offering you a hand up, they offer you a hand out the door. *Some "Church Folk"*, won't save you. Instead of praying with and for you, they are talking about you and literally putting you in the grave.

Jesus also warned us of these types of *"Church Folk"* sitting in high places. The Scribes and Pharisees also called *"Vipers"*- sucking the blood out of the people's veins, so that they live but are spiritually dead. They teach the laws of Moses (Ten Commandments) but do not live by them. Many outwardly appear righteous, but inside are full of hypocrisy and lawlessness. Jesus said, *"Woe to you, scribes and Pharisees, hypocrites!"* Matthew 23:1-33 Church Folk Involved in a Killing!

CONCLUSION

Jesus was indeed ready for Calvary's Cross. Even so, it must have really pulled on the strings of his heart to know that there were Church Folk Involved in his Killing.

As soon as Christ was fastened to that old rugged cross, he prayed for those who crucified him. "Father, forgive them; for they know not what they do" Luke 23:34.

God has forgiven all of us and now, we must continue to be more like his beloved son. We must be christians, saints of the Most High God, following after Christ Jesus and not to be ever characterized as *"Church Folk"*.

Remember this...

> God sent His Son and they called Him Jesus,
> He came to love, to heal and forgive.
> He bled and died to pay my pardon,
> An empty tomb is there to prove my Savior lives!
> Because He lives I can face tomorrow,
> Because He lives all of my fears are gone,
> Because I know, I know saints, He holds the future,
> And life is worth the living, just because He lives!

An Obedient Child Of God

SCRIPTURE: Ephesians 6:1-4
SUBJECT: An Obedient Child of God

INTRODUCTION:
Throughout these United States of America, children are making headline news:

1. Just recently, two twelve year old girls lured a friend into the woods and stabbed her nineteen times, leaving her there to bleed to death. God gave this child the strength to drag herself to safety and get help from a passerby.

2. Seventeen year old Trayvon Martin was shot and killed, while he was talking to his girlfriend on his cell phone, by the neighborhood watchman. Was it the old stereotype "walking by being black" or the hoodie that made him a victim of this senseless act?

3. A single mother, who was nine months pregnant, drives to a car dealership parking lot late one night, places a gun to her stomach, fires a shot, and kills her unborn child.

4. Vincent Parker, a sixteen year old honor student said he pepper sprayed his mother,

then stabbed and beat her with a crowbar and baseball bat. When his father came home later he was also beaten with the crowbar and stabbed. The mother died at the scene, and the father died at the hospital. Vincent further stated, "he just got mad and went off" after his father confiscated his iPod.

There is a common thread in all these stories. Each of these stories, includes a child of God, the good, the bad and the ugly!

The Apostle Paul, in this great epistle to the Ephesians gave us foresight for the times to come. Paul stressed that we should be followers of God as dear children who are redeemed by the Son and sealed by the Holy Spirit. We are called to be children who were once blind but now walk in the marvelous light of Jesus Christ!

Ephesians 6:1-4 New King James Version (NKJV)

1. Children, obey your parents in the Lord, for this is right.
2. "Honor your father and mother," which is the first commandment with promise:
3. "That it may be well with you and you may live long on the earth."
4. And you, fathers, do not provoke your children to wrath, but bring them up in the training and admonition of the Lord.

Today we will discuss (2) two points:

1. The Responsibility of the Children to the Parents
2. The Responsibility of the Parents to the Children.

Just maybe, by what some call "the foolishness of preaching", we can save one child of God!

VERSE #1:

> "Children obey your parents in the Lord for this is right."

The Apostle Paul placed great emphasis on the word Obey, which means to follow the commands of, to be obedient in following given instructions of the parent, in the Lord. (Repeat)

Now the parent does not have to be holier than thou, but the command or the instructions are to be righteous. The instructions may not be what the child wants to hear at that time but it's what God wants.

I believe Paul said it best in Colossians 3:20 "Children obey your parents in all things for this is well pleasing to the Lord."

VERSE #2:

> "Honor your father and your mother which is the first commandment with promise."

Honor: To give high respect. This respect is to be given to your parents as commanded by God himself in the Ten Commandments.

And what are the Ten Commandments?

The first (4) Commandments govern our relationship with God.

1. Trust God.
2. Worship God only.
3. Use God's name in ways that honor Him.
4. Rest on the Sabbath Day and think about God.

Now the 5th thru the 10th Commandments speak of our relationship to other people.

1. Respect and obey your parents.
2. Protect and respect humane life.
3. Be true to your husband or wife.
4. Do not take what belongs to others.
5. Do not lie on others.
6. Be satisfied with what you have.

The Ten Commandments are not as hard as you think, are they?

And besides Jesus said, "If you love me you will keep my Commandments." (John 14:15)

VERSE #3:

> "That it may be well with you and you may live long on the earth."

God promised us that if we kept the 5th Commandment that not only would you live long but also live prosperously:

- Who among you have retired from a Job?
- Who owns their home and other properties?
- Who has lived for almost 90 years?

Disobedience of the Commandments, brings on punishments. A few examples are:

- Dying young
- Bad behavior
- Bad health
- Unfortunate circumstances

Young people, there comes a point in one's life when you must come into the realization that you are in that situation or particular circumstance not because of your parents, peers, the principal of your school, the police department, or your Pastor.

You're where you are in life, some times because of you! Yes, You!

You make choices in life. You can choose to do good, or you can choose to do evil. You can choose to follow Christ or you can choose to follow Satan.

I guarantee, if you choose to follow Satan you will end up where God has prepared for Satan; the Lake which burns with fire and brimstone.

I've got good news. If you choose to follow Christ and His Commandments, you will be blessed to the right of the tree of life, and enter through the gates of that fair city of God!

Verse #4: "And fathers provoke not your children to wrath but bring them up in the admonition of the Lord."

The father is the parent responsible for setting the pattern for the child's obedience in the family. Any disciplining that the mother gives is an extension of the father's authority in the home.

Sisters, you might be saying, "Well Pastor that sounds good, but there's no father in my home. I don't know the last time I saw my baby's daddy."

Moms if there's no father in the home, you are the head of the household, and your responsibility is to be that spiritual leader until a male role model can assist you.

"Provoke not your children to wrath"

What is Paul saying there? If you over discipline your child they may react in an outburst of rage and become violent.

The father should bring up the child in corrective discipline in the Lord. In others words, raise your children to fear God not you!

To bring them up involves (3) basic principles:

1. The father is responsible for taking care of the child as long as the child depends on the father. (it got quiet in here) The child should be nourished, and taken care of in a tender, loving way. Children are little human beings, with feelings and emotions, just like adults. Parents for God's sake, talk to your children! "What's the matter baby? How was your day in school? Did anyone upset my baby today? Who messed with my baby girl?"

2. Mothers, I refuse to let the enemy mess with my child. That's why I pray! Parents, keep on praying, keep on fasting. Don't give up, don't give out and for God's sake, don't give in! The devil is a liar, that's your baby!

3. The father is responsible for all that a child needs for his/her development: physically, mentally, financially, and last but not least, spiritually!

The father/father figure is God's choice to discipline the child when he/she does not obey as God has commanded. A father that does not discipline his child is a father who is undisciplined himself; therefore disobedient to the Word of God!

Parents, a child's disobedience should not be tolerated! (Repeat)

Proverbs 13:24 says, "He who spares his rod hates his son, but he who loves him disciplines him promptly."

Proverbs 22:15 says, "Foolishness is bound in the heart of a child but the rod of corrections shall drive it far from him."

In other words, it's timeout for "time out". You better get back to the old fashioned way your parents and grandparents raised and disciplined you, before your children start doing "real time" in the county jail.

CONCLUSION

Parents, raising your children will not be an easy profession. It is a lifelong, rewarding experience. Our children are precious gifts from God. We are just stewards over them. I compel you to give your children, in the spirit, back to the Lord. Ask for his divine help in doing this great task of parenting.

Children, listen and obey your parents in the Lord. Don't shorten your very bright futures. Jesus loves you very much! He loves all the little children, red, yellow, and black or white, they are so precious in his sight.

And how do I know this, for the bible tells me so…

Before there was redemption, before justification, and salvation, Jesus sat on the right hand of God the Father, sitting high and looking low, pleading our cause with the Father.

I could just hear Him saying, "Father please do not destroy them. What can I do to save them?"

Then God looked at His beloved Son, face to face, Spirit to Spirit and said, "Son, they're just no good. Their wickedness is too great. Even the thought of their hearts is evil continually. I must destroy man whom I have created from the face of the Earth."

Jesus kept on pleading for us, "Please Father, there must be something I can do?"

Then I could just hear God say, "There something you can do Son"

- You will have to step down Son, from your throne of glory.
- You will have to step down Son, to the courts of Pontius Pilate.
- You will have to step down Son, to the Mount of Calvary.

- You will have to step down Son, to ashes to ashes, and dust to dust.
- You will have to step down my beloved Son, to the very pit of Hell.

Then I could just hear the obedient voice of Jesus saying, "Father, not my will, but thou will be done."

Jesus died young people, not just for your grandparents, not just for your parents, but he died for your generation too.

And on the 3rd day, He rose from the dead, for all humanity and generations to come!

So from now on, if anyone asks you who your role model is, you tell them that his name is Jesus Christ; the only perfect example of "An Obedient Child of God".

And when your so called friends try to put you down because you love the Lord and obey your parents, hold your head up high and stick your chest out and you tell them this...

> I'm a child of the King! I am God's child, for I am born again of the incorruptible seed of the Word of God, which lives and abides forever!
> I am forgiven all my sins and I am washed in the blood of the Lamb!
> I'm more than a conqueror!
> I am firmly rooted, I am built up,
> I'm strengthened in the faith, overflowing with joy and thanksgiving!
> Why? Because I'm the apple of my Father's eye...
> An Obedient Child of God!

How Deep Are You In The Spirit?

SCRIPTURE: Ezekiel 47: 1-6 verses
SUBJECT: Allowing the Holy Spirit to Take Control!

INTRODUCTION:

The prophet Ezekiel's name means "God Strengthens" or "Strengthened by God". He had a prophetic ministry that showed a priestly emphasis and concern with: 1. Temple of God, 2. Priesthood, 3. Sacrifices, and last but not least, the Shekinah (the glory of God), which today is recognized as the Holy Spirit.

Ezekiel, was privileged to receive a number of visions of the power and the plans of God. Ezekiel was careful and rather artistic in his oral and written presentations. Our text demonstrates for example that Ezekiel has a vision of the restoration of the temple of God and prophesied that the glory of the Lord would return to the temple. Which brings us to the question of the hour, how deep are you in the Spirit?

DR. JACQUELINE HARDY HARRIS

Sermon

EZEKIEL 47:1-6
(NEW KING JAMES VERSION)

1   Then he brought me back to the door of the temple; and there was water, flowing from under the threshold of the temple toward the east, for the front of the temple faced east; the water was flowing from under the right side of the temple, south of the altar. 2 He brought me out by way of the north gate, and led me around on the outside to the outer gateway that faces east; and there was water, running out on the right side. 3 And when the man went out to the east with the line in his hand, he measured one thousand cubits, and he brought me through the waters; the water came up to my ankles. 4 Again he measured one thousand and brought me through the waters; the water came up to my knees.

Again he measured one thousand and brought me through; the water came up to my waist. 5 Again he measured one thousand, and it was a river that I could not cross; for the water was too deep, water in which one must swim, a river that could not be crossed. 6 He said to me, "Son of man, have you seen this?" Then he brought me and returned me to the bank of the river.

EZEKIEL 47: 3

Then when the man went out to the east with the line in his hand, he measured one thousand

> cubits, and he brought me through the waters; the water came up to my ankles."

The man with the line (measuring tool) in his hand, is our Lord and Savior Jesus Christ, who is perfect, therefore the only righteous one who can measure where you are in the Spirit. The water represents the Holy Spirit Water came up to my ankles; have you been to VA Beach? It's is rated the top 10 beach in the country. Have you noticed that when you are in the water around your ankles you are able to run in and out of the water very easily? Reminds me of individuals who run in and out of the church.

Anything can upset them and cause them to leave the house of God; they even sit in the back making it real easy to leave the church unnoticed; No staying power! Saying stuff like, "They hurt my feelings so I just left girl." Ankle Deep, it's real easy to run in and out of the church!

EZEKIEL 47: 4

> Again he measured one thousand cubits, and brought me through the waters; the water came up to my knees."

Water to your knees you can still run in and out of the church, just not as fast as ankle deep These individuals tend to have a "form of Godliness but deny the power there in". Fall on their knees to pray and before they can get up begin to doubt God. Knee Deep, they don't want to be involved with anything in the Church, but cutting their eyes at anyone else who is being used by God in the church. Knee Deep ain't deep enough!

EZEKIEL 47: 4

> Again he measured one thousand and brought me through; the water came up to my waist.

- To the waist, I'm feeling real good now, the water is high enough to keep me from running or walking.
- Rooted and steadfast in the Word and Will of God
- These individuals have the fruits of the Spirit:

Love, Joy, Peace, Long suffering, Kindness, Goodness, Faithfulness, Gentleness and last but not least: Self-Control

Saints, most of the church is waist deep in the Spirit. That's not that bad, but we can all do better. In this position, the vital organs (heart, lungs, brain) which control the entire body, are still outside of the water. You don't understand a word I'm saying.

Let me see if I can put it another way. That which controls your sexual being is still outside of the water. If you really want to be kept by God, you've got to get a little deeper in God. I believe the scriptures said there must be a "renewing of your mind" (Romans 12:2). You keep wondering how you got tangled up in that mess with somebody you really don't even like. Girlfriends just because you saw those hazel eyes, that wavy hair, six pack stomach and "two guns" (muscular arms) to hold you tight does not mean that he is the right one for you. That guy might not know Jesus if he stepped on his toes! My brothers, you also looked at her with that brick-house shape and silky black hair running down to her "baby's got back"; but these characteristics doesn't show that she's saved or sanctified! Handsome but not holy, beautiful but not blessed. I know I'm right about this. Waist deep means that you are still looking for love on all the wrong faces and in all the wrong places!

There is no way you can keep yourself! You need the sustaining power of the Holy Spirit. You have to love the Lord thy God with all your heart, with all your soul and with all your mind!

Waist Deep, just ain't deep enough!

EZEKIEL 47: 5

> "Again he measured one thousand, and it was a river that I could not cross; for the water was deep, water in which one must swim, a river that could not be crossed. He said to me, "Son of man, have you seen this? Then he brought me and returned me to the bank of the river."

Saints, the Lord showed me something, in a river of water, the water just might get in your ears. Maybe here, you begin to really hear God's Word.

In a river of water, the water sometimes gets in your eyes. Possibly you were blind but now you see.

In a river of water, the water for some reason or another always gets in your mouth and up your nose. At this level, you just can't say or even think like you use to do. There becomes a renewing of your mind.

In a river of water, the water captures your heart and you cry out like the songwriter, "It's in my heart to serve the Lord!"

In a river of water, I mean when the Holy Spirit really starts filling you with its keeping power, there's no way on this side of heaven that anyone or anything can run you out of the house of God!

In a river of water, the Holy Spirit reminds you, that there is Joy in the house of the Lord! There is Peace in the house of the Lord!

The Holy Spirit reminds you, there is Deliverance in the house of the Lord! There is Healing in the house of the Lord!

Your soul boldly says, I was glad when they said unto me let us go into the house of the Lord!

Saints, let me tell you something, ain't nobody going to make me leave the house of the Lord!

Just like David, the Lord, anointed my head with oil, my cup runneth over, surely goodness and mercy will follow me all the days of my life and I will dwell in the house of the Lord forever and ever!

CONCLUSION

Ezekiel said these last profound words: Ezekiel 47: 6 "He said to me, "Son of man, have you seen this?" Then he brought me and returned me to the bank of the river."

This portion of scripture speaks to all the saints of God. We must seek out and compel the lost to come to Christ while there is still time. You see saints we all have one more river to cross, but we can not make it there alone. We're going to need our Lord and Savior, Jesus Christ, and the sustaining power of the Holy Ghost. Jesus is the only one who can safely bring us back to the banks of that old river of Jordan!

I challenge those of you that have been dipped deep down in the cleansing water of the Holy Spirit, to go get God's lost sheep and bring them back into the house of the Lord. This is where they first found Jesus and was touched by His finger of Love!

Go and tell them the Shekinah Glory of God is in this tabernacle of praise! Tell them the Word of God is preached in this house! Tell them that the Anointing Power of the Holy Spirit flows in here, like a mighty river, from the front door to the back door, from the pulpit and in and out of the pews. Tell them we're not playing Church over here, we're serious about this thing. Tell them that we are wrapped up, tangled up, overflowing in the Spirit of the Lord!

Saints I go to the old hymns of the church that stir up the Spirit of the Lord like...

COME HOLY SPIRIT HEAVENLY DOVE

> Come Holy Spirit, Sweet Heavenly Dove,
> With all thy quickening powers;

DR. JACQUELINE HARDY HARRIS

Kindle a flame of sacred love, in these cold
hearts of ours.

Look how we grovel here below,
Fond of these earthly toys;
Our souls how heavily they go, to reach eternal
joys.

So, Come Holy Spirit, Sweet Heavenly Dove
With all thy quickening powers;
Come shed abroad a Savior's love, and that
shall kindle ours!

The question is, How Deep are You in the Spirit?

I Know I've Been Changed!

SCRIPTURE: Mark 2: 1-12
SUBJECT: Jesus Forgives and Heals a Paralytic

INTRODUCTION:
When we are sick, we seek a medical doctor; someone who can skillfully help us through our physical condition by prescribing medication, therapy, or surgery. There are many fields of medicine.

Today, our text tells us of an individual with a sickness of cerebral palsy. Cerebral Palsy is a condition caused by brain damage around the time of birth and marked by a lack of muscle control, especially in the limbs. How many of you know that not all illnesses are unto death? This individual just needed to be brought to a miracle worker named Jesus!

Yes, I'm talking about Jesus Christ, a physician who never lost a patient. Christ is the only doctor who is capable of healing the mind, body and soul. He needs no credentials; his cases are documented world-wide. He healed the sick, opened blind eyes, opened deaf ears, muted mouths, cured the demon possessed, made the lame rise up and walk, healed withered hands, and raised his best friend Lazarus from the dead.

Jesus is the only doctor known, who fed five thousand with just a few fish and five loaves of bread, calmed the raging sea and walked on water. As the comedian Steve Harvey said, "He needs no introduction". He is more than qualified to be our Physician!

In Mark 2:17 Jesus later proclaimed, "Those who are well have no need of a physician, but those who are sick. I did not come to call the righteous, but sinners, to repentance." Our Lord and Savior knew that some people (*Scribes/Pharisees*) cared more about their physical bodies than about their souls.

Nevertheless, this man with palsy and his friends pressed their way to come see this miracle worker called Jesus. The word had gone out in that fair city of Capernaum, that men, women, boys and girls would cry out "I Know I've Been Changed!" in the presence of Jesus.

MARK 2: 1-12 NEW KING JAMES VERSION

1. And again He entered Capernaum after some days, and it was heard that He was in the house. 2 Immediately many gathered together, so that there was no longer room to receive them, not even near the door. And He preached the word to them. 3 Then they came to Him, bringing a paralytic who was carried by four men. 4 And when they could not come near Him because of the crowd, they uncovered the roof where He was. So when they had broken through, they let down the bed on which the paralytic was lying. 5 When Jesus saw their faith, He said to the paralytic, "Son, your sins are forgiven you." 6 And some of the scribes were sitting there and

reasoning in their hearts, 7 "Why does this Man speak blasphemies like this? Who can forgive sins but God alone?" 8 But immediately, when Jesus perceived in His spirit that they reasoned thus within themselves, He said to them, "Why do you reason about these things in your hearts? 9 Which is easier, to say to the paralytic, 'Your sins are forgiven you,' or to say, 'Arise, take up your bed and walk'? 10 But that you may know that the Son of Man has power on earth to forgive sins"—He said to the paralytic, 11 "I say to you, arise, take up your bed, and go to your house." 12 Immediately he arose, took up the bed, and went out in the presence of them all, so that all were amazed and glorified God, saying, "We never saw anything like this!"

Sermon

This miserable man, needing to be carried. He was in a suffering state. It was kind of those who carried him and teaches the compassion that should be in mankind toward their fellow brothers/sisters who are in distress.

PARALYTIC WAS CARRIED BY FOUR MEN

Most of us think that this could never happen to us. We believe that we are whole and have no need of a physician, but truthfully, we all have been carried at one point in our lives:

1. Mom "carried" you for nine months. Some of you are still being carried by your mothers.

2. Your teachers "carried" you through school. Some of you should have been booted out, but you were in sports.
3. Job/Supervisor/Co-worker "carried" you at work. They really should have fired you a long time ago.

In one way or another, we all have been "carried". Someone has assisted us through this life. I know for a fact that the good Lord "carried" all of us. Somebody say Amen!

How many of you know that this paralytic, who was carried by four men, needed help for another sickness? Sin. I've come to this conclusion, Sin (iniquity) is the cause of all our pains and sicknesses, and the way to remove the effect of sin is to take away the cause.

5   When Jesus saw their faith, He said to the paralytic, "Son, your sins are forgiven you."

To be pardon of our sins strikes at the root of all diseases. Christ proved his power to forgive sin, by showing his power to cure the man sick of the palsy. For sin is the disease of the soul. When it is pardoned, it is healed.

If you noticed, Jesus never said what the paralytic's sins were. He just said, "Son, your sins are forgiven you."

We can learn a lot from Jesus. Many churches are embarrassed to embrace a recovering drug addict, alcoholic or prostitute who comes seeking help. Some churches are even reticent to allow an unemployed person or someone who was divorced to train for a position of leadership. I'm so glad Jesus looked beyond this paralytic's faults and saw his needs. He needed a Savior, he needed a Redeemer, he just needed to be needed!

Another point, I'd like to make is that Jesus was deeply moved by the friends and this sick young man's faith. "Now faith is the substance of things hoped for, the evidence of things not seen. Hebrews 11:1". Have you ever hoped for something for a long time? Have you ever visualized something that others did not? Maybe your best friends thought maybe you had lost your mind, but they decided to go along with you because you just didn't give up? Have you ever ventured to persevere with no visible evidence of success in sight?

My brothers and sisters, the paralytic was looking for a miracle that only God could give! God had worked miracles for others. Surely, he would do it for him! Unable to get through the front door because of the crowds, they pressed their way, tearing a hole in the roof, strapping the paralytic to his sickbed and lowering him down to this great physician Jesus Christ.

CONCLUSION

Sunday in and Sunday out, we the ministers of the Lord extend The Invitation to Christian Discipleship followed by the the Altar Call. You've probably wondered, why? Over two thousand years ago, Jesus commanded us to compel them to "Come". He did not just want to *save* us but to also *heal* us and make us whole.

The songwriter Donnie McClurkin sang a song that stated that he called God holy. He is not only Holy, but Faithful Savior and Healer.

The paralytic came to Jesus, weary, worn, sad and in need of healing. Carried by friends, on a sickbed, he was yearning for a change in his life. He was sick and tired of being sick and tired. Have you ever been where this young man was?

My brothers and sisters, I encourage you to do just what he did...

Come to Jesus, for there is Power in the presence of the Lord. There is peace in the presence of the Lord. There is redemption in the presence of the Lord. There is forgiveness in the presence of the Lord. There is healing in the presence of the Lord!

I believe the songwriter said it best...

HYMN #403 WHAT A WONDERFUL CHANGE IN MY LIFE

What a wonderful change in my life has been wrought,
Since Jesus came into my heart!

I have light in my soul for which long I have sought,
Since Jesus came into my heart!

Since Jesus came into my heart, Since Jesus came into my heart,
Floods of joy o'er my soul like a sea billows roll,
Since Jesus came into my heart!

The paralytic stood up, gathered up and folded his sickbed and boldly proclaimed, *I Know I've Been Changed!*

Evangelize!

SCRIPTURE: Matthew 28: 18-20
               Acts 1: 8
SUBJECT: The Gospel Proclaimed

INTRODUCTION:

> Give us a watchword for the hour
> A thrilling word, a word of power;
> A battle cry, a flaming breath,
> A call to conquest or a call to death;
> A word to rouse the church from rest,
> To heed the Master's high behest.
> The call is given, ye host arise,
> The watchword is EVANGELIZE!
> To fallen men, a dying race,
> Make known the gift of gospel grace.
> The world that now in darkness lies,
> Oh Church of Christ, EVANGELIZE!

MATTHEW 28: 18-20

(KING JAMES VERSION)

(18) And Jesus came and spake unto them, saying, All power is given unto me in heaven and in earth. (19) Go ye therefore, and teach all nations, baptizing them in the name of the Father, and of the Son, and of the Holy Ghost:

(20) Teaching them to observe all things whatsoever I have commanded you: and, lo, I am with you always, even unto the end of the world. Amen.

ACTS 1: 8 (KING JAMES VERSION)

(8) But ye shall receive power, after that the Holy Ghost is come upon you: and ye shall be witnesses unto me both in Jerusalem, and in all Judaea, and in Samaria, and unto the uttermost part of the earth.

EVANGELIZE: TO PROCLAIM THE GOOD NEWS OF THE GOSPEL.

At the Christian Education Conference in Daytona Beach, the Rev. Dr. James M. Proctor was teaching a class on Evangelism. He stated that people are brought into the church by the following ways:

- 2% by advertisement
- 6% by the Pastor
- 6% by organized Evangelistic Outreach Ministry
- 86% by friends and family

In other words, there is tremendous value in you, going out and telling somebody how good Jesus is to you!

Sometimes, even I get a little confused about the power of evangelism. I often ask myself, "What's the use in me evangelizing?" Why not just send those 86% out there, praise God." (Smile)

I've learned over the years that God is very precise and clear in His word. He gave us (5) reasons why we should all evangelize:

1. God has commanded us to do so in Matthew and Acts.
2. Evangelism demonstrates our Love for God. Christ said, "If you love me you'll keep my commandments".
3. Sharing our faith is God's chosen method to tell all people about Him, Jesus Christ, our Lord and Savior. Psalm 107: 2 it says, "Let the redeemed of the Lord say so!"
4. God desires to save all people. It says in His word, "The Lord is not slack concerning His promise, as some count slackness, but is long-suffering toward us, not willing that any should perish but that all should come to repentance."
5. Someone shared his or her faith with us. It may have been a church school teacher, a God fearing Pastor, a praying grandmother, grandfather, an aunt or uncle who fell on bended knee and prayed for you. It could have been a nobody like me, trying to tell everybody about somebody who can save your soul!

What should we say when we Evangelize?

Actually we have but one thing to share with the unsaved and that is the Gospel of Jesus Christ.

And what is this great Gospel?

God so loved the world that he gave his only begotten Son and whosoever believeth in him should not perish but have life eternal. This same Jesus came down Forty and Two generations, he was conceived by the Holy Spirit, born of the Virgin Mary, suffered under Pontius Pilate, was crucified, was dead, was buried, but on the third day he rose from the dead with all power in his hand and as I speak he sits on the right hand of God the Father Almighty. And guess what he will come again, and judge the living and the dead!

This is the Gospel of Jesus Christ! If we confess with our mouths, and believe these words in our heart, we are saved!

Now last but certainly not least, how can we be successful in sharing this great Gospel of Jesus Christ?

You must have Power! Power!

This power comes from the Holy Spirit. You must be a clean vessel.

This cleansing comes only from the Holy Spirit. You must be born again!

God reminded Isaiah the prophet, "Be clean you who bear the vessels of the Lord"

One of the greatest Evangelists in biblical history, the Apostle Paul said, "Our gospel did not come to you in word only but also in Power and much assurance!"

* You must dwell with God, before you can tell of God!
* You must know before you can show!

CONCLUSION

Missionaries, there is no trouble too great, no humiliation too deep, no suffering too severe, no love too strong for God.

Preachers/Pastors, There is no labor too hard.

Stewards, There is no expense too large, if it is spent in the effort to win one soul!

God loves the soul more than all creation. He fashioned it after his own image, and made it like unto himself.

Every soul had departed from God and gone astray but God brought the soul back again with a price, and our Lord and Savior Jesus Christ paid that price in full.

When a million eternities have each lived their endless ages and rolled by into the unthinkable past, and Father Time is no more, the soul of man will still be living. It is a conscious personality, endowed with perpetual life.

God said, "He who wins souls is considered wise"

The Bible says: "Those who are wise shall shine like the brightness of the firmament, and those who bring many to righteousness, like the stars for ever and ever."

You are the salt of this earth, but if the salt loses its flavor, how shall it be seasoned? You are the light of this world!

You are like a city that sits on a hill, you cannot be hidden.

MISSIONARIES...

Nor do you light a lamp and place it under a basket, but you wretch it way up high on a lampstand so that it can be seen throughout the whole house!

So let your light so shine before men, women, boys and girls that they may see your good works and glorify the Father who sits in heaven.

I said I wasn't going to tell anyone, but I couldn't keep it to myself!

I said I wasn't going to sing, dance or shout about it, but I couldn't keep it to myself!

I had to tell somebody that the Lord has been good to me!

Oh, Church of Christ, Evangelize!

Epilogue

I believe today more than ever in the saving grace of God's unyielding power. My heartbeats hasten towards those called to do the work of God and those who aspire to preach the gospel. I summons the floodgates of heaven, asking for a rainfall over your ministry, the words that come from your mouth and the motivations of the depths of your soul. May God use the contents of this book to build your kingdom and your heart. I give this to you as my greatest love.

REVEREND DR. JACQUELINE HARDY HARRIS

Endnotes

www.archives.gov/files/press/exhibits/dream-speech.pdf
- AMEC HYMNAL

About the Author

REV. DR. JACQUELINE HARDY HARRIS, RETIRED DEPUTY SHERIFF | GOSPEL PREACHER

Rev. Dr. Jacqueline Hardy Harris is the second oldest daughter of Reverend Roosevelt and Dorothy Hardy's ten children. During her formative years in the Miami Dade School System, she was active as a cheerleader, modern dancer, choreographer, bi-racial committee member, member of the chorus and member of the modeling troupe, in addition to maintaining the National Honor Roll.

After graduating from South Dade High School in 1973, she was employed with Coral Reef Hospital as a medical secretary.

After making a decision to pursue her childhood dream of becoming a police officer, she attended the Miami Dade College Police Academy, and graduated in 1981. She was the first African American female officer assigned to the Kendall District, and within a year, she was promoted to detective, and tasked with working undercover details in vice, narcotics, robbery and homicide cases.

Rev. Dr. Hardy Harris continued to matriculate studies at The Miami Metropolitan Police Institute - 610.5 hours Police Training/Administration, Florida Department of Law Enforcement - Foreign Language/Narcotics and Investigation Law Enforcement, University of North Florida - Sects, Cults and Deviant Movements, St. Petersburg College - Community Policing, The African Methodist Episcopal Church Board of Examiners Five Year Ministerial Theological Studies - Itinerant Elder, and she was accepted at Regent University for studies in Theology and Criminal Justice.

In 1990 Rev. Dr. Hardy Harris answered her calling to become a servant of the Lord. After five years in the African Methodist Episcopal Church Board of Examiners Ministerial Studies, she was ordained as an Itinerant Elder.

On Saturday, October 12, 1997, after her first ordination as an Itinerant Deacon, Rev. Dr. Hardy Harris was appointed by the Right Reverend Frank C. Cummings, Presiding Bishop of the Eleventh Episcopal District to serve as the pastor of Allen Chapel A. M. E. Church in Key Largo, Florida.

As the first woman of God to shepherd the Allen Chapel family, she was sent by God to evangelize, revive, restore and rebuild through the Word of God. She organized the First Black History Day, spiritually named "Soul Food Sunday" because of her love for youth and family. She also spearheaded the "Annual Youth Day" and "Friends and Family Day". Rev. Dr. Hardy Harris served without a salary for her entire tenure of love at Allen Chapel.

In August of 2003, while dually serving as a police officer and pastor, Rev. Dr. Hardy Harris wed her loving and supportive husband Brian, a native of Virginia. She's the mother of Eric, who is also a minister, graduate of Florida State University (1999 World Champions Football Team) and retired professional "true center" for the Arizona Rattlers Arena League. Rev. Dr. Hardy Harris has nurtured two nieces by marriage as her own daughters: Kelia (Liberty University-Criminal Justice) and Andrea (Roanoke College-2013 Graduate Bachelor of Science degree with a major in Biology). She's also a doting grandmother of two grandchildren: Jeremiah and Aaron.

In January 2005, Rev. Dr. Hardy Harris fulfilled a successful career as an honorably Retired Deputy Sheriff, with over Twenty-four years of service with the Miami Dade Police Department. Rev. Dr. Hardy Harris states that the most rewarding part of her career as a police officer was Community Policing and spearheading a Girls Basketball League of over 100 youth!

On May 6, 2006, The Right Reverend Adam Jefferson Richardson, Presiding Bishop of the Second Episcopal District-Virginia Annual Conference, appointed Reverend= Dr. Hardy Harris to pastor Campbell's Chapel the First A. M. E. Church of Virginia Beach, Virginia. She was the first woman of God sent to shepherd this historical church that was over 146 years old!

On May 14, 2011, during the 145th Session of the Virginia Annual Conference; The Right Reverend Adam Jefferson Richardson, Presiding Bishop, appointed her to

Bethel A. M. E. Church, in the beautiful mountains of Roanoke, VA. Within six months of serving as the pastor at Bethel A. M. E. Church, Rev. Dr. Hardy Harris developed a church web site, encouraged Bethel men to form Sons of Allen (Men's Ministry), began steps in the formation of a Deaconess Board and co-hosted with Reverend Christine Ziglar of Mt. Zion A. M. E., the 2011 Portsmouth Richmond Roanoke District Conference in Roanoke.

On December 25, 2011, Presiding Elder James P. Beatty assigned Reverend Dr. Jacqueline Hardy Harris to pastor Greater Ebenezer A. M. E. Church in Richmond, Virginia. The former pastor Rev. Dr. Monica Spencer so eloquently stated, "How appropriate that the Lord has sent Greater Ebenezer a precious gift during this Advent season in the person of Reverend Jacqueline Hardy Harris who comes bearing many spiritual gifts and talents." Reverend Dr. Hardy Harris is regarded for her passionate love of The Lord, charismatic ways, abundant faith, joy in preaching, "songbird" voice, affinity for developing youth and cultural programs, as well as her administrative capabilities.

On Saturday, October 12, 2013, Reverend Dr. Jacqueline Hardy Harris was conferred in ad eundem, a Doctor of Divinity degree from Virginia Triumphant College and Seminary. She is truly a soldier in the army of the Lord!

On May 23, 2014 Bishop William P. DeVeaux appointed Reverend Dr. Jacqueline Hardy Harris to the pastoral charge of Mt. Zion A. M. E. Martinsville, as the first woman of God to shepherd another historical A. M. E. church.

After a monumental journey of service, on May 13, 2016, Reverend Dr. Jacqueline Hardy Harris received her Certificate of Retirement from Bishop William P. DeVeaux, Presiding Prelate of the 2nd Episcopal District -Virginia Annual Conference of the A. M. E. Church. To God be the glory for the great things He has done!

www.ingramcontent.com/pod-product-compliance
Lightning Source LLC
Chambersburg PA
CBHW030301080526
44584CB00012B/398